KV-638-307

The Changing Politics of Gender Equality in Britain

The Changing Politics of Gender Equality in Britain

Edited by

Esther Breitenbach
Alice Brown
Fiona Mackay and
Janette Webb

Consultant editor: Jo Campling

First published 2002 by
PALGRAVE
Houndmills, Basingstoke, Hampshire RG21 6XS and
175 Fifth Avenue, New York, N. Y. 10010
Companies and representatives throughout the world

PALGRAVE is the new global academic imprint of
St. Martin's Press LLC Scholarly and Reference Division and
Palgrave Publishers Ltd (formerly Macmillan Press Ltd).

ISBN 0–333–803043 hardback

Library of Congress Cataloging-in-Publication Data

The changing politics of gender equality in 20th century Britain/edited by Esther Breitenbach ... [et al.].
    p. cm.
    Includes bibliographical references and index.
    ISBN 0-333-80304-3
    1. Women–Government policy–Great Britain–History–20th century.
    2. Women's rights–Great Britain–History–20th century. 3. Sex discrimination against women–Great Britain–History–20th century.
    4. Equality–Great Britain–History–20th century. I. Breitenbach, Esther.

HQ1236.5.G7 C47 2001
305.428'0941'0904–dc21   2001036852

10   9   8   7   6   5   4   3   2   1
11   10   09   08   07   06   05   04   03   02

Printed and bound in Great Britain by
Antony Rowe Ltd, Chippenham, Wiltshire

Dedication

In memory of Val Feld, Member of the National Assembly for Wales and former director of the EOC in Wales. A tireless campaigner for gender equality and social justice for all, she is sorely missed in Wales and beyond.

Er cof am Val Feld, Aelod o Gynulliad Cenedlaethol Cymru a chyngyfarwyddwraig y Comisiwn Cyfle Cyfartal yng Nghymru. Ymgyrchydd di-flino dros gyfartaledd i fenywod a chyfiawnder cymdeithasol i bawb, gwelir ei heisian yng Nghymr a thu hwnt.

Contents

List of Tables and Figures

Tables

Figures

Acknowledgements

This collection has its roots in discussions which took place through an Economic and Social Research Council-funded seminar series in 1997 and 1998. We gratefully acknowledge the ESRC for its support for the seminars and for our research project on Gender and Transitions in the Local State (R000/23/6545), which ran concurrently. We are grateful also for the support of the Equal Opportunities Commission for our initial pilot work on women and local government.

We would like to thank all those academics and equality practitioners who contributed to the series of six seminars on Gender Relations and the Local State at the University of Edinburgh. We are grateful to Lindsay Adams of the Unit for the Study of Government in Scotland for her efficiency and hard work in organising the seminars. We owe much to those who gave papers at seminars, chaired sessions, acted as respondents to papers, who actively participated in the discussions, and made the series such a stimulating interchange of ideas. These include: Erica Davies, Wendy Stokes, Laura Woodruff, Suzanne Chisholm, Joni Lovenduski, Susan Halford, Angela O'Hagan, Sonia Liff, Neil Wooding, Sue Ledwith and Gerry Stoker. Most of all we would like to thank the contributors to this collection for their hard work and their patience in waiting for the fruits of their labour to reach the printed page.

We would also like to thank Consulting Editor Jo Campling, for her advice and enthusiasm about the project, and all those at Palgrave.

Notes on the Editors

Esther Breitenbach is a Teaching Fellow in the Department of Social Policy at the University of Edinburgh, and is currently on secondment to the Women and Equality Unit in the Cabinet Office. Her contribution to this collection is made in her capacity as a member of the Department of Social Policy and does not represent the views of the Women and Equality Unit. She has written extensively on women and gender issues in Scotland, and has co-edited with Eleanor Gordon two volumes on Scottish women's history. She is co-editor with Fiona Mackay of *Women in Contemporary Scottish Politics: an Anthology* (Polygon at Edinburgh, 2001).

Alice Brown is Professor of Politics and Co-Director of the Governance of Scotland Forum at the University of Edinburgh. She has written widely on Scottish politics and women and politics and is co-author of a number of books including: *New Scotland, New Politics?* (Polygon at Edinburgh, 2001): *The Scottish Electorate: the 1997 General Election and Beyond* (Macmillan, 1999); and *Politics and Society in Scotland* (Macmillan, 1996 and 1998).

Fiona Mackay is Lecturer in the Department of Politics, University of Edinburgh. She has written about women and politics and gender and public policy. She is author of *Love and Politics: Women Politicians and the Ethics of Care* (Continuum, 2001) and is co-editor with Esther Breitenbach of *Women in Contemporary Scottish Politics: An Anthology* (Polygon at Edinburgh, 2001).

Janette Webb is Reader in Sociology at the University of Edinburgh. She is interested in gender relations, work and organisations. She has published papers on relations of power and authority in organisations and is co-author with D. Cleary of *Organisational Change and the Management of Expertise* (Routledge, 1994). She is currently writing a book on *Organisations and the Self*.

Notes on the Contributors

Barbara Bagilhole is Senior Lecturer in Social Policy at the University of Loughborough. Her publications include *Equal Opportunities and Social Policy: Issues of Gender 'Race' and Disability* (Addison-Wesley Longman, 1997).

Angela Coyle is Professor of Sociology at City University. She is interested in gender relations, equality policies and organisations. She has carried out research to evaluate the impact of equality initiatives on women's employment in public and private sector, and has recently worked on the implications for nurses of the new primary care arrangements. She has published books and articles on women and work.

Ian Forbes is Professor and Head of the School of Politics at the University of Nottingham. He has written widely on the interface of theory and equality policy with respect to gender, race and disability.

Ellen Kelly is currently the Equalities Manager for City of Edinburgh Council and has worked on equality issues in local government for many years. Her chapter was written in a personal capacity.

Gail Lewis is Senior Lecturer in Social Policy at the Open University. She is interested in the relations of dominance and subordination constituted through the interweaving of categories of 'race' and gender, and in the implications of such power relations for the enactment of equality policies. She has published widely in the field of critical social policy. Her most recent book is *Rethinking Social Policy*, edited by Gail Lewis, Sharon Gewirtz and John Clarke.

David Mason is Professor of Sociology, Associate Dean for Research and Head of the Graduate School in the Faculty of Human Sciences, at the University of Plymouth. He has published extensively on labour market and equal opportunity issues. Recent work includes research into the recruitment of minority ethnic nurses and on diversity in the armed forces. His publications include *Theories of Race and Ethnic Relations* (Cambridge University Press, 1986) jointly edited with John Rex, and *Race and Ethnicity in Modern Britain* (Oxford University Press, 2nd edition, 2000).

Janet Newman is Senior Lecturer, Public Policy at the University of Birmingham. Her research interests focus around analyses of public service change. Her books include: *The Managerial State*, co-authored with J. Clarke (Sage, 1997); *Shaping Cultural Change in Local Government* (Pitman, 1996); and *Gender, Culture and Organisational Change*, co-edited with C. Itzen (Routledge, 1995).

Teresa Rees is Professor at the School of Social Sciences, University of Cardiff, and the Equal Opportunities Commissioner for Wales. She is author of *Women and the Labour Market* (Routledge 1992), *Mainstreaming Equality in the European Union* (Routledge, 1998) and *Women and Work: 25 Years of Gender Equality in Wales* (University of Wales Press, 1999).

Marion Scott headed the Women's Equalities Unit at the London Borough of Islington from 1988 to late 1997. She is currently working in the voluntary sector in the area of women and information technology.

Mandy Wright is Assistant Director, Employment Advice and Equalities at the Employers' Organisation for Local Government (formerly the Local Government Management Board) and has worked on equality issues in local government for many years. She is writing in a personal capacity.

1
Introduction: The Changing Politics of Gender Equality

Esther Breitenbach, Alice Brown, Fiona Mackay and Janette Webb

The beginning of the twenty-first century is an appropriate time to reflect on the progress that has been made towards gender equality and to consider the prospects for further advancement. This edited collection draws on experiences of the 1980s and 1990s, but has been brought together in a period following a fundamental change in the British political landscape. The election of a Labour government in 1997, committed to a programme of constitutional change and modernisation, has provided new opportunities and new structural spaces in which the politics of gender equality can be pursued. It is within this context of change that our contributors have reviewed past policies and practices before exploring the opportunities and challenges for the future.

The contributions in this volume are the outcome of discussions that took place through a series of seminars, the theme of which was gender relations and the local state.[1] A key aim was to engage practitioners in a dialogue with academics about the links between research, policy and action with respect to gender equality policy. In the event, it became clear that boundaries between equal opportunities initiatives and policies at different levels of government from the local to the supra-national, between public and private sectors, and between gender and other equality categories, were permeable. As a result, the scope of discussions was broadened. These interconnections between levels of government and governance, between policies and initiatives, and between equality categories, are illustrative of politics and practice on equality issues in contemporary Britain.

A number of interrelated themes are explored, which are, broadly speaking: the way in which the gender equality 'project' is shaped by political conditions and political change; the differing political

1

opportunity structures that exist for feminists and other equality
activists to make effective interventions within the state and at different levels of governance; assessments of the strengths and weaknesses
of different approaches to equal opportunities, both conceptual and
practical; and the extent to which bureaucracies and organisational
cultures can facilitate or inhibit the promotion of equal opportunities.
The recurring theme of bureaucracy and organisational culture is characteristic of the shift towards equal opportunities becoming professionalised during the period under examination, and primarily driven by
actors inside government and other organisations, rather than by
elected political representatives or equality activists.

  While 'equal opportunities' is widely used to refer to a set of laws,
policies and practices, it is itself a contested definition, and may be
interpreted in many ways. It is frequently used as a useful shorthand to
encompass the range of procedures, actions and initiatives that have
evolved and developed, a usage that is reflected in the contributions to
this book. Additionally, through analysis of equality initiatives in the
UK, the book aims to contribute to a greater conceptual clarity concerning meanings of equal opportunities and related terms, and concerning the interrelationships between equality categories or identities.
It raises issues that are of relevance to audiences outside Britain and
engages with wider debates about the most appropriate legislative and
institutional frameworks for advancing gender and other equalities, the
role of policy machinery and policy development, and the part played
by political opportunity structures.

  Changes in institutional, political and economic contexts create specific political opportunity structures within which equalities politics
and practice operate and develop. Political will (or, indeed, political
won't) remains an important variable for equality politics which suggests that attention should be paid to formal politics as well as the
dynamics of organisational change and the informal politics of social
movements. Broadly speaking, all political parties in Britain have a
'stance' which is supportive of equality and equal opportunities (however defined and understood), although parties of the Right are least
likely to be proactive.

  Differences in definition and understanding do matter, however.
Almost as soon as equality legislation was put in place in Britain and
policy proposals had begun to be developed, the economic, political
and institutional terrain underwent a sea-change with the incoming
Conservative government of 1979. During the 1980s and 1990s
there were fundamental shifts in political discourses about welfare,

citizenship and the role of the state, and in thinking about the role and function of state bureaucracies. These shifts took place within a changed economic climate of public spending cuts and fiscal constraints. Clarke and Newman (1997) argue that during this period the liberal-welfarist postwar settlement was disrupted and a new (unstable) settlement constructed. These trends had important implications for gender relations and for equalities work, not least their marginalisation on the mainstream political agenda.

These system-level contexts and prevailing ideologies have shaped the contours and boundaries of equality debate, policy and practice in the UK. Dominant liberal values tend to a minimalist and procedural model of equal opportunities which focuses upon the individual rather than social groups. Equal opportunities in recruitment and career promotion has been the main focus of practitioner work, with an emphasis upon legal compliance, and formal rules and procedures. Equal treatment and formal equality has been supplemented by weak positive action for members of targeted groups. This is what Cockburn (1989) characterises as the 'short agenda' of equal opportunities in contrast to the 'long agenda' of social and organisational transformation. However, more radical and innovative policies have also been developed: this work around empowerment and service delivery has taken place at local rather than national level in the face of indifference, and sometimes hostility, of successive Conservative central governments between 1979 and 1997.

In addition to the influence of domestic government philosophy and discourses, the changes that have taken place in the European and international political sphere also impact upon equality policy at the various levels of government and on the politics of gender equality. For example, globalisation and increasingly complex forms of multi-level governance mean that equality politics, strategies and policies are played out in different but interconnecting levels of governance and varied institutional settings. Increasingly, campaigns by activists and policy initiatives by governments and other agencies have an international dimension: in this respect the United Nations has played a key role in facilitating international networks of NGOs and in encouraging states to take action through conventions, global conferences and platforms for action. At the European level, Teresa Rees (1998) underlines the increasing importance of the European Union as a site within which equalities concepts and strategies are contested, shaped and promoted. Within the UK, the relevant levels include national, devolved and local sites and involve state bureaucracies, public, private and voluntary sector organisations, political parties, trades unions, lobby groups, civil society organisations and social movements (see Ian Forbes' useful figure which sets out some of the levels, relevant actors and examples of issues p. 22).

Prior to constitutional reform in 1999, the UK could be characterised as a centralised state with power concentrated in the Westminster Parliament and the national government of the day. However, this pictures belies the degree of power which was geographically dispersed in practice. For example, significant administrative – if not political – devolution existed through the Offices of the Secretary of State for Scotland and the Secretary of State for Wales. During the troubled existence of Northern Ireland, the Province has experienced periods of both devolved government and Direct Rule from Westminster. At local level, although local government is a 'creature of statute' with no constitutional status, and its power and influence have steadily been eroded over the 1980s and 1990s, it retains a degree of policy discretion and some autonomy in respect of patterns of service provision and service delivery. In part this discretion and variety result from the political status and legitimacy of local government as another tier of directly elected government.

Gender equality and equal opportunities policy machinery have also existed at a discretionary level in local government. Women's Committees, Equal Opportunities Committees and Race Equality Committees – and their attendant specialist units and officers – have been an important site for the development and promotion of equality in the 1980s and 1990s and have been the focus of a number of academic studies (see, for example, Breitenbach and Mackay, 2001; Bruegel and Kean, 1995; Edwards, 1989, 1995; Halford, 1988, 1992; Lieberman, 1989; Lovenduski and Randall, 1993). They are an important institutional context within which a number of contributors to this volume discuss the achievements and failures of local equalities activism.

In some parts of the UK local government has demonstrated a structural capacity to institutionalise new demands for equality, has seen itself as a site for social justice, and has developed links with and supported feminist and other equality organisations. The ways in which there has been continual adaptation of the institutionalisation of these demands has provided the groundwork for a more generalised mainstreaming approach that, within a changed political climate, is being adopted in a widespread way. During a period in which there was an absence of central government commitment to enhancement and development of women's and other equality policy machinery, experience at local

government level has taught equality activists and practitioners many
of the lessons that have been learned at national level in other countries (see, for example, Stetson and Mazur, 1995).

Additionally, if we understand politics in a broad sense as relating to
sets of power relations and struggles over material resources and to discursive contests of meanings, categories and symbolic orders, then politics can be located in a variety of settings. There is agreement amongst
contributors to this collection about the political nature of gender
equality and equal opportunities projects more generally. However,
there are differences of focus emanating from different ideas about the
nature and form of politics and political action and differing conceptions of power. Some look primarily at the formal politics of political
parties and institutions, governments and states and mainstream political discourses; others focus upon the internal politics of bureaucracies
and organisations. The informal politics of community activism and
social movements is a third arena of importance (see, for example,
Bagguley and Hern, 1999; Chanan, 1992; Lovenduski and Randall,
1993) and is implicit in many of the discussions although not directly
addressed here. We suggest that each of these levels of politics is interconnected and that a multi-levelled and multi-layered approach allows
a greater understanding of the complexity of the 'equality project'.

Policy directions

Anti-discrimination legislation in the UK has been developing over a
period of more than thirty years, since the enactment of the first Race
Relations Act in 1965. The 1970s saw the enactment of equal pay and
sex discrimination legislation, and amendment of race relations legislation. In 1995 the Disability Discrimination Act became law. The need
to comply with European law has brought amendments to equal pay
and sex discrimination legislation and extended its scope, and
European Directives have enhanced the rights of women workers. A
range of other legislation also underpins gender equality and women's
rights, whether laws on social security and taxation embodying principles of equal treatment, laws on maternity rights and minimum wage
legislation which have improved the position of women in the labour
market, or remedies against sexual harassment and domestic violence
(see Bagilhole, 1997, for a 'map' of UK equalities legislation; and
Gregory, 1999, for an evaluation of this legislation). It is anticipated that
the incorporation of the European Convention on Human Rights into
British domestic law[2] and the commitment to equality of opportunity

embodied in the Treaty of Amsterdam, will have an impact on equal opportunities and equal rights, though it remains to be seen how extensive this will be.

UK equality legislation has been criticised for being both piecemeal and confusing, and as reflecting in part a minimalist and reactive approach to equality laws and European challenges, particularly during the Conservative governments of the 1980s and 1990s. It has been described as being rooted in liberal ideology, with a focus on the individual and the protection and enhancement of individual opportunities. Critics have argued that, given the limited scope of the legislation, it is hardly surprising that the changing gender balance at work, particularly at higher occupational levels, is so gradual, and that a substantial pay gap between men and women at all levels still persists. None the less, the existence of legislation, however limited, signals some form of commitment to values of equality of opportunity. It has provided a basis for the development of procedures and practices, and a platform from which further policy development and campaigning could take off.

A significant development in the late 1990s and 2000s has been the widespread acknowledgement of institutionalised racism following the publication of the Macpherson Report in 1999 on the murder of London teenager Stephen Lawrence and the subsequent conduct of the Metropolitan Police in investigating the crime.[3] While the inquiry had a specific focus, its findings have had a much wider significance. The Macpherson Report introduced the concept of *institutional racism* meaning that institutions have a collective responsibility for the failures arising out of direct and indirect discrimination, including prejudice, ignorance, thoughtlessness and racist stereotyping. Many of its recommendations have been seen as applicable to all institutions and public organisations throughout Britain and have led to significant rethinking of institutional practices. The concept is being further developed by some organisations to cover gender, disability and sexual orientation under the umbrella term, *institutional discrimination*.

Subsequent amendments have been made to race relations legislation which take on board key recommendations of the report. The Race Relations (Amendment) Act 2000 outlaws race discrimination in public bodies not previously covered by the 1976 Act. The Act also imposes a general duty on public bodies to work towards the elimination of unlawful discrimination and to promote equal opportunities and good race relations.

In Northern Ireland the legislation creating the Assembly (Northern Ireland Act 1998) has also imposed a duty on all public bodies to promote equality of opportunity. They are required to produce equality schemes, and to consult with relevant equality groups on these. These shifts can be interpreted as strengthening the focus on group disadvantage in both legislation and policy development.

In recent years mainstreaming gender equality has emerged as a dominant policy approach, and finds a powerful advocate in Teresa Rees, who also recognises that her vision is as yet far from the reality. Though not necessarily addressed explicitly by all contributors, it is clear that there is a range of views on mainstreaming, from scepticism to positive support. Mainstreaming is the approach currently favoured by the UN and the EU, and it has received government endorsement at national and devolved levels in the UK as well as support from relevant statutory equality agencies. Similarly, a generic approach to equal opportunities committees and units is also currently favoured in local government, though sometimes for cost-cutting reasons. The mainstreaming approach to gender equality is most advanced in Canada and the Nordic countries, and it can be argued that mainstreaming in its 'strong' version, defined as entailing a systematic inclusion of a range of groups, has much to offer (see Mackay and Bilton, 2000). However, it is not yet clear what this approach will deliver, nor to what extent it can adequately account for the range of groups that aspire to equality.

Rees has characterised the changing approaches of the EU in the past three decades as 'tinkering' (1970s), 'tailoring' (1980s) and 'transforming' (1990s), with the dominant focus of each decade being respectively, Equal Treatment, Positive Action and Mainstreaming. As she notes, equal treatment does not produce equal outcomes, and equal treatment legislation failed to make much impact on gender inequalities in pay. Criticisms of the limitations of this approach led to positive action measures. These in turn facilitated the development of networks of women's organisations, which helped to identify common structural problems facing women in the labour market. The mainstreaming approach to gender equality within the EU emerged together with a critique that labour market policies paid insufficient attention to gender inequalities as a cause of patterns of employment and unemployment, or to labour market developments and policies as productive of inequalities (Rees, 1998).

These successive policy approaches are also in evidence within a British context. Many of the contributions in the collection comment on the limitations of earlier approaches, but also caution against simply dismissing or discarding them. An 'equal treatment' legislative framework and positive action measures remain necessary, if limited, instruments for the promotion of equal opportunities. While there is a general pattern of evolution of policy development from a generic procedural approach within employment practices to a more complex and strategic approach which both recognises diversity and difference and attempts to change attitudes and cultures throughout organisations, these approaches have not necessarily meant a replacement of one by the other. Thus, equal opportunities employment policies coexist with 'managing diversity', and 'positive action' coexists with mainstreaming. Specific procedures and practices for taking action in relation to specific behaviours coexist with attempts to change attitudes and promote cultural change within organisations. Coexistence does not necessarily imply coherence, however, and there are tensions between both the analyses and the principles underlying different approaches.

Changing political, policy and organisational contexts have confronted equality practitioners and activists with a changing terminology of equal opportunities. 'Equality' and 'equal opportunities' are capable of many interpretations. To add to this fluidity of definition is the more recent discourse of social exclusion and inclusion. Again, concepts that have had their genesis in the EU have come to prominence in government policies aimed at tackling poverty and social inequalities, both at UK and devolved government level. This approach has also found favour within some local authorities. Critics, including Bagilhole, have argued that there is a danger of 'social exclusion' being too narrowly defined through a focus on labour market integration as the route to social inclusion. This poses particular problems for women, who have caring responsibilities and intermittent labour market participation, and for disabled people who may not be able to take up employment, or suffer exclusion as a result of discrimination.

A major tension in both discourses and principles of equality is between that of the individual and the group. A number of contributors have noted that the legislative framework and certain types of policy approaches are based upon an individualistic liberal ideology. By contrast there is a broad consensus among contributors that approaches that recognise group-based disadvantage and inequality should be favoured over approaches that focus on the individual and conceptions of individual merit that fail to recognise historical disadvantage, institutional discrimination and structural inequalities.

Though there is a broad consensus about the need to recognise the lack of homogeneity within and between groups, and that equal opportunities policies have to take account of these differences, there is less consensus in this collection about the commensurability of the objectives of different equality groups. Lewis argues that the active constitution of inequalities within organisations in everyday social interactions undermines an 'easy commensurability' of objectives amongst constituencies. A number of contributors argue that equality activists and practitioners should seek ways of creating new alliances and common ground, while recognising diversity and fluidity of identity, but it is also recognised that the creation of such alliances is fraught with difficulty and thus limits the capacity of equality practitioners to effect change.

Organisational change

A major focus of academic research has been the gendered nature of bureaucracy, and the scope for feminist interventions and those of other equality groups within state organisations (see, for example, Connell, 1987; Halford, 1992; Walby, 1997; Witz and Savage, 1992). Studies have investigated the success and failure of equal opportunities policies in changing the position of women and other groups within the workforce, and the impact of equal opportunities policies on service provision. Accounts of attempts to promote equal opportunities through the creation of bureaucratic structures and procedures agree that progress is uneven and that change is often contradictory in its effects. Gains have been made, but progress is often halting and slow, and reversals can also occur. Some of the reasons advanced for this are the incorporation of equality practitioners and 'femocrats' by bureaucracies, de-radicalisation and de-politicisation of equality agendas through institutionalisation, and the inherent tendency of bureaucracies, both governmental and non-governmental, to seek to manage consensus and risk and to render conflict illegitimate (Bruegel and Kean, 1995; Cockburn, 1991; Coyle, 1995; Stone, 1988). Similar themes and issues recur throughout this collection which is characteristic of the shift towards the professionalisation of equal opportunities.

A related debate centres on human resources strategies within both public and private sector organisations, within which the strategy of 'managing diversity' has been prominent (Jewson et al., 1995; Kandola and Fullerton, 1998; Kandola et al., 1995; Thomas, 1991). Mason (chapter 5) argues that in crossing the Atlantic, 'managing diversity' has developed a more individualistic approach, which poses the question as to whether a collective version of 'diversity' can be used to address problems of group disadvantage. Coyle (chapter 7) notes too, in her examination of the NHS, that employers' preferences for such approaches represent a move away from a focus on the position of particular groups, thus inhibiting recognition of gendered hierarchies within the NHS, which persist despite feminisation of the health professions. 'Managing diversity' is seen to go hand-in-hand with the 'new managerialism' that has penetrated public services in the 1980s and 1990s, with its emphasis on cost-efficiency and the adoption of business practices (Clarke and Newman, 1997).

Against this backdrop of new managerialism and new bureaucratic structures in the public sector is positioned a new set of political opportunities and threats in the form of the 'new' politics of the post-1997 Labour government. Whilst it can be argued that New Labour represents continuity in terms of economic policy, limited public spending and an attachment to market mechanisms, it represents change in terms of its explicit commitment to social justice and democratic renewal.

'New Politics' and opportunities for the equality project

The government's stated aim is to provide the kind of environment in which the economy can flourish while at the same time meeting social need. A related theme is concern to re-engage those who are alienated from the political process and to include the voices of those who are often unheard. This can be interpreted as a response to a perceived 'crisis of democracy' which is not confined to the UK, and which is tied up with concerns about lack of public engagement with politics and a decline in traditional forms of political participation. At the level of rhetoric at least, the government has indicated its desire to involve communities in decisions that affect their lives and to make public bodies more representative of the communities they serve – in short, to make politics more meaningful to ordinary people.

New vocabularies of democratic renewal and social justice have offered opportunities. Democratic renewal has provided feminist campaigners with leverage to improve the levels of women's representation in political institutions, both old and new (Brown, 1998). Constitutional change, leading to the restructuring of political systems, and to the creation of new levels or tiers of government, has created new possibilities for equalities work. High proportions of women were elected to both the Scottish Parliament and the Welsh Assembly. New equality policy and machinery has been established at central and devolved levels of government and a broad-based equalities agenda – relating to gender, race, disability, sexual orientation and other dimensions of difference – is emerging. In public life more generally, renewed efforts have been made through the offices of the Commissioner for Public Appointments to address the under-representation of women and other excluded groups in the community. The Equal Opportunities Commission has also added its weight and influence by endorsing the theme of widening participation in public life and proposing reforms to strengthen the legislative framework.

It is within these developments that the term 'new politics' has been conjured up. It is an umbrella term that tries to encapsulate a different approach to politics and the sharing of power in society with a view to engendering a more inclusive political culture. In the British context it has been extended to include reform of the House of Lords, the introduction of freedom of information legislation, the modernisation of parliament and the civil service, processes of constitutional change and the establishment of new institutions with their associated new electoral and parliamentary systems, and greater equality of representation for women and others.

Whilst the political climate for equalities has undoubtedly improved and new structural spaces have opened up, the question is asked about the extent to which there is continuity and to what degree different priorities and agendas can be discerned. In general, contributors express caution about the extent to which the Labour modernisation project offers substantive support for equalities, but many of the chapters also give a sense of fluidity: of there being things left to play for. Newman (chapter 6) argues that 'residual' meanings of equality dominate in current discourses and practices. Forbes asserts that the Labour leadership's vision of equality can be positioned at the minimalist end of the spectrum. Bagilhole points to the 'stigmatising practices' which emerge from social welfare reform. It is evident that, although there are certainly opportunities, there are also problems. In a climate in which interest groups are marginalised in favour of direct connection with 'the citizen', Forbes alerts us to the danger that the equal opportunities movement will be discounted as a 'sectional interest'. Newman also cautions that the 'public' has been reconstituted in a simplistic and homogenising way, with little sensitivity to gender, race or other dimensions of difference. Nevertheless, practitioners writing in this collection, such as Wright, Scott and Kelly, are cautiously optimistic about current developments, which are seen to provide new spaces in which to take work forward; on the other hand, academic assessments are generally more pessimistic.

There is, however, a common theme of the existence of both opportunities and dangers for equality practitioners and the 'equality project' more generally. There is simultaneously radical potential and the risk of minimalism, tokenism and containment. Ongoing struggles over meanings are crucial in this respect, and these discursive contests will, to some extent, shape the practical outcomes. So, for example, mainstreaming may develop into a managerial tool for managing consensus and provide an opportunity to disband specialist units, or it may present a means by which fundamental cultural change can be achieved in governments and other organisations, and new cultures of equality and diversity can be fostered. Similarly, democratic renewal may result in the minimal change needed to restore legitimacy to discredited political institutions, or may result in enhanced participation, access and voice.

The centrality of contests over meaning and categories is a feature of both practitioner accounts and academic discussions. A number of contributors draw upon the work of Bacchi (1996) who has described such contests as 'category politics'. Bacchi has coined the phrase 'category politics' to describe the central role of concepts and categories in political practice, particularly in respect of the relationship between politically mobilised social groups and the state. Such politics requires the use of identity categories (for example, 'black', 'women') and conceptual categories (for example, 'equality' and 'equal opportunities') to justify claims for access to political and other resources. She highlights the power of 'insiders' – mostly white men – to name, misname and rename for political purposes and the struggle between various actors to control the meaning of 'essentially contested concepts' such as equal opportunities. In this respect it is not the content of categories but rather the political significance of categories that is most important. Category politics is in a constant state of flux. This presents both opportunities and dangers for feminists and other equality activists: meanings can be appropriated and reappropriated in ways never intended by the original categorisers. The benefits and drawbacks of trying to 'fit' equalities into mainstream agendas and successive managerial fashions is illustrated in practitioner accounts in this collection.

Conclusions

The political nature of the equality 'project' is stressed time and time again in this collection, although the understanding of politics may differ. The depoliticisation of equalities work in the 1980s and 1990s as it became institutionalised is also generally accepted; and the relative inactivity of social movements and party political activists noted.

Many contributors argue there is a need for the re-politicisation of the equalities agenda. Some see the impetus coming from grassroots activism – through new social movements, workplace politics, political parties and community groups. Newman, for example, argues that there are enough groups with reason to contest current economic and socio-political 'settlements' to enable broad alliances and suggests trade unionists, anti-racist activists, women's movement groups and 'old' Labourites as potential allies.

These prescriptions for political action are tempered by concerns about the limits of collective action and widespread recognition that the very notion of group identity is itself problematic. There is uncertainty about the form political action might take at a time when the meaning, purpose and limits of collective politics and purposive political action have come under increasing theoretical scrutiny. At one level these postmodern preoccupations can seem to present an insuperable challenge to 'category politics', and to modernist rationalist approaches to the promotion of equal opportunities, and to preclude the possibility of sustained political action based on group identity. Related to this is the role of conflict and consensus in equality politics. At the conceptual level this is played out in different discussions about the meaning, possibility and desirability of consensus (seen as relating to outdated, overdeterministic 'modern' politics) versus contentions of the incommensurability of different differences and the implausibility of political consensus (seen as a postmodern approach to politics). At a practical level this is evident in debates about the possibility for alliances to be made by groups who may have conflicting needs and the scope for solidarity through difference.

Most contributors use elements of both modernist and postmodernist approaches: a case of modernist optimism tempered by postmodern pessimism. They concur with Forbes' position that the equal opportunities project can and has to incorporate elements of both modernist and postmodernist approaches, to be eclectic and pragmatic, and to avoid the extremes of either. For example, ideas with a universal application can be employed: that we share a human condition, and all have a claim to be free from harm and to enjoy human dignity. However, the need for understandings of equality as complex, contested and fluid is well acknowledged in this collection.

The implications for political action and practice are seen as less clear, and contributors are to varying degrees optimistic and pessimistic about the potential for solidarity through difference. Equality politics is played out at different and interconnected levels and in a variety of settings within a dynamic and complex process of social and political change which offers both opportunities and constraints and leaves many questions of the possibilities for progress towards greater equality for a range of groups unresolved. There are no easy answers or prescriptions and, overall, the collection gives both a strong sense of the possibilities for purposive political action and change as well as the potential for stalemate and uncertainty. To what extent such 'complex equality' can be embraced by the policy-making process is a challenging question. As Mason argues there is an inherent danger of 'ossification and reproduction of categories' that create exclusion, a dilemma which he regards as integral to the policy process. What does seem clear is that equality politics shares some of the characteristics of what Forbes describes as 'agonal politics': difficult, shifting, contested and provisional.

There are several threads that run through the book. Equal opportunities is viewed as a political project and the ways in which discourses, ideologies and organisational cultures seek to depoliticise it, represent a threat to the success of this project. This project is being advanced at multiple levels of governance in ways that are interrelated. Thus the political commitment demonstrated at these different levels, and the policy framework conditioning equal opportunities, combine to produce particular forms of activity at particular times, and may favour different sites of intervention at different points. Political and constitutional changes in Britain since 1997 have created new political opportunity structures for gender and other equality activists, and have widened the scope for intervention at different levels of governance. Discourses and definitions of equality and equal opportunities remain contested, and while the general climate may be more favourable for equality politics, resistance to change is likely to continue. Because there remains a need for a wider understanding of the complexity of the factors underpinning inequalities experienced by a range of groups in contemporary society, and a need for the development of effective alliances across a range of groups, the project of equality too often suffers from being reduced and contained, with its meaning being diluted and oversimplified. However, it is precisely because of this complexity that pursuit of equal opportunities goals can be multifaceted, and advanced differently within different contexts and organisations at different times. For this reason, despite the many shared understandings of the nature and meaning of the equality project evident in this book, assessments of the potential of current strategies and of future success vary widely.

Taken together, the contributions provide both a rich and stimulating account of the recent past and the fluid present and offer a provocative set of predictions and prescriptions about the future. This collection gives an insight into the specific evolution of the gender equality 'project' in a British context. However, it also relates to themes, concerns and dilemmas which are common to thinking and working in this area in many Western liberal democracies and at different governmental levels. The meanings of equality, the types of demands made by different groups of women, and by men and women in marginalised groups, and the political processes seen as appropriate to the creation of greater equality are thus in a state of flux. Equality activists and practitioners and academic commentators at least share a position that will refuse a bland and reductionist version of equal opportunities, or that will be satisfied with superficiality or token gestures. The challenge, therefore, is to take these complex understandings of equality into the political arena in such a way that they can be better understood, and equality more fully realised.

Summary of chapters

There follows a brief outline of chapters. Chapters 2 to 5 focus upon developments within the context of the national or supranational. They discuss political and policy frameworks, debates and discourses, and equal opportunities practices and policies within both public and private sectors. Chapters 6 to 8 focus on the level of the organisation. They analyse the dynamics of and obstacles to change within organisations – in this case all public sector organisations, but ones into which 'new managerialist' practices have been imported from the private sector. We end with the local level. Chapters 9 to 11 examine experience at local level, namely local government initiatives on equal opportunities, and offer a practitioner perspective on evaluations of success and failure and prospects for the future.

Ian Forbes (chapter 2) argues that the pursuit of equal opportunities is an irredeemably political project, and examines the factors which condition its success as such, including the nature of political regimes, dominant discourses of rights and dominant political ideologies, and political opportunity structures. Combining elements of modernist and postmodernist perspectives on equal opportunities, he argues for an appreciation of a concept of complex equality within political fora, a concept which of necessity will have to be fought over and for.

Teresa Rees (chapter 3) provides an account of the emergence of mainstreaming equality as the dominant policy approach within the EU, the limitations of previous generations of equal opportunities policies which mainstreaming aims to overcome, and the potential this approach might have for building gender equality into the operation of different levels of governance.

Barbara Bagilhole (chapter 4), noting the changing conceptualisations of 'equal opportunities', offers a critique of the concept of 'social exclusion', which originated from the EU and has become prominent as a way of framing equality and anti-poverty policies at central, devolved and local government levels. Too narrow a definition of 'social exclusion' can be stigmatising and divisive, in particular through a focus on paid work and labour market integration as a solution to exclusion. Conversely, she argues, a broader definition of social exclusion can facilitate recognition of diversity and alliances between groups.

David Mason (chapter 5) offers a critical analysis of the approach of 'managing diversity' and the particular ways in which it has been adopted within a British context, illustrating the tensions between an individual and a group focus. Though perceptions of group difference can be based on stereotyping, a collective version of 'diversity' can be used to address problems of group disadvantage, whereas the individualist version focuses only on the empowerment of individuals.

Janet Newman (chapter 6) discusses the impact of 'new managerialist' practices and discourses on equal opportunities, showing its contradictory consequences for equality issues and inadvertent consequences in providing opportunities for women and ethnic minorities. Though 'new managerialism' has by no means wholly displaced older welfarist ideologies, its continuing prominence within public sector organisations, for Newman indicates a future of marginalisation of equal opportunities.

Angela Coyle (chapter 7) scrutinises organisational change within the NHS, concluding that women are already marginalised within new decision-making structures, and that rather than leading to a significant shift in power relations between women and men organisational change has only altered the ways in which gender relations are expressed. The NHS in particular has suffered from the lack of a strategic alliance of women constructed around a common purpose, and has not been the focus of 'grass-roots' feminist or race equality activism or cultural challenge.

Gail Lewis (chapter 8), drawing on her analysis of relationships within organisations at the micro-social level, shows how inequalities are actively constituted and reproduced within organisations, as well as reflecting the inequalities apparent in social relations outside organisations. This process whereby individuals position and reposition themselves as subordinate or dominant in relation to others undermines the capacity for solidarity and alliance between different groups with claims to equality.

Marion Scott (chapter 9) charts the changing attitudes to women's units in local government, and the changing emphasis over time of the work of such units. She underlines the capacity of women's units to adapt and to make use of opportunities, arguing that women's units in many local authorities have responded creatively to the changing local government agenda. None the less developments such as mainstreaming may be double edged, and may be used by managers to depoliticise equalities work, and thus mainstreaming is afforded only a cautious welcome.

Mandy Wright (chapter 10) assesses the achievements of equalities practitioners in local government, surveying the evidence of decrease in the gender pay gap and decrease in gender segregation within occupations in local government, and the increase in the proportion of councillors who are women. While the overall picture may be one of slow progress, she argues that local government demonstrates enormous variability, from a minimalist tokenistic stance towards equal opportunities to a maximalist position where strategies of managing diversity and mainstreaming are being effectively implemented.

Ellen Kelly (chapter 11) discusses the opportunities offered to equalities practitioners by the introduction of 'Best Value' regimes into local government, in particular the stress on quality of service provision, and the need for authorities to evaluate users' views of services. Both these foci may prove helpful in allowing equality groups and communities of interest to put forward the case for the integration of their needs into the framework of service delivery in local government. Given that Best Value is being developed in a wider context of support for mainstreaming of equality from devolved and central government, and that knowledge of equal opportunities is more widespread than in the early 1980s when equal opportunities initiatives in local government first started up, Kelly concludes that equalities practitioners might reasonably be hopeful about outcomes.

Notes

1. The editors gratefully acknowledge support from the Economic and Social Research Council for funding the seminar series *Gender and the Local State* which ran from 1997 to 1998.

2. The Human Rights Act 1998 became effective in England and Wales from October 2000. All legislation passed by the Scottish Parliament since its inception in 1999 has had to comply with the European Convention of Human Rights.
3. The inquiry chaired by Sir William Macpherson was commissioned by the Home Office in response to allegations of racism within the Metropolitan Police Force in its investigation of the racist murder in South London of black teenager Stephen Lawrence in 1993. It found that 'the investigation was marred by a combination of professional incompetence, institutional racism and a failure of leadership by senior officers' (Macpherson, 1999: para. 46.1).The Race Relations (Amendment) Act 2000 fulfils a recommendation made in the Macpherson Report and represents a significant strengthening of race equality legislation.

References

Bacchi, C.L. (1996), *The Politics of Affirmative Action: 'Women', Equality and Category Politics*, London: Sage.

Bagguley, P. and Hern, J. (eds) (1999), *Transforming Politics: Power and Resistance*, Basingstoke: Macmillan.

Bagilhole, B. (1997), *Equal Opportunities and Social Policy*, Harlow: Longman.

Breitenbach, E. and Mackay, F. (2001), 'Keeping Gender on the Agenda – the Role of Women's and Equal Opportunities Initiatives in Local Government in Scotland', in Breitenbach and Mackay (eds) *Women and Contemporary Scottish Politics: An Anthology*, Edinburgh: Polygon.

Brown, A. (1998), 'Deepening Democracy: Women and the Scottish Parliament', *Regional and Federal Studies*, Vol. 8, No. 1, Spring.

Bruegel, I. and Kean, H. (1995), 'The Moment of Municipal Feminism: Gender and Class in 1980s Local Government', *Critical Social Policy*, No. 44/45, Autumn.

Chanan, G. (1992), *Out of the Shadows. Local Community Action and the European Community*, Dublin: European Foundation for the Improvement of Living and Working Conditions.

Clarke, J. and Newman, J. (1997), *The Managerial State*, London: Sage.

Cockburn, C. (1989), 'Equal Opportunities: The Short and Long Agenda', *Industrial Relations Journal*, Vol. 20.

Cockburn, C. (1991), *In the Way of Women*, Basingstoke and London: Macmillan.

Connell, W. (1987), *Gender and Power: Society, The Person and Sexual Politics*, Stanford: Stanford University Press.

Coyle, A. (1995), *Women and Organizational Change*, Discussion Series No. 14, Manchester: Equal Opportunities Commission.

Edwards, J. (1989), 'Local Government Women's Committees', *Critical Social Policy*, No. 24, Winter.

Edwards, J. (1995), *Local Government Women's Committees*, Aldershot: Avebury.

Gregory, J. (1999), 'Revisiting Sex Equality Laws', in S. Walby (ed.) *New Agendas for Women*, Basingstoke: Macmillan.

Halford, S. (1988), 'Women's Initiatives in Local Government: Where Do They Come from and Where Are They Going?', *Policy and Politics*, Vol. 16, No. 4.

Halford, S. (1992), 'Feminist Change in a Patriarchal Organization: the Experience of Women's Initiatives in Local Government and Implications for Feminist Perspectives on State Institutions', in A. Witz and M. Savage (eds) *Gender and Bureaucracy*, Oxford: Blackwell.

Jewson, N., Mason D., Drewett, A. and Rossiter, W. (1995), *Formal Equal Opportunities Policies and Employment Best Practice*, Department for Education and Employment, Research Series No. 69, London: DfEE.

Kandola, R. and Fullerton, J. (1998), *Diversity in Action: Managing the Mosaic*, London: Institute of Personnel and Development.

Kandola, R., Fullerton, J. and Ahmed, Y. (1995), 'Managing Diversity: Succeeding where Equal Opportunities have Failed', *Equal Opportunities Review*, No. 59, January/February, pp. 31–6.

Lieberman, S. (1989), 'Women's Committees in Scotland', in A. Brown and D. McCrone (eds) *The Scottish Government Yearbook*, Edinburgh: University of Edinburgh.

Lovenduski, J. and Randall, V. (1993), *Contemporary Feminist Politics: Women and Power in Britain*, Oxford: Oxford University Press.

Mackay, F. and Bilton, K. (2000), *Lessons from Experience: Lessons in Mainstreaming Equal Opportunities*, Edinburgh: Governance of Scotland Forum, University of Edinburgh.

Macpherson, Sir W. (1999), The Stephen Lawrence Inquiry, Home Office, Cm 4262-I.

Rees, T. (1998), *Mainstreaming Equality in the European Union*, London: Routledge.

Stetson, D. M. and Mazur, A. (eds) (1995), *Comparative State Feminism*, London, Sage.

Stone, I. (1988), *Equal Opportunities in Local Authorities*, London: HMSO.

Thomas, R. Roosevelt, Jr. (1991), *Beyond Race and Gender: Unleashing the Power of Your Total Workforce by Managing Diversity*, New York: AMACOM, American Management Association.

Walby, S. (1997), *Gender Transformations* London: Routledge

Witz, A. and Savage, M. (1992), *Gender and Bureaucracy*, Oxford: Blackwell.

2
The Political Meanings of the Equal Opportunities Project

Ian Forbes

This chapter critically explores the equal opportunities project in the context of an apparent decline in the salience of equal opportunities as a creative and purposive policy orientation. This context is shaped by challenges to the contemporary relevance of equality of opportunity, changes to political structures and practices, developments in the theoretical underpinnings of equal opportunities practice and public initiatives in relation to women and social justice. In order to understand both the current situation and the forces that will shape the future, the political meanings of the equal opportunities project are analysed first in terms of the strengths and weaknesses of modernist accounts of political reality, and second as a conflict between modernist and postmodernist approaches to politics. Given the prospects for the equal opportunities project, a generic approach to equality of opportunity is proposed as a means of responding to the erosion of equal opportunities as a political project.

The pursuit of equal opportunities is an irredeemably political enterprise. As an enterprise that requires commitment and activity in both the public and private realms, it invites political analysis common to other areas of resource allocation and distribution. However, equality of opportunity also problematises the foundations of political analysis, since the equal opportunities project is an important site of contestation for the meaning of politics, for the goals of politics and for the possibilities for political action.

At the theoretical level, equality of opportunity plays host to all the key debates around the grand themes of justice and equality, and involves the deployment of various interpretive political theories and analytical tools. In practical terms, equal opportunities is also intensely political and politicised. This is also true of the existing political context, or political opportunity structure, within which the politics of the equal opportunities project is played out. The nature of any regime heavily constrains the way that equal opportunities can be political and can be pursued. Most of the proponents (and analysts) of equal opportunities live in a stable political order characterised by a modern state system, representative government and a liberal rule of law, accompanied by a civil society dominated by capitalist property relations, Judaeo-Christian morality, and patriarchal and familial social relations. At the level of public policy, this gives rise to a distinct set of questions about and meanings of the political, ranging from law-making, to institution-building and to practical policies, as well as symbolic orders, discursive realms and political activity, with all the attendant assumptions about people and power that are entailed.

   Within this, conceptions of the political are employed at every turn, but these very conceptions of the political are brought into question principally because equality of opportunity means a commitment to a particular kind of change. Indeed, this change agenda of equal opportunities animates and makes political every aspect of equal opportunities. At the very least, it exposes the contradictions within existing political orders, reveals that political concerns are not confined to the public domain and shows that 'the private' is an arena for debates, ranging from privacy to the private sector and to privatisation.

Political approaches to equality of opportunity

Thus equality of opportunity has political ramifications within the formal and informal, the public and the private, and the state and civil domains of politics, and manages to problematise those domains. Enmeshed at every turn and at every level in the intricacies of political, economic and social reality, the politics of equal opportunities is played out at sites that range from the international stage to the individually private interaction. Table 2.1 shows these sites, with indications of the organisations that are active at each level and examples of the kinds of issues that are on the different agendas.

   Within this extensive range of equal opportunities politics, recurring themes and concerns are observable. These reflect the confluence of the universality of key aspects of the situation of women throughout the world, the political structures and processes that are available to deal with (or ignore) them and the differing approaches to equality politics itself. For example, a concern with 'rights' appears at a number of levels. These 'rights' may be in respect of individuals, and derive

Table 2.1   The sites of equal opportunities policies

Political level	Organisations	Examples of issues
International Society	United Nations, International non-governmental organisations	International human rights, Rape as a war crime
The Region	European Union, North American Free Trade Association	Human rights, Refugees, Asylum, Social dumping
The State	Constitution, Law, The justice system	Equality and representation
Government	Executive, Legislature, Administration, Equality commissions	Representation, Reproductive choice, Employment equality
Party Politics	Political parties, The 300 Group	Participation, Representation and power
Pressure Groups, Social Movements	Feminist movement, National Organisation of Women	Civil rights, Identity, Liberation, Empowerment
The Civil Sector	Voluntary sector, Non-governmental organisations, Schools	Social justice, Social exclusion and equal chances
The Private Sector	Industry and finance	Glass ceilings and walls, Child care, Equal pay
The Public Realm	Central and local states, Media	Personal safety, Pornography, Access
The Private Realm	The family, Relationships	Domestic violence, Rape in marriage, Sexuality, Child care

from a liberal legal discourse. However, they may equally be framed within a collectivist tradition, and refer to the social and economic rights of groups and peoples rather than individuals. This means that it is important to support the knowledge that the equal opportunities project is political with a grasp of the political approaches that actively seek to construct our understanding of and dictate policies for the project. Table 2.2 gives a representation of the major ideological positions. Although the table identifies three positions, there is in practice a considerable degree of overlap along a bounded spectrum of possibilities. Excluded are the positions that oppose equality of opportunity in any

Table 2.2   Political dimensions of equal opportunities

Ideological disposition	Conservative	Liberal	Radical
Values	Hierarchy and stability	Liberty and endeavour	Equality and empowerment
Precept	Meritocracy	Diversity	Difference
Change	Equal treatment = equality of opportunity	Equal treatment and equal access = equality of opportunity	Equal outcome = equality of opportunity
Public Policy	Non-specific (gender-'blind') law, Pro-family law and 'free' markets allowing private initiatives	Specific equality rights law, Improved access and education	Specific group equality and anti-discrimination law, Re-education, Compensation, Redistribution
Policy Process	Persuasion, Market forces and individual action	Individual action Equality institutions monitored and backed by the state	Group action, Equality institutions, Public responsibility Direct state intervention
Change Agencies	Individuals and firms	Individuals, Government agencies	Government and its agencies Groups
Protest and Influence	Elite lobbying	Lobbying of Government Political entryism	Direct action

form and those that advocate violence or propose apartheid to achieve political ends.

A number of crucial antinomies underpin the choices facing the equal opportunities practitioner: methodological individualism versus methodological holism; rights versus entitlement; *laissez-faire* versus intervention; and equal treatment versus equal outcome. Unsurprisingly, it is not a simple matter to map party political positions onto the three-way division set out above. First, parties are comprised of groups that take diametrically opposed views on gender equality, and the policy stance will vary according to the strength and effectiveness of those groups. Second, the policy implications, in terms of immediate economic cost and political risk, vary significantly, especially in relation to state intervention and equality of outcome. This can also prompt a caution that is indistinguishable from conservatism in governments with otherwise liberal and radical credentials. By contrast, a commitment to the free market can be as radically corrosive on an hitherto entrenched privilege as any explicit governmental intervention.

Nevertheless, the three approaches outlined in Table 2.2 do provide some broad insights. Radical approaches derive strength from more closely reflecting the demands of women's pressure groups and seeking to find ways to actualise the values of equality and empowerment. The radical predisposition to accept the necessity of structural as well as processural change to achieve outcomes, however, can increase the possibility of social and political conflict, impose costs on a new set of 'losers' and be prohibitively expensive. By contrast, the conservative is prepared to acknowledge the need for fair and equal treatment within the confines of a valid existing order, and will devote time and energy to persuade employers, for example, to recognise merit regardless of sex. No responsibility is accepted for a continuing structural inequality that is in effect strengthened by the minor changes that result. The liberal approach is the most popular with government, since there is considerable scope for laws that instantiate formal equality, for a reliance on the liberating potential of education and individual achievement and for the persuasive efforts of equality commissions. This approach is also limited by a reluctance to countenance policies that favour groups over individuals or to consider fundamental structural change.

Knowledge about the ways that equal opportunities are political and politicised does contribute to our understanding. What is needed further is a political analysis that illuminates and assists in the primary task of developing that understanding in order to facilitate the efforts to change the world. This seems a tall order in the light of the preceding account of the many facets of politics. An additional complication arises through the existence of more than one way to conduct political analysis. In the remainder of this chapter, we examine two analytical approaches that compete for our attention and favour and present us with political choices. Broadly speaking, the approaches are modernist and postmodernist. These, in my view, are not rigidly defined terms that delineate mutually exclusive terrains of political reality and analysis. Rather, they are here regarded as portmanteau terms that allow contrasts and comparisons to be made between two distinct sets of analytic as well as descriptive propositions about politics.

The dominance of political modernism

Most people engaged in the equal opportunities project use a modernist frame of reference (Collins, 1992; Mithaug, 1996; Roemer, 1998). This includes proponents, practitioners and critics of equal opportunities in a liberal society. When I have used the modernist frame, I have tended to think in terms of three broad arenas, namely principles, prescriptions and processes. Without a principles base, there would be no motivation to develop and pass prescriptive laws; without processes to carry out the legislative intent and enforce compliance with the prescriptions, the outcome would be abject failure. On reflection, I see a further dimension. As well as principles, prescriptions and processes, there are people. These include claimants for and distributors of vital resources, supporters of the equal opportunities project, and those disadvantaged by oppression and discrimination.

This account reflects a modernist interpretation, in that it sees politics as 'the constrained use of social power' (Goodin and Klingemann, 1996: 7). Within that notion of politics, equal opportunities can be understood in terms of the models that have been advanced by thinkers and within distinct policy frameworks. In other words, the 'nature and sources of constraints' and 'the techniques for the use of social power' within those constraints can be analysed. This has been somewhat in parallel to the work of Nick Jewson and David Mason (1986), in particular the way that they drew out some of the conceptual antinomies of equal opportunities policies and produced the minimalist/maximalist axis as a means of understanding. Looking again at this area, I am struck by the changes that have taken place and which, to some extent, have overtaken earlier analyses. The battles to get equal opportunities on to the political and administrative agenda are now supplanted by debates between experienced equal opportunities professionals on implementation strategy and best practice, especially in regard to service delivery. Also, the collectivist tenor of radical approaches has lost cogency (and therefore influence) in a post-Fordist world of temporary part-time work for women, the spread of privatisation and the lurch toward new public management. Activists have themselves redefined the nature of collective action by deserting the fora of formal politics in favour of new social movements and single-issue politics. In the process, they have developed new themes and directions associated with difference and cultural relativism that present new challenges to the social and political order, even as it undergoes significant change. To observe this is to be reminded of the fascination of equal opportunities. It is an area that cannot easily be dismissed, as some seek to do, as straightforward and uninteresting.

Considered from a theoretical and public policy perspective, all the ideological approaches to equal opportunities reflect the same modernist framework. Politics, when it is foregrounded, is seen as the rational pursuit of general goals (often sponsored by parties and their affiliates) through the possession of government power and through the agency of an instrumental and objective administration. However limited one might find such a view of politics, this account does permit us to identify key actors, and these political actors certainly behave as if this view of politics is accurate and can produce results. It is also clear that there are real resources at stake, and that there are separate levels of political action (see Table 2.1).

Throughout a political system so described, party political activity is in general accordance with standard ideological frameworks, leading to preferences for some interpretations and solutions over others. Administrations occupy a distinct realm and operate according to known rules and practices. Some people can choose to be participants in this accessible and publicly accountable process. Official lobbying organisations will offer knowledge and expertise for paid political work to exercise influence in the interests of business and industry. Voluntary organisations will use exactly the same techniques on behalf of others whose needs are for protection and recognition. This political system can be 'understood' by the public, permitting the mobilisation of bias and resource mobilisation, and sometimes the public might even get what it wants.

This modernist version of the political as the rational pursuit of general goals through established political and administrative mechanisms has it strengths. Seen this way, there is a formal political opportunity structure, with established loci of power, well-trodden routes around the structure, recognised modes of communication and entreaty, pivotal actors and a set of possibilities constrained by political orientations, legislative frameworks, funding cycles, climates of opinion and expectation and the electoral cycle. This conventional view does not entail a particularly static view of politics, since change can occur in any element, with sometimes dramatic shifts in the overall political opportunity structure. New leaders – when they bring a different ethos – can have a significant impact on the political opportunity structure. For example, the neoliberal social conservatism of Margaret Thatcher and Ronald Reagan respectively displaced Britain's postwar consensus on social welfare and undermined America's long commitment to affirmative action. The public, or more specifically interest groups, are supplicants in this structure. They choose how to engage at any one time, and their success will be in part dependent on their skills, information and timing. Just as US elections are accompanied by wholesale changes to the governing elite, the change of government in Britain in 1997 had a dramatic effect on the political opportunity structure for women, and for constitutional reformers. Suddenly, different forms of knowledge, interpretations and ideas can be in demand, validating alternative views and turning previously excluded groups of activists or academics into insiders and official 'experts'. In the British case, the movement for constitutional reform incorporated the drive for improved participation and representation of women, demonstrating that political activity can be worthwhile if it can be sustained even when the political opportunity structure is adverse.

This reading of the political has been an important one for equal opportunities. It bespeaks a Weberian state exemplified by its bureaucratic structures and processes, with official jurisdictional areas wherein important social relations are regulated by rules and laws. Underlying this is the idea that such a state represents progress, since it embodies systems that stand in 'extreme contrast to the regulation of relationships through individual privileges and bestowals of favour' (Weber, 1970: 198). This describes a shift from pre-modern ways of conceiving of social relations to the modern, where deliberative action is based on an appreciation of a fundamental equality between humans and the appropriateness of reason. In the face of pre-modernist practice, and in the context of a choice between the pre-modern and the modern approach, it is to be expected that equal opportunities practitioners will align themselves with this kind of modernism, and see that approach as an advance. After all, individual privileges and bestowals of favour are confronted by equal opportunities practitioners every day as problems to overcome. Associated with this preference for modernist conceptions of social relations is a substantial acceptance that the means to tackle these practices often involves rules and procedures that are bureaucratic in nature. Bureaucracy in this sense is a bulwark against the private deals, nepotism and arbitrary decisions that characterised pre-modernism. These advantages are set against the problems with bureaucracies, such as resistance to change and dilution of policy aims. This is a politics that permits progress by rational means towards agreed and universal goals. For many equal opportunities proponents, it is a politics that is patently worth engaging in, especially when the political opportunity structure is amenable. When it is not, then efforts can be made to change the structure, change access tactics or prepare for a change that is seen as inevitable.

The common ground for all these positions is a procedural approach to equality of opportunity, based on a simple or formal view of equality between the nature of women and men and a liberal view of justice within a stable structure of authority and hierarchy. To reiterate Weber's contrast between the modern and pre-modern state, this common ground represents progress defined as improving the life chances of disadvantaged groups and a fairer and more transparent allocation of resources, goods and services. It is unsurprising, therefore, that this low level of equality of opportunity has become embedded in the modernist body politic, and enjoys steady levels of public support. It is now a middle-ground issue that cannot be ignored. So this understanding of equality of opportunity has attained a certain respectability and status within the modernist frame of reference. 'Modernisers' in politics regard support for this version of equality of opportunity as routine, as beyond the need for debate or defence. This kind of equality of opportunity serves as a badge of right thinking in relation to women, ethnic minorities and disabled people. It is a 'common' equality of opportunity.

The political limits of modernist equality of opportunity

However, equality of opportunity has elements that are not accepted in the middle ground. The clearest example of this is the way that arguments have notoriously and tediously raged over quotas for most of the twentieth century. Also, the minimalist/maximalist dichotomy is continuously rehearsed not just between but also within established ideological positions. These arguments, however, should not disguise the fundamentally modernist nature of this politics of equal opportunities. In modernist politics, the equal opportunities project is conducted as a search for consensus. Consensus is sought via reasoned communication, where reliance is placed on the force of the better argument. Affirmative action, as a means to achieve equality of opportunity, provides a good example of this claim.

Affirmative action involving quotas and elements of compensatory justice is a controversial proposal, one capable of dividing even those groups on whose behalf this policy might be introduced (Bacchi, 1996; Cahn, 1995). It threatens the existing consensus enjoyed by common equality of opportunity, exposes the lack of consensus on changes that will produce many new winners and some new losers, and makes a consensus difficult if not impossible to build between those with very different ideological predispositions. Essentially contested ideas like liberty and equality are counterposed in such a way that they become associated with antagonistic, irreconcilable policies. Liberty rules out intervention in favour of groups and renders equal opportunities policies powerless against inequality, while equality insists upon intervention that must offend against powerful versions of natural justice and individual rights. Rather than address the efficacy of affirmative action policies, affirmative action itself becomes the site for ideological last stands, locking in those who count the commitment more important than anything else, and alienating many others.

Thus the political argument is not about affirmative action, or compensatory justice, or liberty, or state intervention or efficiency, or about equal treatment versus equal outcome. The underlying issue is the possibility of consensus over a public policy. The consensus model seeks agreement reached after communication, negotiation and compromise. All parties to the agreement are regarded as committed. Modernist proponents of affirmative action are divided into maximalists and minimalists on a number of scales, including the basis of the type of consensus they seek, the threshold for the perception of consensus, the identification of the relevant parties to a consensus, and the duration and scale of threats to or an absence of consensus.

This, however, is not everyone's idea of equal opportunities, of politics, or of the way forward. In fact, this modernist view of politics has a geography containing the dominating features of big government, formal institutions, mass parties, fixed ideological points on the compass and a limited range of policy options. The public is regarded as an undifferentiated whole, subject to macro-policies based on universalising assumptions about needs that can be satisfied by a combination of government action and economic growth. Political activity is a competition for scarce resources, with plural inputs leading to broadly plural outputs within a set of rational procedures to deliver just and legitimated outcomes.

Implied in the modernist view is a conception of a strong and effective state that is served by this form of politics. However, as Gerald Clarke (1998: 50) has pointed out, the countermobilisation of pressure groups and voluntary organisations is a direct demonstration of the 'shortcomings of state performance'. Using the insights of Migdal's *Strong Societies and Weak States* (1998), he has observed in modern states 'a duality of state strength', whereby the penetration of society by the state is nothing short of extensive, but the power to produce goal-oriented change seems much diminished. This insight into the capacity of states resonates with attempts to achieve equality of opportunity goals. Successive surveys and analyses of women's position in society, of racist behaviour and of discrimination against disabled people show that government aspirations are not matched by significant progress. When we add to this insight the claim by Fitzpatrick (1995: 699) that there is an 'old politics', where 'power wielded by governments is ever more divorced from the interests and demands of ordinary people', it is possible to conclude that state capacity is characterised by a matrix of effectivity and inability that is not reflected in government assumptions concerning political demands and the ability to deliver policies to meet them.

How does equality of opportunity fit into this analysis? Is it a goal that cannot be achieved, and is it still relevant to the expressed interests of the people? John Schaar's (1967) classic criticism of equal opportunities remains persuasive to many observers. He argued that it had no useful impact on inequality, but served only to reinforce the status quo. His account attaches blame to the inadequacy of the concept and its practice. It is argued here, however, that it is the concept of the political that may be inadequate.

Clarke's (1998) two explanations of the politics of change and the state may offer an additional way of understanding the endurance of a concept apparently so flawed. If we adopt de Tocqueville's perspective on the nature and purposes of politics, political engagement is its own virtue for the self and for others. We need the constant articulation and representation of political interests, in order to have our political demands mediated and for the political order to be sustained. Political activity itself is important, regardless of the issue or objective. On this reading, equal opportunities is the kind of idea that can come to the rescue of the problem of the modern state. Equal opportunities is much more than a political policy to achieve a sectional interest. It offers a means of political engagement for generalisable social ends. By drawing activists into the political realm, it strengthens civil society through practical involvement of citizens with the mechanisms of interest articulation and representation. These are political goods in themselves, and are attached to worthwhile political goals. In brief, the pursuit of equal opportunities is capable of animating both actors and processes. Inequality may not be comprehensively eradicated, as Schaar requires, but progress will be made, leaving a strengthened polity wherein further political activity is possible. This analysis has purchase at all levels, from international action through to local politics.

A Gramscian perspective, however, sees politics very differently. For Gramsci, structure is more important than process. Rather than a set of processes, politics is regarded as 'the manifestation of systemic contradictions' (Fitzpatrick, 1995: 703). Gramsci was critical of political activity that would institutionalise existing patterns of social contestation. He also thought it possible but undesirable, on the whole, to add to his pithy list of political dimensions and demands (class hegemony, equality, social justice). In Gramscian terms, the equal opportunities project – whatever its merits – is likely to be a burden on consciousness rather than a progressive force. The problem for Gramsci is that the fundamental struggle in relation to class is always in danger of being obscured by minor concerns (for example, gender equality). Equal opportunities can be seen to add to the burdens of understanding and action for those seeking real (i.e. structural) change to the major pillars of an unequal society.

If Gramsci's account is followed, then Schaar's (1967) conclusions hold: that the equal opportunities project has been successful in articulating and representing interests, much in the way the de Tocqueville would have approved, but at the cost of diverting political awareness and energies from the systemic sources of inequality. This still represents something of a success, in modernist terms, since institutions and practices have been manipulated to bring about piecemeal progress in relation to at least some of the symptoms of systemic contradictions. At base, however, it is a self-defeating exercise, and according to followers of Schaar's argument (for example, Baker, 1987), it should be abandoned, at least by those with a serious intention to address inequality.

There are many who disagree with Gramsci's attempt to keep the political agenda relatively free of elements that are not strongly linked to class analysis. Others think that the state, whatever its problems, can be used to make further progress. Philip Nanton (1995), for example, argues that successful equal opportunities implementation is really a matter of social regulation. The modernist reading of his argument is that there is more to the politics of equal opportunities than political manoeuvring for resource mobilisation and emancipatory legislation. There are mechanisms of social control that are appropriate and constructive, that will allow us to achieve the long-term aims of structural and cultural change. This relies upon 'the notion of a public good' (Nanton, 1995: 209) in order to justify subjecting people to deterrence and compliance.

Nanton is proposing social regulation as a means of producing changes in the deep-seated sources of discrimination, and suggesting the means to do it. In other words, individuals are treated as a means to the public good end, and the state is relied upon to bring it about. On the social regulation issue, it is instructive to consider Elshtain's

(1992) remarks on the general dangers of modernist management in the contemporary state:

> Highly institutionalised forms of government, increasingly bureau-cratised and dominated by technologies that facilitate centralized control, daily erode space for genuine political action, for beginning something anew, for creating and sustaining social forms that allow human beings to be at home in the world. (Elshtain, 1992: 118)

By implication, social regulation becomes more about state control and less about the political intention that led to it, and ultimately makes the world worse. Furthermore, it would tend to lock into place the prevailing perception of equality of opportunity and privilege only some of the existing claimant groups. In any event, she points out that since 'war is immanent within the form of the modern nation-state' (Elshtain, 1992: 118), it is a strange choice of apparatus to use in the pursuit of equality goals.

Policy promise and implementation failure

Political analysis of the infrastructure of the modern state further undermines any predilection for relying on the power of the state and the belief in rational, achievable solutions to the political project of equal opportunities. Public administration has been seen as a vehicle specially devised on sound Weberian and Millian principles of rational-ity, organisation, efficiency and accountability. Its purpose was system-atically and impartially to steer the implementation of macro-political equal opportunities policies agreed at the centre of the political appara-tus. Rather than a fine-tuned vehicle for the smooth implementation of universalist public policies, public administration has become a vehicle that is very costly to operate, has a habit of stalling, works only under quite restricted circumstances and is increasingly unsuited to a dramati-cally changed social and political terrain. In late modernity, public administration needs instead the characteristics of a versatile off-road vehicle. Peters and Wright (1996: 630 *passim*) have sketched out charac-teristic elements of the new political geography with which public administration must negotiate. They reveal that two principal changes have undermined the modernist model of public administration.

In the first place, privatisation, competition and subcontracting have eroded the single base for implementation enjoyed by the classical mode of public administration. This means that the *self-sufficiency* of public administration has ended, since it is no longer the monopoly supplier of the public good (the converse of the state as legitimately having the monopoly of coercive authority). *Uniformity* is another casualty of the development of modernism (perhaps it should be regarded as its realisation). There is no longer an equal sharing of burdens and benefits, as a result of decentralisation, deconcentration and a focus on client satisfaction. Other knock-on changes have secondarily affected the capacity for public administration to deliver policy implementation. *Autonomy* for lower echelon workers has increased, and the moves to *empower* clients have introduced new forces and new possibilities that are increasingly difficult to manage. Structurally, there has been a *diminution* of the link between bureaucracy and democracy, at a time when, crucially, there has been a *normative loss* of the public interest ethos that supported the smooth implementation of policy.

Such characteristics of public administration have a specific application for equality of opportunity policy because such policy relies on some universalist precepts and is intended for uniform application across political space and time. For these reasons, it is possible to recognise that modernist versions of the efforts to attain political goals in society do express important truths. Pluralist conceptions highlight the way that people can become productively involved and achieve their objectives. Politically, this supports the passage of legislation and activities to realise the objectives of legislators and interest groups alike. Some forms of discrimination in some sections of society at some times for some individuals and some groups are addressed. However, the skilled practitioners of the pluralist arts tend to be confined to political orders and the middle class in particular, and the distribution of political progress and benefits reflects this bias within the system. In Gramsci's terms, universal ends are not being served. Instead, sectional interests are being met, and a particular political order, structure and pattern of interaction between citizen and state are reproduced. That pattern excludes not only class considerations and change to the deep structure of capitalist society, but also leaves untouched patriarchy. The very competency of the state is brought into question.

These observations are meant to indicate some of the reasons for the limits to the modernist political project of equality of opportunity, despite its dominance. It is not suggested here that the modernist equal opportunities project is dead. Rather, it is the strength and persistence of modernism that is of concern. It is an attractive approach, given its capacity to explain a great deal within modernist state structures and politics. It also offers possibilities for immediate action to remedy observable problems. However, these attractive features and strengths disguise three problems. First, the modernist account relies upon and enforces a narrow view of the political. Second, some actions and some groups are excluded. Third, there is a lack of reflexivity about the nature of the modernist approach and the implications of being the dominant discourse. It is just these issues that have been addressed within the postmodernist framework.

The postmodern political project

In political and administrative terms, the postmodern political project lies at the margins of the modernist enterprise. In response to the rigidities and simplicities of modernism, it offers a demanding critique and, at best, an uncertain alternative. Equality of opportunity is implicated in this turn to postmodern readings of politics by virtue of its connection with, among others, the women's movement. Specifically, three core assumptions of the modernist account of equality of opportunity – universalism, consensus and material equality – are challenged by practical political experience and the development of movement politics. Within the women's movement, false universalism came under attack from black feminists, and subsequently the term black has been attacked as being falsely inclusive and ultimately excluding of, for example, Asian identity (hooks, 1984; Modood, 1994). 'Otherness' becomes a cause for celebration, not discrimination. The focus on the false universalism of some equality discourse came to be associated with a rejection of any universalist discourses. This signalled the development of difference and identity politics. It meant the empowerment of self-defined groups, and the legitimisation of particular wants over universally understood needs. There was an end to the privileged discourse and in its place emerged many voices, all claiming standpoint authority. There was a turn to the 'internal' aspects of politics, drawing out the aesthetic, the cultural and the symbolic (Fitzpatrick, 1995: 701). This meant both a critique of existing modernist approaches and a tremendous opening up of political possibilities, as new actors authorised themselves and a more radical agenda was promulgated. Equal opportunities once more could be associated with bottom-up demands rather than top-down solutions. There was mobilisation around single-issue causes rather than the large unifying themes.

On the other hand, in this centripetal 'new politics' of identity 'no a priori lines of conflict are conceivable' (Fitzpatrick, 1995: 699). There is a flight from modernist or regular politics, with its established positions and rules of engagement. This brings into question the second modernist assumption. Not only are there no common grounds for conflict, there is also no basis for consensus. The postmodern view of politics (Lyotard, 1979) is that dialogue may well be important as an exchange between different world-views, but it does not have consensus as its goal. Indeed, consensus cannot be the goal, because consensus is just not available. Without the fiction of a collective universal subject to unite us communicatively (for example), the radically divergent views of the world held by different groups can be incommensurable. It is not necessarily the case that there are common grounds and common understandings that can be shared and be the basis for agreement. If this is so, then it is not possible for all speakers to come to agreement on which rules or metaprescriptions about life and politics are universally valid. This critically undermines the modernist approach to equality of opportunity, which tends towards and often comes to rely upon rules to ensure the proper recognition and treatment of individuals and people.

The third modernist assumption that comes under challenge is the idea that people need to be emancipated from discrimination, and that the key to this emancipation is equality of opportunity in relation to major societal resources and material benefits such as employment and education. Emancipatory politics, as Giddens (1992: 210) calls it, tends to deal in these large issues, in turn requiring a modernist politics populated by interest groups, institutions and law. Postmodern concerns are less about emancipation and more about individuation, realisation of self, the celebration of difference and the construction of identity. Non-material benefits are sought. This reflects a much more personal set of expectations of society and the political, and a concern with 'life politics' that does not trade in the kind of equalities that can be translated readily into law, or even good practice.

The fourth question is about politics itself. Postmodern politics is unlike the 'old' politics of constrained use of power, which saw power as a possession or substance. As Laclau puts it (in Fitzpatrick, 1995: 703), the new politics is 'a politics of conflict, flux, dispersion and dislocation'. This politics has no common grounds to set up conflict and move to dialogue on the way to consensus. It is aimless and purposeless, in the control of no one and no thing.

Postmodern politics is characteristically non-teleological, creating a freedom from the need for articulated and programmatic social and political goals. This means that new spaces for political activity are opened up to those who have previously lacked a voice, were denied acknowledgement in a political system that requires language competence, had no access to key players or a familiarity with unwritten rules, nor the ability to mobilise appropriate resources. Instead, protest can be self-validating and political legitimacy self-referenced.

With such a different conception of politics, the modernist tools and institutions are also likely to be irrelevant. Political parties cannot hope to represent and mediate – certainly in the short term – the myriad and often contradictory demands made upon them and come to be seen as institutionalised barriers to the new agenda and emergent claimant groups. Government and administration are similarly seen as antagonistic to postmodern political movements, since they constitutionally embody universalist values and rationalist assumptions about implementation. Under this kind of onslaught, any conception of equality of opportunity soon begins to stand for nothing in particular, as demands become as infinite as the number of solutions that are rejected.

Prospects for the equal opportunities project

It was noted earlier that equal opportunities have always had to respond to the prevailing environment. The account above of the modernist and postmodernist perspectives on equal opportunities does not presume that these are mutually exclusive alternatives for theorists or practitioners. Rather, they are both partial pictures. They capture important sets of political realities and reflect but also conceal social and political developments, all of which are of key concern to the equal opportunities project. As a consequence, that project currently faces at least four sets of challenges, according to the prevailing political opportunity structure.

In Britain, the political project must respond to the large-scale changes in the political opportunity structure, brought about by the incoming government and its agenda for constitutional reform and decentralisation. At a second-order level, there are new ministries and new political actors in central government that are seeking to implement a political agenda well honed (if not always a soundly developed) during the years in opposition. Underlying this, at the ideological level, is the impact of 'New Labour' and 'The Third Way' (Blair, 1998). This new ideological approach does not fit with the ideology of an equal opportunities project that has been constructed under the ideological agenda created by Conservative thought and rule. Nor does it relate to the model developed at the level of local authorities. Blair's 'Third Way' 'moves decisively beyond an Old Left preoccupied by state control, high taxation and producer interests' (1998: 1). Unless it is responsive, the equal opportunities project is in danger of being associated with 'old' approaches, and perhaps with the previous regime, with damaging consequences.

It is clear that the political constituency in the United States and in all European countries has changed, sometimes dramatically. The most important postmodern insight is that the change amounts to fragmentation. The recognition and validation of difference makes disparate what once could be appealed to in terms of solidarity and a common reaction to oppression. Difference politics means a specialisation and particularisation of demand. Identity politics extends the possibilities of political postmodernism to all groups regardless of their moral standing or relation to oppressive practices. The need for identity is easily manifested as a self-referencing claim for validation, for rights and for resources, with a downgrading of judgements about the varying circumstances and oppression experienced on a systematic basis by different groups. The intensification of claims to meet identity wants, backed up by a rhetoric of rights, increases the pressure on already scarce resources available to tackle discrimination. Equal opportunities practitioners were once charged with delivering emancipation and opportunities by the dismantling of barriers and tackling discrimination. Now they are front-line workers who have to adjudicate between rival identity claims, and ration their resources. The project, in other words, has become complicit with political and bureaucratic control. It can be associated with the denial of identity needs and can be seen as unresponsive and irrelevant to its own political constituency. Finally, the regionalisation of the political constituency places strains on the ability to maintain communication and equity between the regions within and between states. This threatens the ability to communicate and draw on the support of others in substantially similar circumstances. At worst, forms of discrimination derived from nationalistic forces will become more significant at the very moment when unified responses are more difficult to achieve.

The third set of challenges arises from changes in the organisation of equal opportunities politics. The rise of new social movements and their impact on political activity has been well documented, as has the increased focus on single-issue politics. Other changes are mentioned above, such as the shift away from attempts to remove or reform unsatisfactory political structures to a pursuit of the cultural and aesthetic dimensions of possible life-worlds beyond modernist politics. This is exemplified by the contrast drawn by Giddens (1991) between 'emancipatory' and 'life' politics. At the same time, one of the products of the equal opportunities project since the major legislative initiatives of the 1970s is the emergence of committed, experienced and trained equal opportunities professionals. They have entered and become an established part of the bureaucracies of the public and private sectors just as those mechanisms have come under challenge. They have become a 'producer interest' at the very moment when the importance of that form of interest is being dismissed.

Finally, the equal opportunities project finds itself not just subject to the debates concerning modernism and postmodernism, but is also implicated in the political pressures and theoretical concerns that gave rise to those debates. Moreover, the project has to devise policies and address their practical consequences. The conceptualisation of the political is something with which those involved with equal opportunities have long been involved. In the same way, the conceptualisation of the possible and of the overall aims of the project have been under continuous discussion. A more recent problem is the challenge over consensus and conflict. Under a regime that is hostile to anything more than a minimalist approach to equal opportunities, consensus-building among interest groups and public administrators is an astute tactic. However, a changed political opportunity structure can allow the impossibility of consensus between groups to become an issue. To add to the complexity, the competencies and practices of the state are in flux and under pressure for further alteration. In general, the assumptions of universality and of the capacity not to mention the willingness of the state to intervene in large-scale social and political policy engineering have less purchase. As a result, the responsibilities and challenges facing the equal opportunities project have changed, as have expectations about what can (and ought to) be achieved.

The generic case for the equal opportunities project

If there is to be a case for the equal opportunities project, then it must be an approach that manages to address serious and long-standing equality problems in imaginative and effective ways. To achieve that, it must avoid the limitations inherent in the extremes of modernism and postmodernism as I have presented them. Modernism has a restricted view of politics and an over-developed sense of its power to bring about systematic change. It therefore privileges rationalist and legal positivist political understanding and action, despite the demonstrable weaknesses and failure to achieve the substantive change promised. In the process, it crowds out and delegitimises other approaches. Postmodernism, on the other hand, has a wider grasp of the political and an acute awareness of the conditionality of political understanding and action. The focus on difference highlights the nature and extent of oppression and the importance of power, but in so doing it too easily emasculates political will, to the point at which any action at all may be precluded.

Instead of dismissing one or both approaches, it is necessary to do what equal opportunities practitioners have long done, which is to be eclectic and pragmatic. If carried out in a clear and defensible manner, the objective of an account that draws upon the strengths of these two accounts of politics where they are most relevant can be realised.

Suspicion about universalism is appropriate, but that does not mean that ideas with a universal application cannot be employed. Thus, from the point of view of equal opportunities, we all live in a state, we all have a claim to be free from harm and to enjoy human dignity. This is a simple equality, but one that goes beyond the liberal idea of people being similar (but unequal). We share a human condition, rather than possess a human soul or body of rights. There is both an equality and a difference between subjects seeking to establish identity as a means to realise the need to be recognised. As Touraine puts it, 'we are equal only because we all want to be different' (1998: 170). From a postmodern perspective, we should nevertheless be wary of solutions that seek programmatically to apply these rubrics, imposing a particular way of life associated with one experience of those values. Complex equality is needed to apply these values for differentiated individuals and groups, according to circumstance and time. The optimism of the modernist to shape society and people on the basis of an agreed plan needs to be tempered by the pessimism of the postmodernist who does not believe that our goals can even be adequately expressed, much less given to institutions to administer. That means an opening of the political forum to debate and dispute, and multiple paths to self-realisation. This is more like an agonal politics, where satisfaction for all is never guaranteed, and there are endless contests over meaning and resources. For an agonal politics to be effective, there must be restraint and even an appreciation of the tragic nature of some political contestation. Some disputes are not amenable to consensual resolution. There is no point denying this, and being drawn to options including separation or violence. Nor, however, does that mean that efforts to search for a solution should cease, even if it is only for the current participants. This is one answer to the claim that economic redistribution is the foundation stone of equal opportunities' solutions. It may well be, but there are good historical reasons to argue that it may not be enough. If the argument on this point needs go on, then so too must a range of equal opportunities' actions that have relevance in the short term.

The non-universalist component of equal opportunities is something that has already begun to develop, but is still in its infancy. This is the politics of identity and difference. It requires a move beyond the standpoint authority position, which may be an important step in terms of earning recognition and gaining a voice, but can only be a step towards the exploration of otherness and the potentialities of political identity. Those committed to equal opportunities have choices in this, in relation to an understanding of the possibility of the political position they currently occupy, and the strategies they adopt. If it is the case that the rationalist, hierarchical and heavily institutionalised social system of a modernist world is being undermined by its own failure and the emergence of other possibilities, then the old antinomies of liberty versus equality, and equality versus difference no longer have such a tight hold. In that case, the equal opportunities project can begin to manage the material as well as non-material aspects of equality and identity alike, without being forced to choose between them. As Touraine argues:

> It is only once the social system begins to weaken under the pressure of permanent changes and of the growing independence of the economy from institutions and mechanisms for social control, that social actors can claim equality of opportunity as well as respect for their cultural and psychological identity. (1998: 175)

Even this view, however, leaves a perennial problem for the equal opportunities project. The requirement for 'the social system' to weaken raises the question of the compatibility of the pursuit of that end with the pursuit of the ends of individuals and groups. Nevertheless, from an agonal perspective the equal opportunities political project must be about making a difference wherever difference matters.

The future for the equal opportunities project

The question of the capacity of the modern state and the division over the consequences of strategies to introduce change is a crucial aspect of contemporary politics across Europe and America. It affects in particular the way that politics and progress are expressed by government. The last period of Conservative government (1979–92) was not unique in its rejection of interest articulation and public service in favour of privatisation and the market as the solution to a better society, but there was still a steady creep of much equal opportunities activity consistent with de Tocqueville's approval of interest articulation. Does this mean that the politics of identity and class struggle are fully represented in the equal opportunities project? Further, does the 'Third Way' promoted by the Labour government under Prime Minister Blair integrate the disparate facets of the equal opportunities project? To both questions, the short answer appears to be no.

Nevertheless, Blair's politics is important. It represents something of a challenge to equality of opportunity as it has developed in Britain. It may be as great a challenge as the one brought about by Thatcher and Reagan. Blair appears to have a conventional approach to equal opportunities. He wants 'a transformation in the role of women', enabling them – 'in the name of equality of opportunity – to fulfil their full potential according to their own choices' (1998: 6). Given his track record, he can be described as a minimalist, as a liberal reformer, especially as he immediately follows the fine words above with socially conservative references to the need to strengthen the family. In practice, he avoids public policies (but not always foreign policies) that threaten consensus or have insufficient consensus. Hence he distanced himself from the Labour Party's use of affirmative action to create women-only short lists for marginal constituencies even before it was successfully challenged at an industrial tribunal in the run-up to the 1997 general election. Following the decision of the tribunal, he jettisoned the policy immediately. His approach to consensus demonstrates that his idea of politics is a version of modernism. However, Blair is not obviously an adherent of de Tocqueville. Blair appears to be convinced that the traditional political mechanisms are either moribund because they are insufficiently connected to disparate and sometimes inchoate social forces, or they are inappropriate because they reflect inflexible interest groups with an outdated agenda for political action. The Third Way is about forging new connections with the populace that are unmediated by the rather tired and predictable routes into government that have existed for some time.

Twenty years ago, British government was said to be in crisis, suffering overload by dint of its felt responsibility to meet the wealth and weight of demands made upon it by powerful producer interest groups and myriad pressure groups. New Labour is intent on avoiding what it sees as the mistakes of previous administrations in this respect, and employs a strategy with three components of interest here. Each component can be said to be a part of an overall objective related to empowerment. The first is to change the constitutional framework such that local and regional access to political systems is maximised. The local political opportunity structures will change, providing space for empowering those who want to develop local community initiatives. These structures may well be more receptive to local equal opportunities activism. The limits of effectiveness will be conditioned by the local ideological climate and the political and economic resources available at these non-national levels. In this respect, Britain is doing no more than emulating the decentralisation common to federal structures in the US and many European countries. The second component is intended to allow citizens to possess and exercise rights at national and supra-national levels. This empowers citizens as individual bearers of rights. At the national level, the third element of the strategy has two main elements. First, macroeconomic policy is designed to carry the burden of providing equality of opportunity (understood in material and, possibly, educational terms). Second, some of the large interest groups are being sidestepped in favour of a more direct connection with the needs and wants of the public.

This is a modernist politics with some new twists. Methodologically, it reflects a preference for qualitative over quantitative analysis. Paying attention to the expressed needs of individuals will bring to light a different set of priorities and perspectives that will seem fresh. It introduces a new voice and will do much to assist the government in accessing and assessing public understanding and perception of the government's legislative and policy intentions as well as the performance of the government and its policies. In terms of public relations it makes a great deal of sense, and bespeaks a professional approach to the business of governing. But this reaching down to the grassroots and deliberately bypassing established routes of influence comes as something of a shock. The new listening culture is instituting new rules and privileging new actors, precisely on the basis that they are not implicated with existing formal and organisational attempts to exploit the political opportunity structure.

Ultimately, however, this is a modernist enterprise, and both the Gramscian and the power critiques appear to have a good deal of force. Authority is not relinquished to non-governmental sources, and only 'common' equality of opportunity is on the agenda. As far as the equal opportunities project is concerned, this is a retrograde step. It challenges an equal opportunities movement that has developed its priorities through work, through political and administrative institutions, through challenge, through evaluation and through trial and error, and is based in an engagement with a wide range of groups and positions. It has drawn strength and claimed credibility on the basis of its sources in and connections with groups in society, and for its ability to deliver services and outcomes. Moreover, the movement has developed a reflexivity about equality of opportunity. This amounts to a set of strengths that will be necessary, since, once again, equality of opportunity will have to be fought for and over in the new political fora, lest the agenda for change be ignored or diverted, with the predictable and systematic consequence that voices will continue to go unheard, discrimination and harassment will grow and needs will be unmet.

References

Bacchi, C. (1996), *The Politics of Affirmative Action*, London: Sage.
Baker, J. (1987), *Arguing for Equality*, London: Verso.
Blair, T. (1998), *The Third Way: New Politics for the New Century*, Fabian Pamphlet 588, London: Fabian Society.
Cahn, S. (ed.) (1995), *The Affirmative Action Debate*, New York and London: Routledge.
Clarke, G. (1998), 'Non-Governmental Organizations (NGOs) and Politics in the Developing World', *Political Studies*, Vol. 46: 36–52.
Collins, H. (1992), *The Equal Opportunities Handbook*, Oxford: Blackwell.
Elshtain, J. B. (1992), 'The Power and Powerless of Women', in G. Bock and S. James (eds) *Beyond Equality and Difference*, London: Routledge.
Fitzpatrick, T. (1995), 'Seeming Contradictions: Parliamentary and Extra-Parliamentary Politics of Opposition', in J. Lovenduski and J. Stanyer (eds), *Contemporary Political Studies*, vol. 2, Belfast: Political Studies Association of the UK.
Giddens, A. (1992), *Modernity and Self Identity*, Oxford: Polity Press.
Goodin, R. E. and Klingemann, H-D. (1996), *A New Handbook of Political Science*, Oxford: Oxford University Press.
hooks, b. (1984), *Feminist Theory: From Margin to Center*, Boston: South End Press.
Jewson, N. and Mason, D. (1986), 'The Theory and Practice of Equal Opportunities Policies: Liberal and Radical Approaches', *Sociological Review*, Vol. 2.
Lyotard, J-F. (1979), *The Postmodern Condition*, translated by G. Bennington and B. Massumi (1984), Manchester: Manchester University Press.
Migdal, J. (1988), *Strong Societies and Weak States: State–Society Relations and State Capabilities in Third World Countries*, Princeton; NJ: Princeton University Press.
Mithaug, D. (1996), *Equal Opportunity Theory*, London: Sage.
Modood, T. (1994), 'Political Blackness and British Asians', *Sociology*, Vol. 28, No. 4.

Nanton, P. (1995), 'Extending the Boundaries: Equal Opportunities as Social Regulation', *Policy and Politics*, Vol. 23, No. 2. pp. 203–12.

Peters, B. G. and Wright, V. (1996), 'Public Policy Administration, Old and New', in R. E. Goodin and H-D. Klingemann (eds), *A New Handbook of Political Science*, Oxford: Oxford University Press.

Roemer, J. (1998), *Equality of Opportunity*, Cambridge, Mass: Harvard University Press.

Schaar, J. (1967), 'Equality of Opportunity, and Beyond', in J. Chapman and R. Pennock (eds), *Nomos Six: Equality*, New York: Atherton Press.

Touraine, A. (1998), 'Can We Live Together, Equal and Different?', *European Journal of Social Theory*, Vol. 1, No. 2, pp. 176–8.

Weber, M. (1970), 'Bureaucracy', in H. H. Gerth and C. Wright Mills (eds), *From Max Weber: Essays in Sociology*, London: Routledge and Kegan Paul.

3
The Politics of 'Mainstreaming' Gender Equality

Teresa Rees

'Mainstreaming' or integrating gender equality into policy and practice has become politically fashionable at a variety of levels of governance across Europe. First mooted as an approach to equal opportunities at the United Nations World Conference on Women held in Nairobi in 1985, women's organisations have put mounting pressure on government institutions to take equal opportunities policies more seriously. This began at a time of increasing concern about a 'demographic time bomb' which would mean more use would need to be made of women – the 'untapped resource'. In the event, the time bomb failed to explode but there has been, nevertheless, growing recognition that women have a more significant role to play in the labour market. They are the majority of the new labour market entrants, the economically inactive, the unemployed and low-skilled (OECD, 1994). Hence the business case for a more effective approach to equality was combined with more vociferous concerns about social justice that equal treatment in the law had failed to remedy. Mainstreaming offered a new, long-term strategic approach to gender equality. It is now the official policy approach of the European Union (EU) (CEC, 1996), the Council of Europe (Council of Europe, 1998), the United Kingdom (UK) government and the devolved governments in Scotland, Northern Ireland and Wales. It is also an increasingly common discourse in local authorities. Mainstreaming, however, means different things to different people. This chapter examines approaches being taken to mainstream gender equality at a variety of levels of governance.

It is particularly timely to be considering the rhetoric and reality of mainstreaming. First, as a consequence of devolution in the UK, new political institutions have been established which have integrated equality into the design of their remit and procedures. Second, more than five years have passed since the United Nations Fourth World Conference on Women held in Beijing in 1995, where mainstreaming was identified as one of ten items on a 'Platform of Action' for gender equality (Women's National Commission et al., 1997). The representatives of the non-governmental organisations, equality agencies and women's groups in the voluntary sector who attended that conference made a commitment to encourage their respective governments to implement this agenda. At the Beijing Plus Five conference in 2000, progress in implementing the Platform of Action since the 1995 conference was reviewed. Finally, the Human Rights Act 1998 came into force in the UK in October 2000, placing responsibilities on all public authorities and bodies conducting public functions to ensure that they are acting in compliance with European Convention on Human Rights (Spencer, 1999).

How is the concept of mainstreaming being operationalised in the UK and to what extent have the Scottish Parliament and National Assembly for Wales been shaped by this new approach to gender equality? What steps are being taken by the European Commission (EC) to implement the EU's commitment to mainstreaming, and with what results? And how are these patterns and policies affecting what is happening at the local level? Is it all so much rhetoric, or are there significant changes in approach? This chapter examines three levels of governance in turn, exploring the rhetoric and reality of mainstreaming.

The fact that mainstreaming is being discussed at such a variety of institutional levels and across so many countries does not necessarily mean, of course, that there is any consensus as to what the concept entails. On the contrary, it is clear that there are many competing definitions. Moreover, lack of understanding and lack of expertise have been identified by the EC as two major problems impeding the implementation of mainstreaming as a strategic approach towards gender equality (CEC, 1998). However, a broad working definition for the purposes of this chapter is that mainstreaming is the integration of gender equality into all policies, programmes and projects.

In my own view, mainstreaming ideally should involve identifying how existing systems and structures cause indirect discrimination and altering or redesigning them as appropriate. In the case of gender equality, this means addressing the ways in which political institutions reinforce the breadwinner-homemaker gender contract (Duncan, 1996a). This is a far more radical interpretation of mainstreaming than the one that characterises most political institutions. It requires expertise, awareness and training in equal opportunities at a more sophisticated level than can usually be found in organisations, even those which regularly provide equal opportunities training for staff involved in recruitment procedures. Such training in gender mainstreaming would include an understanding of equality in its fullest sense, by addressing sets of disadvantage experienced through direct and indirect discrimination on the grounds of sex. This approach could also integrate equality on the grounds of race, disability, age and sexual orientation. Monitoring and evaluation are vital and attention to equality issues should be built into individual and department performance review mechanisms and procedures. Mainstreaming in this way could arguably have profound implications for organisations and their culture as well as for systems and structures of policy design and delivery. However, this hypothetical model of mainstreaming bears little resemblance to what is happening in the field. Few existing bodies committed to mainstreaming appear to be engaged in cultural and organisational change along these lines.

Organisations that assert their commitment to mainstreaming gender equality appear to be engaged in some or all of a range of activities. At one end of the spectrum, they may simply be seeking to develop some gender awareness across departments. This may take the form of gender impact assessments of new policies or gender audits on pay. At the other extreme, some talk of full-scale integration of equal opportunities, from policy formulation through to implementation, monitoring, evaluating and reporting. Hence, gender equality becomes the 'responsibility of all'. However, this approach has its dangers. In some local authorities, for example, it has, paradoxically, led to the dismissal of specialist equality personnel and units on the grounds that equality should not be ghettoised. The Equal Opportunities Commission (EOC) in Britain has warned against dispensing with equality experts in the name of mainstreaming in its framework for mainstreaming gender equality in local government (EOC, 1997). No organisations that I know of are engaging in the yet more radical redesign of the organisation and its culture that gender mainstreaming might legitimately imply, described above. This may well be because, for the most part, the complexity of equal opportunities is not appreciated and the expertise is not available in-house. The agenda is the short-term one of ameliorating some immediate recruitment or retention problem or fostering a good image as an employer, rather than the longer-term one of addressing structural change (Cockburn, 1989).

There are further differences in interpretation and emphasis in terms of two crucial dimensions of mainstreaming. The first concerns internal and external focus. Some organisations see mainstreaming as an internal human resource management tool, designed to ensure fair and effective policies in recruitment: some extend this to include promotion and patterns of work organisation. Others go beyond this to consider the gender equality dimensions of the external delivery of goods and services, the business of the organisation. The second dimension concerns whether mainstreaming is seen as exclusively a matter of gender equality or equality more widely. Mainstreaming for some includes integrating equality on the grounds of race and ethnic origin, disability, age and sexual orientation, in line with ideologies of inclusiveness. For others, it starts and stops with gender equality.

This chapter begins with an account of the history of mainstreaming in the EU. This is followed by a brief review of the situation in the UK before focusing on the National Assembly for Wales and finally local government in Wales. The setting up of the Scottish Parliament and the Welsh Assembly provided an opportunity for gender equality to be integrated into the design of buildings, the drafting of standing orders, the setting of the business agenda and the overseeing of public services. To what extent were these opportunities grasped?[1]

Mainstreaming gender equality in the European Union

Since the 1970s, the EC has arguably acted as a catalyst to the development of equal opportunities law and policies in most of the member states (Duncan, 1996b; Rossilli, 1997). It is possible to identify three phases in the EC's approach to gender equality, roughly corresponding to the last three decades: equal treatment in the 1970s (which I call 'tinkering'), positive action in the 1980s (which I call 'tailoring'), and mainstreaming in the 1990s (which I call 'transforming') (Rees, 1998). Equal treatment is essentially a legal redress to treat men and women the same. Positive action recognises that there are, in fact, differences between men and women and therefore measures are needed to address the disadvantages experienced by women as a consequence of those differences. Mainstreaming (ideally) begins by understanding how institutions and their cultures sustain and perpetuate inequalities through privileging the breadwinner homemaker gender contract and seeks to transform them to allow equality based on difference.

The commitment to equal treatment of men and women in pay was enshrined in Article 119 of the 1957 Treaty of Rome which set up the forerunner of the EU. However, little notice was taken of it by the then member states. Indeed, it was not until the 1970s that three crucial equal treatment Directives were introduced, which were designed to ensure that member states brought in their own binding legislation to honour that commitment. Member states had also to set up a sex equality body to enforce the legislation if they did not already have one (hence the setting up of the Equal Opportunities Commissions in Britain and Northern Ireland respectively in 1975). Later Directives in the 1980s and 1990s were designed to plug various gaps (for example, equal treatment in social security) and encourage a balance between home and work.[2]

Equal treatment does not, of course, produce equal outcome. The assumption was that women would need to be treated the same as men: men were taken as the yardstick or the norm. The legislation did not have a dramatic effect on the pay gap, partly as a consequence of rigid patterns of gender segregation. Women were identified as 'disadvantaged' in a labour market principally organised around breadwinners. The identification of these shortcomings led to some criticisms of the liberal, equal treatment approach. The 1980s saw the first of the EC's positive action measures for gender equality designed to address this disadvantage. Medium Term Action Programmes for Equal Treatment of Men and Women were established, together with support for training and employment projects through New Opportunities for Women (NOW) and a series of transnational expert networks. These initiatives are very small-scale compared with other Commission programmes, but they facilitated women's groups to network with each other across the EU and led to the identification of common structural problems facing women in the labour market across the member states.

In the early 1990s, in the context of demographic change, the underutilisation of women in the workforce was identified as a barrier to economic competitiveness. A number of organisations began to debate the 'business case' for developing women's skills. For example, in 1993, the 'Social Dialogue' of employers and trade unions organisations at EU level produced a *Joint Opinion on Women and Training* (CEC et al., 1993). This was significant in that social partners play a key role in the development of policy at the EU level. The EC, unusually for a civil service, makes proposals for legislation and action programmes to the Council of Ministers and the European Parliament. Support from the social partners is crucial if such proposals are to receive approval. The European employers and trade union organisations are, in any case, consulted in the long process of securing approval for proposals. Hence, given that they themselves had put women's training needs on the agenda, and that there was a strong interest in the issue within the Women's Lobby of the European Parliament, the time seemed politically favourable for a more pro-active approach to gender equality such as mainstreaming. The addition of countries with a more sophisticated understanding and radical approach to equality to the EU, such as Sweden in 1995, helped to raise awareness. The late 1990s were characterised by a comprehensive drive on mainstreaming as the main EU approach to equal opportunities (Rees, 1998). Some of the key landmarks of the 1990s are set out in Table 3.1. They are then discussed under broad headings.

Table 3.1   European Union: landmarks in mainstreaming

1994	Dec.	• Council of Ministers identifies equal opportunities as a priority at Essen Summit
1995	Sept.	• UN Fourth World Conference on Women, Beijing • Group of EC Commissioners on equal opportunities set up • Inter-service Group on equal opportunities set up
	Nov.	• Communication on External Aspects of Human Rights Policies
	Dec.	• Council Resolution on equal opportunities in Development Cooperation
1996	Feb.	• EC's *Mainstreaming Communication* adopted
	Dec.	• Council Resolution on equal opportunities and Structural Funds
1997	Jan.	• First EC *Annual Report* on equal opportunities
	Feb.	• Inter-service group on equal opportunities agrees *Strategy Paper*
	Sept.	• Resolution of Parliament endorsed *Mainstreaming Communication*
	Oct.	• Amsterdam Treaty widens equal opportunities commitment
	Nov.	• Luxembourg Employment Summit (equal opportunities one of 4 pillars) • Group of 29 'mainstreaming officials' designated • EC *Guide to Gender Impact Assessment* published
1998	Mar.	• First EC *Progress Report on Mainstreaming*
	May	• *National Action Plans for Employment* published
	Aug.	• Second EC *Annual Report* on equal opportunities
	Sept.	• Austrian Presidency identifies equal opportunities as a priority • EC proposal for Council regulation on mainstreaming in development policies
	Dec.	• Vienna Summit: Review of Action Plans
1999	Mar.	• EC Communication on *Women and Science*
	April	• Third EC *Annual Report* on equal opportunities

The EC's communication on mainstreaming

An influential OECD report pointed out the key significance of women to the labour market and advocated integrating gender equality into labour market policies in 1994 (OECD, 1994). Despite this, the EC published in the same year a White Paper, 'Growth, Competitiveness, Employment', to shape the framework for the EU's economic policy for the foreseeable future. It was based on an analysis of the labour market that took little heed of its gendered dimension beyond identifying women as a disadvantaged group (EC, 1994). Shortly after its publication, 'seven wise women' were invited by the Commission's Equal Opportunities Unit to prepare a 'feminist critique' of the White Paper (EC, 1995). The authors argued that the analysis that underpinned the framework of policy in the White Paper ignored or dealt inadequately with sex inequalities in education, training and the labour market. Hence, it was fatally flawed. As a consequence, policies that flowed from the analysis were bound to fall short of meeting their stated aims. The authors claimed that integrating equal opportunities has to reach beyond the rhetoric expressed in the White Paper:

> [It] ... means more than making references to women's employment and to equal opportunities. It also means more than just paying special attention to women as a target group as the White Paper does. Analysing from a gender perspective implies that on the one hand gender inequalities should be examined as one of the *causes* of developments in employment and unemployment. On the other hand gender inequality could be *produced by* 'general' labour market developments and policies. The White Paper does pay some attention to the first but not to the latter. (de Bruijn, 1995: 111; original emphasis)

This critique reflected tensions between different interpretations of mainstreaming. It was prepared for the Council of Ministers Summit held in Essen in December 1994, at which gender equality was identified as a priority area for action. The following year, a committee of Commissioners was set up on equal opportunities, chaired by the then president Jacques Santer. This group of five was determined to drive the gender equality agenda forward, and was supported by an inter-service group of senior Commission officials. One of its earliest activities was to seek to establish baseline data on what the various Directorate Generals (DGs) of the Commission were 'doing about equal opportunities'. The responses were very mixed. Some DGs claimed to be addressing equal opportunities as an internal human resource issue; a few also referred to how equal opportunities was being addressed in the way in which they worked. However, the remaining DGs assumed that the request for information had been sent in error, as they did not hold the equal opportunities brief and therefore it had no relevance for them.

This response prompted the Commission to draft a *Communication* to the Council of Ministers which argued for the incorporation of equal opportunities for women and men into all Community policies and activities (known as the 'mainstreaming' *Communication*) (CEC, 1996). It was adopted by the Council in 1996 and endorsed by Parliament in 1997. The *Communication* facilitated Parliament and the Commission to take a more pro-active approach to the promotion of gender equality, principally through insisting that equal opportunities was highlighted in all EC co-funded activities,

Hence, Council Resolutions were passed on mainstreaming equal opportunities into the European Social Fund (one of the main methods through which the Commission co-funds training and employment projects in the member states) and in development cooperation. All DGs are now expected to mainstream equality. A group of 29 officials across the Commission has been charged with special responsibility for this (the 'gender mainstreaming officials'): they report to the inter-service group. One of the first activities of this group was to publish a guide to gender impact assessment (EC, 1998c). Annual reports are presented on equal opportunities for women and men (EC, 1997; 1998a; 1999, 2000) and on progress on the follow up to the mainstreaming *Communication* (CEC, 1998).

The task of finding progress to report was clearly a challenging one. Most 'progress' is reported by the Commission as having taken place in just four DGs. First, following the December 1995 Council Resolution on equal opportunities in development cooperation, there have been attempts to mainstream equality in this area of activity (DGIB and DGVIII). The Commission's *Communication* on the EU and the External Aspects of its Human Rights Policies of November 1995 identifies women as 'potentially vulnerable' and as essential contributors to the democratic process. DGV (Employment, Social Affairs and Industrial Relations) promoted mainstreaming in the guidelines to the member states on the preparation of National Action Plans (NAPs) on employment and in the Structural Funds (both discussed below). DGV also hosted one of the main positive action spaces for women in the Community Initiative EMPLOYMENT: the NOW strand (New Opportunities for Women) until it was replaced by the EQUAL programme in 2000.

The developments described in the progress report on mainstreaming and the various annual reports on equal opportunities are extremely modest and take the form of uncritical accounts of various initiatives. However the EC has acknowledged that much remains to be done in order to implement mainstreaming effectively. In its fourth annual report on equal opportunities for women and men it stated its intention to reinforce Community policy on gender equality via a far-reaching framework programme for 2001–2005 (EC, 2000). As yet there is no systematic evaluation of what these initiatives have achieved, nor have mechanisms yet been put in place to allow systematic assessments to be made. There is little discussion as to whether these initiatives constitute mainstreaming. There is no clearly specified definition laid down for the DGs as to what mainstreaming means. There are no set objectives, nor are there procedures and mechanisms for measuring progress towards achieving them. As a consequence, progress reports will inevitably be limited in their capacity to analyse whether mainstreaming has occurred and if so, whether it makes a difference, and if so, to whom.

The 1997 Treaty of Amsterdam

The various equality dimensions, such as sex, race and disability, are all at different stages on the journey to nirvana where discrimination is completely eliminated. Three milestones on that journey are, first of all, winning the legal right to equal treatment; second, the allocation of budgets for positive action projects; and finally, legal underpinning for mainstreaming in all policies and programmes.

Sex equality is clearly in the lead. The principle of equal treatment was enshrined in the Treaty of Rome as far back as 1957 and underpinned by Directives in the 1970s forcing member states to introduce their own sex equality legislation if they did not have it already. Article 141 of the 1997 Amsterdam Treaty, which was drawn up at the Summit in June 1996, adopted in October 1997 and ratified in 1999, reinforces the legal base for equal treatment for men and women. Moreover, positive action measures for women (such as the Medium Term Action Programmes on Equal Treatment for Women and Men introduced in the 1980s) have a firm legal base in the Amsterdam Treaty. However, the Treaty also includes, in Articles 2 and 3, a formalised commitment to mainstreaming gender equality. It establishes mainstreaming as a 'specific task of the Community as well as a horizontal objective affecting all Community tasks' (EC, 1998: 3). This provides the legal base that will facilitate action on mainstreaming in the future. The official policy of the EC on gender equality is referred to as the 'dual strategy' (CEC, 1998: 9) of positive action and mainstreaming.

Coming up behind gender equality are race, ethnic origin, religious belief, disability, sexual orientation and age. The Amsterdam Treaty established the right to equal treatment on all these grounds in Article 13. However, this needs to be followed up by Directives to have any impact. It remains to be seen which dimensions will then assert a legal lead. Race and ethnic origin have the complexity of citizenship status with which to contend (Mitchell and Russell, 1994): the principle of subsidiarity may prevent much progress beyond positive action measures. Sexual orientation requires a very different approach from gender equality. For example, while routine gender monitoring is seen as an essential tool in mainstreaming gender equality, gay and lesbian groups advise against monitoring on sexual orientation for obvious reasons. The disability lobby is currently in the political ascendancy within many member states, judging by the focus on disability in the National Action Plans on employment, and there are some indications of political movement on age discrimination in the near future in the context of an ageing workforce.

The irony here is that the version of mainstreaming outlined in the introduction would in principle have the capacity to address all these equality dimensions to some extent. By changing systems and structures to accommodate men and women in all their diversity, rather than training 'disadvantaged groups' to fit in with the status quo, differences among men and among women as well as those between them, are more readily addressed. Limiting mainstreaming to gender equality is conceptually flawed given the diversity among women and men (see Bacchi, 1994, 1996)

The Amsterdam Treaty influences what goes on directly in member states but also indirectly through shaping the Commission's own activities, one of which is to co-fund substantial projects through Structural Funds. The next section looks at mainstreaming in the Structural Funds.

Reform of the European Structural Funds

Structural Funds are the major tool by which the EU seeks to achieve its objective of economic restructuring through capital and human resource investment. Resources are allocated to regions and target groups regarded as disadvantaged and in need of support.[3] It has always been difficult to assess the extent to which women benefit from projects supported by these very substantial funds precisely because of the lack of gender monitoring (see Lefebvre, 1993; Rees, 1998). However, equal opportunities has been a horizontal theme of parts of the Structural Funds since 1993, and the 1996 Commission guidelines for the adjustment of the Funds until 1999 incorporated gender equality. Evaluation criteria and monitoring mechanisms are being developed. It is intended that mainstreaming will:

> Permeate the whole implementation process, from the program-ming phase to the reporting ... At all phases of decision making the aim is to have a balanced participation of women and men and to ensure the commitment of competent authorities and bodies to promoting equality between men and women. (CEC, 1998: 18)

The European Parliament signed up to the 1997 *Agenda 2000 Communication* that sets out future priorities and includes a broad strategic approach for the reform of the Structural Funds. A Working Group on Equal Opportunities in the European Structural Funds has been set up. There has been scope for positive action projects for women within the framework of the European Social Fund since 1993, especially for areas where women are under-represented, women without qualifications and women returners. In the revised Structural Funds, the dual approach is being implemented. Equal opportunities for women and men is one of five policy fields on which funds are being concentrated. At the same time, equal opportunities is intended to be mainstreamed throughout the other four policy fields: active labour market policy, promotion of social inclusion, lifelong learning, and anticipating and facilitating economic and social change (CEC, 1998: 14). In proposals for a new regulation for the European Regional Development Fund (ERDF), priority is identified for business creation and the reconciliation of work and family life.

The lack of evaluation tools means that it still not possible to assess effectively the impact of this strengthened emphasis on gender equality. However, a study of Structural Funds carried out in Finland, Ireland, Spain and Portugal reached the conclusion that equal opportunities was 'not sufficiently taken into account in the programming process and in the evaluation of impacts' (EC, 1998a: 12). Assessment of the impact on equal opportunities for men and women is a priority for the mid-term evaluation of the rural development programmes of the Structural Funds.

The Structural Fund reforms include a better gender balance on monitoring committees and more involvement of women's organisations and equality agencies in planning and implementing projects. Member states are asked to conduct gendered analyses of labour markets where the Funds will be operating and to set targets informed by these analyses. Projects will be monitored from a gender perspective. Gender disaggregated statistics and a better representation of women in decision-making committees are seen as tools to help member states achieve this.

One of the more contentious elements of the reforms has been the abolition of NOW in favour of a new Community Initiative, EQUAL, aimed at combating all forms of discrimination. This is an example where a positive action 'space' for gender equality is in effect being lost in the name of promoting equality more generally. This has been much criticised by the EC's Advisory Committee on Equal Opportunities for Women and Men, made up of representatives of gender equality agencies in the member states, and employers' and unions' organisations. It is important to recognise the differences between equality dimensions. The politics of gender equality are quite different from those operating in the field of racial equality that in turn may have little in common with disability politics. Lumping all these dimensions together in one initiative constructs project recipients as vulnerable and in need of support. It distracts attention from underlying power structures and discriminatory institutions, structures and behaviour that give rise to experiences of disadvantage. Remedies to address some of these dimensions may well be inappropriate for others.

1998 National Action Plans for employment

In order to develop the growth, competitiveness and employment of the EU highlighted in the White Paper, the 1997 Luxembourg Employment Summit sought to develop a more focused employment strategy at the EU level. Following the Summit, member states were asked to prepare National Action Plans (NAPs) on employment around four 'pillars': employability, entrepreneurship, adaptability – and equal opportunities. This represented a relatively high profile for the issue of equal opportunities. The Commission prepared 19 guidelines for member states to help them prepare their action plans: those on equal opportunities are set out in Table 3.2. However, when the member states submitted their NAPs on employment in Spring 1998, the

Table 3.2 Commission guidelines on equal opportunities for National Action Plans on employment

---

- Tackling gender gaps – member states to reduce unemployment rates between men and women (guideline 16);
- Reconciling work and family life – increasing care provision (guideline 17);
- Facilitating return to work – reducing obstacles (guideline 18);
- Promoting integration of people with disabilities into working life – special attention to problems faced (guideline 19).

(EC, 1998b: 15)

Commission described the sections on equal opportunities as 'disappointing':

> The content of the NAPs addressing the issue of equality between women and men appears modest and insufficiently detailed … the approach to equality-driven policies in many national action plans is less developed than that to other policy areas. This is reflected in the relatively limited number of new measures proposed, the small budgets attributed (if mentioned), and the limited number of quantitative targets envisaged. (EC, 1998b: 15, 16)

The NAPs tended to spell out existing policies rather than developing new ones or taking a strategic approach to equal opportunities. Again, without targets and evaluation tools, the impact of these policies are difficult to assess. Moreover, the NAPs were highly revealing in that discussion of equal opportunities tended overwhelmingly to be confined to the section on the equal opportunities pillar: little mention is made of gender equality issues in any of the plans laid out for the other three pillars. Clearly the core message of mainstreaming had not taken root! By contrast, the NAPs do mention in their responses to the other pillars, in particular employability, providing more opportunities for people with disabilities and the labour market integration of disadvantaged groups such as ethnic minorities. This reveals a limited conceptual approach to equal opportunities as one of assisting disadvantaged groups better to fit in with the mainstream, rather than identifying and tackling the causes of disadvantage, including discriminatory features of the ways in which the labour market and its institutions are organised. This is one of the fundamental problems with the mainstreaming agenda and has at its roots an oversimplified model of equal opportunities as being about helping vulnerable groups – rather than looking at the social construction and institutionalisation of disadvantage.

Women and science in Europe

One of the areas where women are particularly poorly represented in Europe, and indeed in the US, is in science (Fox Keller and Longino, 1996; Schiebinger, 1989, 1999). Women are severely under-represented among university professors, members of academies and Nobel Prize winners. They also constitute a tiny minority of recipients of EC Research and Development Framework Funds and members of Framework monitoring and evaluation committees. Hence EC-funded science, engineering and technology projects are shaped, conducted, monitored and evaluated almost exclusively by men. Drawing on only half the brainpower of the EU is at odds with the goals of growth, competitiveness and employment.

Following EC policy on mainstreaming equality in all Commission activities, DGXII (the Research Directorate General) produced a *Communication* on women in science in 1999 that identified a specific set of actions (EC, 1999). Crucial to this is the setting up of a 'Gender Watch System': a small unit of dedicated staff with the job of mainstreaming equality into EC science policy. There is a commitment to increase the participation of women on monitoring and evaluation committees for the Fifth Framework research programme, to encourage more women applicants for research projects and to exhort applicants to include a gender dimension in their project proposals. It is still too early to judge the effects of these measures, but if they are successful, given the size of the science budget, they could be influential among a wide range of EU institutions, principally research institutes, universities and industry. A European Technology Assessment Network (ETAN) was set up by DGXII on the topic of women in science. This small group of women scientists, serviced by the Commission, was charged with the task of preparing proposals for policies to improve the situation of women in science at all levels: EU, the member states and the scientific and research communities. The group also made specific recommendations on how gender equality could be mainstreamed in science education, training and employment, and, crucially, in the funding of scientific projects and the shaping of the science agenda (Osborn *et al.* 2000).

Moving towards mainstreaming

Having described some of the ways in which the EC is seeking to adopt a mainstreaming approach to gender equality, this section seeks to assess progress so far. However, the lack of a clear and shared vision as to what mainstreaming means renders this task highly problematic. The lack of stated objectives, targets and monitoring tools also severely limits opportunities to make such an evaluation. Nevertheless, the EC itself has produced two documents that give some indication of where weaknesses lie. The second EC annual report on equal opportunities identified as problems in developing the gender mainstreaming agenda, the need for:

- awareness arising;
- large-scale training to develop gender expertise;
- regular gender impact assessment of policies; and
- gender proofing to guarantee quality of legislative proposals and other policy documents.

(EC, 1998a)

In other words, there are problems of understanding, there is lack of expertise and there are no clear goals specified with ways to measure progress towards achieving them. These themes are echoed in the first report on progress since the adoption of the mainstreaming *Communication*. Here, the EC identifies the three main 'barriers to progress on mainstreaming' as the following:

- lack of awareness of gender issues at decision-making levels;
- lack of human and budgetary resources allocated to these tasks; and
- lack of gender expertise.

(CEC, 1998: 3)

These three factors also appear to be common issues at other levels of governance where attempts are being made to mainstream gender equality. We return to them later in this chapter. Underlying the barriers identified in both reports is the conceptual ambiguity surrounding mainstreaming.

Equal opportunities infrastructure in the UK

The principle of subsidiarity limits the influence of the EU: responsibility for equality policies still rests largely with the member states. In the UK, the infrastructure that delivers equal opportunities policies is made up of an extraordinary confusion of laws and agencies (see Bagilhole, 1997 for a map). Piecemeal responses have been made to accommodate European Directives (for example on employment rights for part-time workers) and the growth in political weight of an equality dimension (such as the disability lobby). The consequences of such an incremental approach, the muddle of bodies and legal arrangements, the hierarchies among equality agencies together with the disparities between the different countries of the UK are bewildering for employers and the public alike and have been exacerbated by devolution. *Context*

Underlying the confusion are some fundamental theoretical issues in conceptualising equal opportunities. A key issue here is the tension between the goal of legislating against discrimination based on an individual's membership of a particular group, and seeking to ensure the human rights of individual citizens. This tension has clear implications for the design of 'remedies'. Group discrimination has given rise to legislation such as the Sex Discrimination Act, the Equal Pay Act and the Race Relations Act, and the creation of equality bodies charged with upholding these laws: the Equal Opportunities Commission (EOC) and the Commission for Racial Equality (CRE). Concern with individual rights has given rise to the European Human Rights Convention, recently implemented by the UK government.

Let us just chart this crowded institutional playing field of equality agencies, bearing in mind the context of devolution. In Britain, there is the EOC, based in Manchester. Its remit was recently extended to include trans-sexualism (gender reassignment). It has small 'regional' offices and committees in Wales and Scotland and a Scottish and Welsh Commissioner but as yet no offices or designated Commissioners for the English regions. The DfEE's (1998) *Financial Management Survey* of the EOC, following its quinquennial review, recommended strengthening the regional infrastructure of the EOC.

The CRE has always had a regional infrastructure through its Race Equality Councils, and has also relatively recently opened offices for Scotland, Wales and Northern Ireland. The Disability Rights Commission established to uphold disability legislation has a budget of about £16 million (compared with the CRE's budget of £12 million which, in turn, is almost twice that of the EOC in GB). A non-statutory code of practice on age discrimination is planned. So there are new kids on the equality block.

However, in Northern Ireland, the three equality agencies on sex, race and disability have been merged with the Fair Employment Commission (which upholds the law in Northern Ireland on political and religious discrimination and for which there is no parallel legislation or institution in Britain) into one Equality Commission. The Fair Employment Commission was the equality agency with the strongest teeth and largest budget, and could insist that employers monitor their workforces on the basis of religion. It welcomed the amalgamation into a single Equality Commission; however, the EOC NI was, at least initially, a reluctant mergee, fearing that it would be a device, in effect, to save resources.

Post-devolution, the new Equality Commission is the key driver of equality mainstreaming (including gender equality). The Northern Ireland Act 1998 introduced a Statutory Duty on public bodies to promote equality of opportunity. All public authorities have been required to prepare an Equality Scheme and to submit this to the Equality Commission for approval. The civil service in Northern Ireland had operated Policy Appraisal for Fair Treatment (PAFT) on new policies for some years (McCrudden, 1996). This was already a much stronger and more widely known mechanism than the operationalisation of guidelines on policy appraisal operating in Whitehall, the Scottish Office and the Welsh Office. The imposition of a statutory duty represents a further strengthening of mainstreaming mechanisms in the Province.

Proposals for a merger of the equality agencies in Britain were live following the election of the Labour government in 1997; indeed, draft proposals for such an agency were produced by the Institute for Public Policy Research (Spencer and Bynoe, 1998). While they now appear to be on a back burner, the Northern Ireland merger is seen by some as a piloting of arrangements for Britain. In addition to the new Northern Ireland Equality Commission, for some time there has been a Standing Advisory Committee on Human Rights, which has now become the Northern Ireland Human Rights Commission. No such parallel body exists in Britain although it has been discussed and seems more likely to come into existence in view of the adoption of the Human Rights Convention.

Meanwhile, the sex equality legislation in GB, introduced in the mid-1970s and amended to accommodate the EC *Equal Pay for Work of Equal Value Directive* in 1986, is badly out of date and unmanageable. Introduced in a rush in order to pave the way for eligibility to join the European Economic Community, it has never worked effectively. Those who have brought cases and won them, a fraction of those who begin down that path, describe the outcome as 'pyrrhic victories' (Leonard, 1987). Having said that, despite its limited budget, the EOC has taken cases to both the House of Lords and to Strasbourg and won them. It tabled proposals to the government for new gender equality legislation in 1998 (EOC, 1998a) which have been rejected although many of the specific issues raised, such as the need for legislation for sexual orientation, may be addressed in the second Labour term of office.

The main strategic approach of the EOC since 1993 has been main-streaming equality, and this is reflected in its activities (see annual reports, most recently EOC, 1998b; EOC, 1999; EOC, 2000). Since the election of the Labour government in 1997, this policy has found more favour and indeed there is now a government sub-committee on mainstreaming to review the gender impact of new legislation. The Women's Unit (now Women and Equality Unit) based in the Cabinet Office, seeks to influence all government departments to mainstream equal opportunities in policy development. They have begun work to develop a Gender Impact Assessment Tool to supplement and thus strengthen existing guidance on Policy Appraisal for Equal Treatment (PAET).

Devolution is another key context within which mainstreaming is being developed. In 1999 two completely new political institutions were established, the Scottish Parliament and the National Assembly for Wales. Regional Development Agencies have also been established in England. The next section focuses on the particular case of mainstreaming and the Welsh Assembly and draws out lessons for future practice.[4]

Mainstreaming equality in the National Assembly for Wales

Wales provides a good test-bed for initiatives in gender equality. Patterns of gender segregation are particularly marked: female economic activity rates are below the GB average, rates of pay are lower than any English region and there are relatively few women in senior positions in work or public life (Aaron et al., 1994; Blackaby et al., 1999; Rees, 1999a). The Welsh Assembly provides a unique opportunity to address these issues at an all-Wales level and to organise politics differently. As with Scotland, a clear intention to avoid the Westminster style of government influenced the design of the building and the operating practices. For example, family-friendly methods of working have been introduced and the policy of mainstreaming equality has been endorsed by the Assembly in the conduct of its business. Moreover, all the publicly funded organisations for which the Assembly has responsibility – Assembly Sponsored Public Bodies (ASPBs) are obliged to provide, on an annual basis, information on their equal opportunities activities.

In Wales, the EOC, the CRE and Disability Wales (1998) successfully lobbied together to ensure that equal opportunities was written into the Government of Wales Act. Sections 48 and 120 make specific reference to the need for due regard to equal opportunities in the functions and business of the Assembly. These clauses were proposed by the equality agencies to seek to 'lock' mainstreaming into the responsibilities of the Assembly. The three agencies then produced a joint set of proposals on how equal opportunities could be mainstreamed in the design and business of the Welsh Assembly for the National Assembly Advisory Group, the committee set up to recommend to the Secretary of State how the Assembly should be organised (EOC, CRE and Disability Wales, 1998). Most (but not all) of the proposals were broadly accepted by the National Assembly Advisory Group and appeared in its recommendations to the Secretary of State for Wales on setting up the Assembly (National Assembly Advisory Group, 1998).[5]

An equal opportunities committee has been set up, chaired by a member of the Assembly's Cabinet. It is one of only two standing committees of the Assembly to cut across substantive areas (the other is on European issues). Its membership includes representatives from all subject committees (such as health and education) who then act as equality champions in their subject areas. The committee produces an annual report on the Assembly's progress in promoting equality of opportunity, as required by the Government of Wales Act. This includes, crucially, the promotion of equal opportunities in all ASPBs, including local authorities. The Assembly is currently conducting a pay review. An Equality Policy Unit has been established in the administration which conducted an equalities audit of all divisions to assess the extent to which they were equality issues (EOC, 2000). The Assembly's strategic plan for Wales for the next decade is based upon three pillars: equality of opportunities, sustainable development and tackling social disadvantage (betterwales.com).

Mainstreaming equality in local government in Wales

There are significant repercussions at the local level of these moves towards mainstreaming in the EU and in the National Assembly for Wales. The granting of Objective 1 status to Wales means that there is considerable interest among a wide range of organisations in accessing European funding for projects. In order to be successful, some account will have to be taken of EC stipulations on mainstreaming gender equality. Indeed, it was at a conference held in Newport, Gwent in 1996 that the (then) Regional Affairs Commissioner, Dr Monika Wulf-Matheis, stated that she would not fund bids that had not addressed the equal opportunities dimension (Wulf-Matheis, 1996). Local authorities and their partners will need to be seen to embrace the mainstreaming agenda and set up tools and mechanisms to deal with gender in European reporting requirements. The question is whether mainstreaming can be neatly side-stepped through rhetoric and astute box-ticking in annual reports and evaluation forms. Will the level of expertise among monitoring committees in Wales, London and Brussels be adequate to judge whether equality is being delivered or fudged?

In addition to the push from EU funding, there is also pressure from the Welsh Assembly, described above. As a result of the equality clauses in the Government of Wales Act, all those organisations in Wales (dubbed 'Quangoland' by Morgan and Roberts, 1993) in receipt of funding from the Assembly have to give annual reports on their progress on equal opportunities. This creates an unprecedented focus on gender equality. And it is not, of course, just local authorities that come into the orbit of the Assembly. The list includes: the NHS (the biggest employer in Wales) and its constituent Authorities and Trusts; primary, secondary, further and higher education; the newly enlarged Welsh Development Agency (with its budget of £200 million); and a variety of other publicly funded bodies.

The local authorities in Wales have, then, a clear reason to focus attention on mainstreaming equality: for many, both their main sources of revenue (the Welsh Assembly and the EC) are insisting on attention being paid to this issue. Equality also is relevant for the Best Value agenda analysed elsewhere in this volume. It is then perhaps not surprising that the Welsh Local Government Association, working with the equality agencies and the Local Government Management Board in Wales, has produced an equal opportunities toolkit for local authorities (WLGA, 1999).

Similarly, Chwarae Teg (Fair Play), a consortium of Welsh employers concerned to promote the quality and equality of women employed in Wales, has been working with technical assistance monies from the EC to pilot work with partners on mainstreaming equality into Structural Fund bids. The main result from the first year of the project was the discovery that the level of understanding of equality issues among the partners was very low indeed. Rather than developing innovative approaches to mainstreaming in projects to be supported by Structural Funds, as intended, there was considerable work to be done on providing a basic introduction to equal opportunities issues and an awareness of existing sex equality legislation (Chwarae Teg, 1998).

It remains early days to assess the extent to which elected Members of the Assembly will use these opportunities to promote mainstream equality in the business of the Assembly and influence local authorities to do the same. However, enabling provisions have been locked into the design of the institution. Moreover, a record-breaking 40 per cent of the 60 members elected to the Assembly are women, a far higher proportion than has ever been returned to local authorities or the Westminster Parliament from Wales. They include some individuals who have been very active in the field of equal opportunities: this means that equality issues, for once, may be relatively high on the agenda in Wales.

Conclusion: problems and prospects

Mainstreaming equality has come to dominate the discourse of equal opportunities at a number of levels of governance. However, it is clear that there is little consensus as to what it means beyond the broad idea of 'integrating' gender equality. Like other approaches to equal opportunities, it is susceptible to being ignored or manipulated. While there are some attempts at different levels of governance to build gender equality into ways of operating and mechanisms of resource allocation, monitoring and evaluation, there is as yet little concrete experience upon which to draw to assess impact. Mainstreaming is, in any case, a long-term agenda, an approach to equal opportunities designed to complement that of equal treatment in the law and positive action.

Despite this, it is possible to draw out what might be some key principles of mainstreaming and to identify tools to implement it as a policy approach (Rees, 1999b). The principles of mainstreaming include what I have called 'visioning', that is, an analysis of how existing systems and structures discriminate, and taking steps to change them. They also include integrating equality into the culture and organisation; regarding the employee as a whole person (who may have family responsibilities); respect and dignity for the individual; consultation with employees and service users on how they experience discrimination, and building ownership of the mainstreaming agenda throughout the organisation. Tools to implement these principles include gender monitoring, gender disaggregated statistics and equality indicators; gender proofing and auditing; awareness raising and training, and drafting in expertise (Sweden has 'flying experts' in mainstreaming, working with government departments). It is also necessary to develop lines of responsibility, through, for example, including equal opportunities in performance review and staff development.

There are elements of these principles and tools in place at some levels of governance but the approach is rather haphazard. A key difficulty is the lack of appreciation of the complexity of the equal opportunities agenda and the level of expertise and training that is required in order to implement mainstreaming. In particular, widening the concern with equal opportunities from one of internal human resource management to one that addresses the allocation of rationed, publicly funded goods and services will require considerable expertise. Experiences of mainstreaming to date illustrate it is essential to have a clear understanding of individual rights, group discrimination and disadvantage, direct and indirect discrimination, issues surrounding sameness and difference, and of the differences and similarities between the equality dimensions in terms of policy principles and tools that are appropriate. Without that understanding underpinning attempts to mainstream gender equality, then positive outcomes will inevitably remain limited.

[handwritten margin notes: Must have clearer understand of Mainstreaming. Better understanding required.]

Notes

1. The chapter draws on research conducted in my capacity as a consultant to the EC on mainstreaming and as the Equal Opportunities Commissioner for Wales but does not necessarily represent the views of either organisation. It was written as devolution was coming into place.
2. See European Parliament (1998) for details of these Directives. There are nine in all. The crucial one is the equal treatment Directive on pay in 1975. This was followed by a series that attempted to plug gaps in the provision of equal treatment, for example among self-employed women, and to address equal treatment in social security. Directives in the 1990s have addressed the health and safety of at work of pregnant and breastfeeding women, parental leave and the shift in the burden of proof in cases of discrimination based on sex.
3. The Structural Fund Objectives for the period 1994–9 were as follows:
   (1) To promote the development and structural adjustment of regions whose development is lagging behind;
   (2) To convert regions seriously affected by industrial decline;
   (3) To combat unemployment and facilitate the integration of young people;
   (4) To facilitate the adaptation of workers to industrial changes in production;
   (5a) To speed up the adjustment of agricultural structures;
   (5b) To promote the development of rural areas;
   (6) Assisting the development for sparsely populated areas.

   The Structural Fund Objectives for 2000–6 are:
   (1) Regions whose developments is lagging behind;
   (2) Regions undergoing economic and social conversion;
   (3) Human resources.
4. For parallel developments in mainstreaming in Scotland, see Mackay and Bilton (2000).
5. Among proposals was one concerning training in equal opportunities for Assembly members; this was rejected on the grounds that this was the responsibility of political parties.

References

Aaron, J., Rees, T., Betts, S. and Vincentelli, M. (eds) (1994), *Our Sisters' Land: The Changing Identities of Women in Wales*, Cardiff: University of Wales Press.
Bacchi, C. L. (1994), *The Politics of Affirmative Action: Women, Equality and Category Politics*, London: Sage.
Bacchi, C. L. (1996), *Same Difference: Feminism and Sexual Difference*, Sydney: Allen and Unwin.
Bagilhole, B. (1997), *Equal Opportunities and Social Policy*, Harlow: Longman.
Blackaby, D. et al. (1999), *Women in Senior Management in Wales*, Manchester: Equal Opportunities Commission.
de Bruijn, J. (1995), 'Equal Opportunities and New Requirements for New Jobs' in European Commission *Follow-up to the White Paper on Growth, Competitiveness and Employment: Equal Opportunities for Women and Men*, Report to the European Commission's Employment Task Force, Brussels: DGV European Commission V/5538/95–EN.
Chwarae Teg (1996), *Women, Players in Regional Development – Conference Report*, Chwarae Teg and Gateway Europe.
Chwarae Teg (1998), *European Equality Partnerships: Integrating Equal Opportunities in the European Structural Funds*, Progress Report, Cardiff: Chwarae Teg.
Cockburn, C. (1989), 'Equal Opportunities: The Short and Long Agenda', *Industrial Relations Journal*, Vol. 20, No. 3, pp. 213–25.
Commission of the European Communities (1996), *Incorporating Equal Opportunities for Women and Men into All Community Policies and Activities*, COM(96)67 final (the mainstreaming Communication), Luxembourg: Office for Official Publications of the European Communities.
Commission of the European Communities (1998), *Progress Report from Commission on the follow-up of the Communication: 'Incorporating Equal Opportunities for Women and Men into All Community Policies and Activities'*, COM(1998) 122 Final, Brussels: Commission of the European Communities.
Commission of the European Communities (1999), *Women and Science: Mobilising Women to Enrich European Research*, Communication from the Commission, COM(1999) 76 final, Luxembourg: Office for Official Publications of the European Communities.
Commission of the European Communities and Social Dialogue (1993), *Joint Opinion on Women and Training*, SEC(93) 1977, Brussels: Commission of the European Communities.
Council of Europe (1998), *Gender Mainstreaming: Conceptual Framework, Methodology and Presentation of Good Practice*, Strasbourg: Council of Europe.
Council of Ministers (1996), 'Resolution on Mainstreaming Equal Opportunities for Women and Men into the European Structural Funds', 2/12/1996, *Official Journal* C 386 of 20/12/1996.
Department for Education and Employment (1998), *Equal Opportunities Commission Financial Management Survey 1998*, London: DFEE.
Duncan, S. (1996a), 'The Diverse Worlds of European Patriarchy', in M. D. Garcia-Ramon and J. Monk (eds) *Women of the European Union*, London: Routledge.
Duncan, S. (1996b), 'Obstacles to a Successful Equal Opportunities Policy in the European Union', *European Journal of Women's Studies*, Vol. 3, No. 4, pp. 399–422.

Equal Opportunities Commission (1997), *Mainstreaming Gender Equality in Local Government: A Framework*, Manchester: Equal Opportunities Commission.

Equal Opportunities Commission (1998a), *Equality in the 21st Century: A New Sex Equality Law for Britain*, Manchester: Equal Opportunities Commission.

Equal Opportunities Commission (1998b), *Making Equality Work: The Challenge for Government, 1997 Annual Report*, Manchester: Equal Opportunities Commission.

Equal Opportunities Commission (1999), *Setting the Agenda for Equality, 1998 Annual Report*, Manchester: Equal Opportunities Commission.

Equal Opportunities Commission (2000), *Equality in the 21st Century, 1999/2000 Annual Report*, Manchester: Equal Opportunities Commission.

Equal Opportunities Commission, Commission for Racial Equality and Disability Wales (1998), *Mainstreaming Equality: The National Assembly for Wales*, Cardiff: EOC.

European Commission (1994), *Growth, Competitiveness, Employment: The Challenges and Ways Forward into the 21st Century – White Paper*, Luxembourg: Office for Official Publications of the European Communities.

European Commission (1995), *Follow-up to the White Paper on Growth, Competitiveness and Employment Equal Opportunities for Women and Men Report to the European Commission's Employment Task Force*, Brussels: DGV European Commission V/5538/95–EN.

European Commission (1997), *Equal Opportunities for Women and Men in the European Union: Annual Report 1996*, COM(96) 650, final, Luxembourg: Office for Official Publications of the European Communities.

European Commission (1998a), *Equal Opportunities for Women and Men in the European Union: Annual Report 1997*, Luxembourg: Office for Official Publications of the European Communities.

European Commission (1998b), *From Guide-lines to Action: The National Action Plans for Employment*, Luxembourg: Office for Official Publications of the European Communities.

European Commission (1998c), *A Guide to Gender Impact Assessment*, Brussels: DGV V/D/5 European Commission.

European Commission (1999) *Equal Opportunities for Women and Men in the European Union: Annual Report 1998*, Luxembourg: Office for the Official Publications for the European Communities.

European Commission (2000), *Equal Opportunities for Women and Men in the European Union: Annual Report 1999*, Luxembourg: Office for Official Publications of the European Communities.

European Parliament (1998), *Women's Rights and the Treaty of Amsterdam*, Directorate General for Research, Working Paper, Women's Rights Series, FEMM 104 EN, Luxembourg: European Parliament.

Flynn, P. (1998), Answer to Written Question E–0631/98, European Parliament (98/C 323/78) *Official Journal of the Commission*, 323/59, 21/10/98.

Fox Keller, E. and Longino, H. E. (1996), *Feminism and Science*, Oxford: OUP.

Lefebvre, M-C. (1993), *Evaluation of Women's Involvement in European Social Fund Co-financed Measures in 1990*, Final report for DGV, Social Europe Supplement 2/93, Luxembourg: Office for Official Publications of the European Communities.

Leonard, A. (1987), *Pyrrhic Victories: Winning Sex Discrimination and Equal Pay Cases in the Industrial Tribunals* 1980–84, London: HMSO.

Mackay, F. and Bilton, K. (2000), *Learning from Experience: Lessons in Mainstreaming Equal Opportunities*, Edinburgh: University of Edinburgh.

McCrudden, C. (1996), *Mainstreaming Fairness? A Discussion Paper on Policy Appraisal and Fair Treatment*, Belfast: Committee for the Administration of Justice.

Mitchell, M. and Russell, D. (1994), 'Race, Citizenship and "Fortress Europe"', in P. Brown and R. Crompton (eds) *Economic Restructuring and social exclusion*, London: UCL Press.

Morgan, K. and Roberts, E. (1993), 'The Democratic Deficit: A Guide to Quangoland', *Papers in Planning Research No. 144*, Cardiff: Department of City and Regional Planning, University of Wales, Cardiff.

National Assembly Advisory Group (1998), *The National Assembly for Wales: Recommendations*, Cardiff: National Assembly Advisory Group.

National Assembly for Wales (2000) *betterwales.com: The Strategic Plan*, Cardiff: National Assembly for Wales.www.betterwales.com.

OECD (1994), *Women and Structural Change*, Paris: OECD.

Osborn, M. et al. (2000), *Science Policies in the European Union: Promoting Excellence through Mainstreaming Gender Equality. A report from the ETAN Network on Women and Science*, Luxembourg: Office for Official Publications of the European Communities: www.cordis.lu/science-society/women/htm.

Rees, T. (1998), *Mainstreaming Equality in the European Union*, London: Routledge.

Rees, T. (1999a), *Women and Work: 25 Years of Gender Equality in Wales*, Cardiff: University of Wales Press.

Rees, T. (1999b), 'Mainstreaming Equality', in S. Watson and L. Doyal (eds) *Engendering Social Policy*, Milton Keynes: Open University Press.

Rossilli, M. (1997), 'The European Community's Policy on the Equality of Women: From the Treaty of Rome to the Present', *European Journal of Women's Studies*, Vol. 4, No. 1, pp. 63–82.

Rubery, J. and Fagan, C. (1998), *Equal Opportunities and Employment in the European Union*, Vienna: Federal Ministry of Labour, Health and Social Affairs and Federal Ministry for Women's Affairs and Consumer Protection.

Rubery, J., Smith, M., Fagan, C. and Grimshaw, D. (1998), *Women and European Employment*, London: Routledge.

Schiebinger, L. (1989), *The Mind Has No Sex? Women in the Origins of Modern Science*, Cambridge, Mass: Harvard University Press.

Schiebinger, L. (1999), *Has Feminism Changed Science?*, Cambridge, Mass: Harvard University Press.

Spencer, S. (1999), 'Delivering Human Rights for Women in Britain', paper presented at the Institute for Public Policy Research seminar *Delivering Human Rights and Equality for Women*, 15 June, London: IPPR.

Spencer, S. and Bynow, I. (1998), *A Human Rights Commission: The Options for Britain and Northern Ireland*, London: Institute for Public Policy Research.

Welsh Local Government Association (1999), *Equal Opportunities Toolkit*, Cardiff: WLGA.

Women's National Commission, Equal Opportunities Commission and Equal Opportunities Commission for Northern Ireland (1997), *In Pursuit of Equality: A National Agenda for Action*, Manchester: Equal Opportunities Commission.

Wulf-Matheis, M. (1996), 'The Structural Funds and Equal Opportunities', in Chwarae Teg (Fair Play) (ed.) *Women, Players in Regional Development*, Cardiff: Chwarae Teg.

4
Divide and be Ruled? Multiple Discrimination and the Concept of Social Exclusion

Barbara Bagilhole

This chapter investigates 'social exclusion' as a policy context within which attempts can be made to respond to problems of multiple discrimination. The complexity of the definitions of social exclusion are explored, and their merits and drawbacks as a potential vehicle for equality projects are considered and evaluated. The chapter compares the narrow discourse of social exclusion which concentrates on 'social integration' through individual economic contribution with the more comprehensive and broad-based discourse of social, economic and political inclusion through the removal of discrimination. The former defines social exclusion through the promotion of a message that paid work is the only contribution to society that is legitimate. This is acknowledged as problematic for the equal opportunities project, particularly for women, ethnic minorities and disabled people. It is argued that the complexity of the various processes of both social exclusion and discrimination against women, disabled people and ethnic minority communities means that neither will, nor can be, reduced or eliminated by single focus policy initiatives. Therefore, the chapter argues for the conceptualisation of social exclusion beyond a narrow focus upon labour market participation. Also, alongside this it advocates an 'integrated' conceptualisation of equal opportunities across the areas where anti-discrimination legislation presently exists (sex, race and disability) as a response to these political developments. It argues for using the context of social exclusion to enable the formulation of integrated equal opportunities legislation which outlaws discrimination against women, ethnic minorities and disabled people, and which includes a single umbrella monitoring and enforcing agency.

Equal opportunities and the political agenda

The major question addressed in this chapter is: How can equal opportunities be advanced within the political agenda of social exclusion? Walby sets out a similar project based around the transformation of gender relations through women's greater and more successful participation in the labour market. She considers the question of 'how to engage with proposed new ways of addressing old problems of injustice' (Walby, 1999: 1).

Equal opportunities as a concept is ultimately political, even though it impacts on most people only as organisational or bureaucratic procedures, and there are many motivating factors for its development (Bagilhole, 1997). Equal opportunities policies did not simply arise because governments decided to legislate or employers to improve their personnel policies. The idea of tapping into other agendas and priorities has long been recognised and advocated as a useful political strategy to further equal opportunities. For example, Wooding (1998) argued that language was crucial when advocating equal opportunities. He suggested that the dominant political language could be used strategically. Certainly, the tracing of the historical development of equal opportunities theory and policy in the UK showed that it has evolved as its major driving forces and catalysts have changed in dominance over time (Bagilhole, 1997). Some examples of the development and adaptation of equal opportunities discourse have been arguments around the 'business case', 'managing diversity' and 'mainstreaming' (see Bagilhole, 1997). Therefore, in its turn the Labour government's dominant discourse of 'social exclusion' demanded attention. For as Gregory warned: 'the single most important factor determining the success or failure of civil rights legislation is political commitment on the part of governments. Statements of principle or good intent enshrined in statute ... undermined by conflicting government policies will be ineffective' (1999: 98).

What connections are there between social exclusion and equal opportunities?

As Lee and Murie (1999) point out, the concept of social exclusion is disputed and there are many definitions within the current discourse. In some of its definitions social exclusion has a lot to offer the equal opportunities community, in terms of a political agenda to embrace. This is because the concept can lend itself to the examination of the dynamic processes that create, reinforce and maintain disadvantage and deprivation for particular groups in society. In this form it goes beyond poverty or economic exclusion to embrace exclusion from citizenship through political, social, and cultural processes and lack of power. As Walker argued, social exclusion was 'the dynamic process of being shut out, fully or partially, from any of the social, economic, political and cultural systems which determine the integration of a person in society' (1997: 8). This definition enables the investigation of disadvantage in the labour market, in welfare service delivery and outcomes, and importantly the influence and contribution of discrimination to exclusion. Also, as Lee and Murie (1999) argued, it allows the consideration of what and who are doing the excluding, and the multiple nature of this deprivation for some people.

However, it can also be argued that, whilst this complexity of the concept of social exclusion can be useful and conducive to the equal opportunities project, it can also hold dangers. Lee and Murie highlighted that in policy terms 'the vagueness of the term arguably increases its practical value ... and enables political acceptability' (1999: 3). At the same time its very vagueness could allow the dominance of the narrow definition of social exclusion: exclusion from the labour market. This could camouflage or distort policies for eliminating inequality by keeping them off the agenda or at least on the backburner. 'Policies designed to integrate people into the workforce will not be relevant to all sections of the population but focus on those of working age and those who do not have demanding unpaid care responsibilities' (Lee and Murie, 1999: 7). Other people who may find these policies irrelevant or at least inadequate can be added; people whose disability limits or prevents their participation in the labour market, and indeed are users of unpaid care themselves; women, disabled people and ethnic minorities, who are disadvantaged in, and discriminated against by, the labour market.

The Labour government elected in 1997 adopted the elimination of social exclusion as one of its priorities and central planks of policy, and established a special Cabinet Office unit for this purpose. However, through its advocacy of policies on the New Deal, it appears to have emphasised a simplistic definition of social exclusion, singularly focused on getting people into paid work. While this emphasis is useful and essential for some groups, for others it remains a problem. As Walby argued, 'the focus on contribution and participation in society through paid work is widely regarded as appropriate for all those whose circumstances allow it. The problems come in determining how the polity is to take account of both the need to care and to be cared for' (1999: 2–3). What is to happen to those who are restricted in the paid work they can do by either unpaid caring responsibilities or the need for care themselves? Added to this, how are they to be valued? Also, single-focused 'Welfare to Work' policies cannot tackle discrimination endemic within the labour market for women, disabled people and ethnic minorities. The equality laws[1] (EPA, SDA, RRA, and DDA) were 'designed precisely to intervene in the market in order to protect vulnerable groups from exploitation' (Gregory, 1999).

A definition of social exclusion based on exclusion from the labour market tends not to mention discrimination or allow room for the inclusion of analysis by social divisions. The divide in society is defined as either being 'included' or 'excluded' as an individual or a geographical area. Also, as Rees has argued, 'inequalities among those in employment are obscured by a focus on the relationship between the employed and the unemployed' and 'the amount of attention paid to those outside the labour market' is diminished (1998: 175). However, employment and unemployment are not distributed equally in Britain. Those in higher-paid, higher-status and higher-powered jobs are more than likely to be white, non-disabled and male (Bagilhole, 1994). Also, as Rees (1998) highlighted, significant aspects of social life are diminished by this discourse of social exclusion. She raises the crucial problem of ignoring unpaid work when trying to deal with equal opportunities for women. But it might be argued that this is an even more serious deficit for disabled people, many of whom rely on unpaid work for their care.

Another important problem which should be signalled for disabled people is the forceful rhetoric around 'rights' going only to those who fulfil their 'duties', and the idea that nothing should be given to those who contribute nothing in terms of productive paid work. The following extract from a speech on social exclusion made by the Prime Minister at the Aylesbury estate, Southwark, illustrates this:

> We should reject the *rootless morality* whose symptom is a false choice between bleeding hearts and couldn't care less, when what we need is one grounded in the *core of British values*, the sense of fairness and a balance between *rights and duties*. The basis of this modern civic society is an ethic of mutual responsibility or duty. It is *something for something*. A society where we *play by the rules*. You can *only take out if you put in*. That's the bargain. (www.open.gov.uk/co/seu/more.html, 1998: 6; my emphasis)

Another deficit in a narrow definition of social exclusion is that it does not include on the agenda the issue of improvement in social security benefits for those not able to work. It has started to construct a division between those able to work and those not able to work, with the latter being considered for improvements in benefit levels but not the former. It is in danger of creating a new deserving/undeserving poor distinction. People are seen as deserving only if they contribute through paid work.

As Lee and Murie highlight: 'the problem of aligning social exclusion with integration through paid employment has consequences for the way in which unpaid work is regarded. The integration of carers and those that cannot take up employment but are deprived requires separate attention' (1999: 8). As Levitas argues, in the government's discourse 'there is little recognition of the fact that society depends upon large amounts of unpaid work, chiefly done by women' (1997: 3), and we should add (as mentioned above), which many disabled people rely upon for their care. Therefore, this chapter will argue that policies to eliminate inequality across the social divisions of gender, 'race' and disability requires both separate attention and the maintenance of the broader conceptualization and discourse of social exclusion.

As Abberley (1996) argues, emphasis on paid work means that disabled people who are unable to work are regarded as less than full members of society. Disablism means that disabled people are in an inferior position to other groups. They are disadvantaged not only in terms of employment, but in housing, finance, transport and education (Bagilhole, 1997). Also, disabled people have been denied access to key political, educational and cultural institutions which could enable them to participate fully in society (Oliver, 1990). This exclusion of disabled people has had profound effects on social relations, resulting not only in the marginalisation of disabled people within labour markets, but from society as a whole (Oliver, 1991).

The government's 'Welfare to Work' agenda has come to dominate many areas of policy, as seen in the targeting of lone mothers. Even specific strategies for disabled people place virtually all their emphasis on making them 'employable'. Harriet Harman, just before her removal as Minister for Social Security, announced a 'Radical Strategy for Disabled People'. One of the cornerstones of the strategy was to 'sweep away the obstacles to work in the benefit rules and system':

> This announcement will give a significant boost to those disabled people who want to work. The Government wants to give

marginalized and excluded people *a hand up not a hand out.* (www.disabilitynet.co.uk/info/employment/harmoutwtw.html, 1998: 2; my emphasis)

What she did not mention in her press release was that even those disabled people in employment are disproportionately represented in lower-status and lower-paid jobs (Barnes, 1991). Before the Disability Discrimination Act 1995, disabled people could legally be refused employment simply because they were disabled, even though their disability was irrelevant to the job they applied for (Barnes, 1991). Most employers maintain stereotypical views of disabled people, such as reservations about their ability to do certain jobs and their level of productivity. Also, because of certain individual impairments, there cannot be total inclusion of all disabled people into the world of productive labour. Optimistic views emerged over the potential of new technology to challenge the view that physical ability was still a useful skill in modern society and to back the social model of disability by showing environmental and attitudinal barriers to be the true source of disability (Finkelstein, 1980). However, to date technology has generally been used to 'correct' the deficits of the impaired individual, rather than impacting on employment barriers. In other words, the question asked is, how can disabled people be adapted to make them suitable for employment? Therefore, attempts to reduce inequality for disabled people in the labour market have failed because they concentrate on the labour supply side of the equation (Oliver, 1991).

Another area of concern for disabled people concerns the Disability Discrimination Act (DDA) itself, which should ensure that those disabled people who can and wish to engage in paid work can do so equally. However, the DDA applies only to employers with 15 or more staff, leaving 92.5 per cent of employers outside the Act. Brian Lamb, Head of Public Affairs at Scope, the cerebral palsy charity, stated that 'many disabled people would remain unsupported by the law, excluded from the workforce and reliant on state benefits' (Brindle, 1998).

A glimmer of hope: a call to claim social exclusion

The previous section, using an analysis particularly around disability, has attempted to show that social exclusion is problematic in many ways for the equal opportunities project, if it is advocated in a simplistic form. In contrast, the more complex discourse of social exclusion appears useful, acknowledging that exclusion may be produced by factors, such as direct or indirect discrimination against women, ethnic minorities and disabled people. There was 'an intrinsic connection between discussion of social exclusion, and concern with inequality ... The discourse in which social exclusion is embedded in British critical social policy is essentially redistributive' (Levitas, 1997: 2). Lister also argued that social exclusion did have a value:

> It is a more multi-dimensional concept than poverty, embracing a variety of ways in which people may be denied full participation in society ... Different dimensions of exclusion can interact and compound each other. For example, black people are not only more vulnerable to poverty than white people but the exclusion that they experience can be exacerbated by racism which undermines their effective rights as citizens. Racism, and other forms of discriminatory and oppressive behaviour and attitudes such as sexism, homophobia and disablism, can, at the same time, operate as mechanisms of exclusion even in the case of those who have adequate material resources. (Lister, 2000: 1)

This discourse of social exclusion can be seen to be useful not only to maintaining but also to developing and enhancing equal opportunities policies within the political agenda. As Walby argued, 'the effective implementation of equal opportunities policies is one of the prerequisites to securing social inclusion ... for women' (1999: 4). This is, of course, also true for disabled people and ethnic minorities. The concept of social exclusion can open up and allow the consideration of how exclusion from one area impacts on and creates exclusion from other areas. As Room argued, social exclusion 'involves the analysis of the mechanisms and relations of the process and the interaction between different elements that lead to exclusion' (1995: 10). This allows, for example, the consideration of how discrimination experienced by a disabled person in one area of life will impact on other areas of their life.

The discourse of social exclusion can encourage the recognition that women, ethnic minorities and disabled people are not homogeneous groups. For example, discrimination experienced by a black person may be extended and changed if they are also disabled or a woman. Thus social exclusion can be associated with, and lends itself to, policies for the elimination of multiple deprivation. The research on different aspects of social exclusion identifies key groups vulnerable to exclusion, in many cases the same groups where legislation seeks to eliminate discrimination: women, disabled people and ethnic minorities. As Lee and Murie argued, 'social exclusion will prove resistant to initiatives that have a single focus and there is general acknowledgement of the need to adopt new approaches to service planning and delivery' (1999: 43). Social exclusion, by encouraging a multiple focus, has a potential knock-on effect on the development of equal opportunities policy. However, to take advantage of this, equal opportunities policy needs to move towards a multiple focus approach itself and away from the present divided focuses on women, ethnic minorities and disabled people exemplified by the single focus Acts in these areas. This chapter will now lay out the advantages for a move to an 'integrated/generic' approach across the social divisions of gender, 'race' and disability.

Multiple discrimination and arguments for an 'integrated/generic' approach to equal opportunities: 'falling between two or more stools, or between the cracks'

An argument for an 'integrated/generic' approach to equal opportunities is that multiple discrimination can be personified in one individual. In reality, social divisions can be manifested in an individual in different ways, with a different impact at different times, and in different circumstances. This highlights the inadequacy of the present legislation. As Gregory argued, 'the piecemeal approach of the last 20 years has left a legacy of unwieldy and complicated laws which provide an uneven and uncertain route to justice for individuals and groups experiencing discrimination' (1999: 105). Given the separation of the discrimination legislation along gender, 'race' and disability lines (SDA, RRA and DDA), where do people experiencing multiple discrimination turn for recourse? Their decision can be crucial to the success of their case. Do black women use the SDA or RRA? Do disabled women use the DDA or SDA? Do black disabled women use the DDA or RRA or SDA? The correct answer can depend more on who is doing the discriminating, and/or who to use as a comparator, rather than the nature of the discrimination.

What we have to deal with is multiple, intersecting and merging layers of identity and experience. For example, research on black women in the National Health Service (Bagilhole and Stephens, 1997) has shown that they may encounter either sexism or racism at different times and in different circumstances, or they may experience one oppression tempered and changed by the other. This is confirmed by statistics which show that women are disproportionately victims of racial harassment (CRE, 1996). One example in the NHS research was of a black nurse told by a male doctor that 'usually he asked his nurses to wear black stockings, but in her case white would be better'. Should this woman take recourse under the SDA or RRA? What are the consequences if he is black?

As Bacchi (1996) demonstrates in her investigation of affirmative action programmes, the designation of target groups, such as women, necessarily defines the rest as men, thereby allowing 'multi oppressed' women to fall through the cracks in many programmes.

Avoiding 'divide and rule'

Another argument for an 'integrated/generic' approach to equal opportunities is that different groups do share certain discrimination in common and may be able to control the powerful 'divide and rule' effect if they can unite on these issues, whilst of course acknowledging and being sensitive to their specialist needs. If we take women, ethnic minorities and disabled people, we see a hotch-potch of theory, policy and practice.

There is a lack of continuity in the use of a variety of language and terminology around oppression, and responsibility for the enforcement of equal opportunities legislation. Even if we look at the single-focused enforcing agencies, we find the Commission for Racial Equality answering to the Home Office, and the Equal Opportunities Commission, and the Disability Rights Commission under the remit of the Department for Education and Employment. All these agencies have different expertise, but it would be more useful for organisations wishing to pursue equal opportunities if they were one umbrella body. Gregory (1999) identified the need for the addition of some form of Equal Pay Commission, given the increasing fragmentation of the labour market and complexity of payment systems. Hastings (1997, cited in Gregory, 1999) argued that implementation of the minimum wage would inevitably have an effect on equal pay; any body set up to monitor its implementation should have a broader remit to include equal pay issues. However, this would add on another complication in the form of yet another enforcing agency. This encourages identity politics and can force people into 'essentialist' categories (Bacchi, 1996).

In contrast, an 'integrated/generic' approach to equal opportunities with one piece of legislation and one enforcing agency could link equal opportunities issues common to 'race', gender and disability, into effective coherent proactive policies. What are needed are both policies and practices to deal with 'shared discrimination' across more than one group, and 'specialist discrimination' experienced within one group. On top of this, 'multiple discrimination' must be addressed, where one person can cross group boundaries, as discussed above, which is possibly the strongest argument for an 'integrated/generic' approach to equal opportunities. As Gregory acknowledged, 'the protection from discrimination enshrined in current equal opportunities legislation is patchy and incoherent, both in terms of the groups protected and the areas of activity covered' (1999: 112). The piecemeal approach is confusing, both for complainants experiencing multiple discrimination and for organisations implementing equal opportunities policies, as the expertise they need is located in separate agencies. These disparate bodies should be brought together under an 'umbrella' equal opportunities law.

An 'integrated/generic' approach would be facilitated by incorporating the present diverse equal opportunities legislation into one piece of legislation which identifies and prohibits disadvantage and discrimination experienced in common by women, ethnic minorities and disabled people, whilst also recognising particular disadvantage in different groups. To be effective, this would need to be proactive legislation which requires equal opportunities practice within organisations by demanding such things as equal opportunities audits, and monitoring of outcomes for women, ethnic minorities and disabled people.

What changes need to be made to the legislation?

Besides the incorporation of the single-focused equal opportunities legislation into a single Equal Opportunities Act, other changes are also needed to make it both pro-active and effective. There have been many suggested changes. First, shifting the responsibility of burden of proof from employees to prove they have been discriminated against to employers to prove they have not discriminated is an essential element of more proactive legislation. There is a precedent for this. The Fair Employment (Northern Ireland) Act 1989, outlawing religious discrimination, required employers to monitor the make-up of their workforce and evaluate recruitment, training and promotion practices. To monitor these procedures a Fair Employment Commission was established, which had the powers to impose positive action, including setting goals and timetables for eliminating discrimination. As Gregory argued, 'the policy of shifting responsibility for dismantling discrimination firmly onto the institutions that reproduce it, and away from individuals who experience it, promises to be both a more efficient and fairer way of proceeding' (1999: 106).

Also, the legislation needs more teeth than the present Acts possess. Gregory argued that the 'time has come for stronger sanctions against organisations that continue to ignore the expertise on offer. They should be required to undertake equality audits and pay audits and to develop programmes for the eradication of any inequalities revealed. An enforcement agency would need to be given the powers and resources to scrutinize this process and to take legal action where necessary' (1999: 106). This enforcement agency would be more effective as an umbrella body containing the present extensive expertise across gender, 'race' and disability.

Scott argued that 'equality requires the recognition and inclusion of differences' (1988: 48). This approach provides the framework for creating a much more imaginative and proactive piece of legislation, which recognises both the common and diverse interests of women, ethnic minorities, and disabled people. For example, if employers were required to prove that their recruitment procedures were fair, it makes sense that this is done for all groups at the same time. Thus a single piece of legislation would not undermine the equal opportunities project, but strengthen it. As Gregory argued, 'feminism is strengthened by its recognition of the different experiences and interests of women and the need for a social movement which ensures that all of them have a voice' (1999: 109). This is also true for ethnic minorities and disabled people, some of whom, of course, will be women.

As Hoskyns argued, 'a recognition of diversity does not necessarily lead to political paralysis; it can provide the basis for solidarity and common action on specific issues' (1996: 110). Moves towards integration have already been made. 'Equality proofing' was introduced into Britain in relation to gender and 'race' towards the end of the 1980s through the initiative of the Ministerial Group on Women's Issues across all government departments. However, there was no mechanism for coordination across departments, whereas a single Equal Opportunities Act and umbrella enforcing agency would have the potential to address these issues, with a single unit to oversee the process of integrating equal opportunities.

Conclusion

This chapter has considered the concept of social exclusion in both its simplistic and more complex forms. It argues that the narrow discourse of social exclusion which limits the agenda to the need for inclusion into paid work is problematic for the equal opportunities project in many ways. However, the broad-based discourse of social exclusion, which allows the consideration of social, economic and political inclusion through the removal of discrimination, is very useful. It is proposed that not only does it allow equal opportunities to be an important and essential aspect of its agenda, but it also encourages the development of equal opportunities towards an integrated approach across gender, 'race' and disability. Thus, an integrated approach to equal opportunities through a single piece of legislation and a single body for its review and implementation can be advanced and developed through the use of the discourse of social exclusion in its complex form.

This would involve the incorporation of the present piecemeal equal opportunities legislation into one Equal Opportunities Act, with one monitoring and enforcing agency encompassing the divided expertise on gender, 'race', and disability. It is argued that through this single Act a more effective, pro-active equal opportunities project could be built which addresses the issues of multiple discrimination and deprivation and the important issue of misleading identity politics, which can lead to groups being divided and ruled.

Note

1. These include the Equal Pay Act (EPA), Sex Discrimination Act (SDA), which deal with gender inequality; Race Relations Act (RRA) and the Race Relations (Amendment) Act, which deal with 'race' discrimination; and the Disability Discrimination Act (DDA), which deals with discrimination against disabled people.

References

Abberley, P. (1996), 'Work, Utopia and Impairment', in L. Barton (ed.) *Disability and Society: Emerging Issues and Insights*, London: Longman.

Bacchi, C. L. (1996), *The Politics of Affirmative Action: Women, Equality, and Category Politics*, London: Sage.

Bagilhole, B. (1994), *Women ,Work and Equal Opportunities*, Aldershot: Avebury.

Bagilhole, B. (1997), *Equal Opportunities and Social Policy; Issues of Gender, 'Race' and Disability*, Harlow: Addison Wesley Longman.

Bagilhole, B. and Stephens, M. (1997), 'Women Speak Out: Equal Opportunities in Employment For Ethnic Minority Women Workers in a National Health Service Hospital Trust', *Social Services Research*, No. 1, pp. 11–25.

Barnes, C. (1991), *Disabled People in Britain and Discrimination*, London: Hurst and Co.

Brindle, D. (1998), 'Anti-bias Measure "Betrays" Disabled', *Guardian*, 9 September.

CRE (1996), *Annual Report*, London: Commission for Racial Equality.

Finkelstein, V. (1980), *Attitudes and Disabled People: Issues for Discussion*, New York: World Rehabilitation Fund.

Gregory, J. (1999), 'Revisiting the Sex Equality Laws', in S. Walby (ed.) *New Agendas for Women*, London: Macmillan.

Hastings, S. (1997), 'The National Minimum Wage and Equal Pay for Work of Equal Value: Will the One Achieve the Other?' Unpublished paper for the ESRC Economics of Equal Opportunities Series, cited in Gregory (1999).

Hoskyns, C. (1996), *Integrating Gender: Women, Law and Politics in the European Union*, London: Verso.

Lee, P. and Murie, A. (1999), *Literature Review of Social Exclusion*, Edinburgh: The Scottish Office Central Research Unit.

Levitas, R. (1997), 'Discourses of Social Exclusion and Integration: From the European Union to New Labour', Paper presented at the European Sociological Association Conference, August, Essex: University of Essex.

Lister, R., (2000), 'Strategies for Social Inclusion: Promoting Social Cohesion or Social Justice?' in P. Askonas and A. Stewart (eds) *Social Inclusion: Possibilities and Tensions*, Basingstoke: Macmillan.

Oliver, M. (1990), *The Politics of Disablement: A Sociological Approach*, Basingstoke: Macmillan.

Oliver, M. (1991), 'Disability and Participation in the Labour Market', in R. Brown and R. Scase (eds) *Poor Work: Disadvantage and the Division of Labour*, Buckingham: Open University Press.

Rees, T. (1998), *Mainstreaming Equality in the European Union. Education, Training and Labour Market Policies*, London: Routledge.

Room, G. (1995), 'Poverty in Europe: Competing Paradigms of Analysis', *Policy and Politics*, Vol. 23, No. 2, pp. 103–13.

Walby, S. (1999), 'Introduction. A new Gender Settlement', in S. Walby (ed.) *New Agendas for Women*, London: Macmillan.

Walker, A. (1997), 'The Strategy of Inequality', in A. Walker and C. Walker (eds) *Britain Divided: The Growth of Social Exclusion in the 1980s and 1990s*, London: CPAG.

Wooding, N. (1998), 'Perspectives on Defining Equality', *Gender Relations and the Local State, ESRC Seminar Series*, July, Edinburgh: University of Edinburgh.

www.disability.gov.uk/ (1998), dispr/summary

www.open.gov.uk/ (1998), co/seu/more.html

5
Equality, Opportunity and Difference: The Limits of the Diversity Paradigm

David Mason

In recent years there has been a growing tendency for equal opportunities to be reframed, if only rhetorically, in the language of diversity. This reframing has, in turn, given rise to divergent reactions. For some, notably human resources managers in the private sector, diversity provides the means to legitimise equal opportunities, transcending old debates about the relative claims of different, more or less disadvantaged, groups and building a business case for action. For others, diversity represents the submerging of the equal opportunities project in individualism and its eventual disappearance in the day-to-day exigencies of the 'bottom line'.

In this chapter I want to review these developments from the perspective of some fifteen years' research into equal opportunities policy and practice primarily, but not exclusively, in private sector organisations.[1] In that time I have been repeatedly struck by the way in which familiar themes recur, often in new guises, and how often old, usually unresolved, debates resurface in new contexts. The last ten years or so have seen the convergence of a number of intellectual, political, economic and business trends which have served to undermine confidence in conventional conceptions of equal opportunities among practitioners and theorists alike. The concept of diversity has at the same time made its way to centre stage. It is characteristically presented both as an inexorable outcome of these same trends and as a potentially radical solution to both old and new equal opportunities dilemmas (see, for example, Kandola and Fullerton, 1998; Kandola et al., 1995; Thomas, 1991).

In what follows I want to trace the origins of this development and to assess the claim that diversity represents a means of transcending both enduring and emergent problems in the design and implementation of equality initiatives. I shall argue that, like other social developments, the diversity concept is potentially Janus-faced in its implications and that embracing it does not absolve policy makers and campaigners from the need to make difficult judgements. I begin by surveying a number of persistent dilemmas that regularly resurface in the equal opportunities literature.

Equality

The first set of recurring dilemmas concerns the nature of 'equality'. There is not space here to do justice to the complex philosophical, political and moral debates surrounding this question (see, for example, Edwards, 1995). Instead, for the purposes of this chapter, I want to concentrate on two issues which have regularly dogged not just intellectual debate, but also day-to-day policy development.

The first concerns the question of whether equal opportunities can be addressed through the medium of generic policies or whether advancing the cause of equity requires different policies and practices in respect of the inequalities experienced by different 'disadvantaged'[2] groups (such as women, minority ethnic groups or the physically impaired).

There is widespread recognition that the precise nature of the disadvantage experienced by different marginalised and excluded groups varies in both character and degree. This fact is characteristically stressed forcefully by political activists. Nevertheless, with limited exceptions, equal opportunities policies in both the private and public sectors have tended to take a generic form. Where differences in the needs of particular groups have been recognised this has tended to be reflected in more or less elaborate targeted positive action provisions (Jewson et al., 1990, 1992, 1995). This contrast is mirrored at government policy level. Despite significant differences in the legislative provisions regarding sex, race and, more recently, disability discrimination (Bourne and Whitmore, 1996), official Employment Department (now Department for Education and Employment) advice on the development of equal opportunities policies focuses on generic recommendations (Employment Department, 1991).

There are often practical reasons for the adoption of generic policies (Jewson et al., 1995). These include pressure on resources that are characteristically limited and often contested within organisations. In addition, there are often variations in the perceived legitimacy of the claims of different groups. This may give rise to the argument that generic policies offer the opportunity to piggy-back the needs of less favoured groups on the acceptance of general principles justified by reference to the better recognised or accepted needs of others.

Over and above these practical considerations, however, the choice of generic policy is often dictated by the more or less explicit embracing by policy-makers of a particular conception of equal opportunities. This brings me to the second recurrent issue I want to touch upon. This is the question of whether the objective of policy is a matter of securing equality of *opportunity* or equality of *outcome*. A stress on outcomes necessarily entails making comparisons between groups. It involves monitoring, measurement and some level of intervention. In its extreme form it would entail positive discrimination in favour of under-represented groups, a practice that is unlawful in Britain. Although the relevant legislation makes provision for more limited positive *action* measures, research evidence suggests that these have by no means been widespread even among organisations apparently committed to equal opportunities (Jewson et al. 1992, 1995; Iganski et al., 1998). Instead, the dominant emphasis has been on equality of opportunity with the proceduralist emphasis characteristic of what has become known as the 'liberal' model of equal opportunities (Jewson and Mason, 1986; Jewson et al., 1995). Here it is argued that equality can be achieved if the skills and qualities of individuals, which are assumed to be randomly distributed in the population, can be matched more precisely to the functional requirements of occupational roles. The emphasis, then, is on bureaucratic regulation of recruitment and selection systems designed to remove unfair and inefficient barriers to the achievement of that aim (Jewson and Mason, 1986; Mason, 1990b).

The limitations of this model are well known and do not require detailed rehearsal here. We may note in particular, however, that this approach takes no account of the way in which extra-labour market issues intrude into this simple matching process such that, for example, the same procedural measures can have quite different consequences for members of different groups. Thus, in some circumstances, promotion procedures which rely upon strict seniority rules may limit the opportunity for discrimination on grounds of ethnicity, as in the case of London Underground in the 1960s and 1970s (Brooks, 1975; Jewson et al., 1990). Yet those same rules would characteristically discriminate against women whose careers tend to be discontinuous (Rees, 1992).

More fundamentally, the very conceptions of skill on which the liberal model is based take no account of the way in which definitions of skill are gendered (Webb and Liff, 1988).

Opportunity

Just as there are persistent confusions and disputes about the nature of equality, there are also a number of contradictions and paradoxes in conventional conceptions of the *opportunity* in equal opportunities.

Traditionally, equality of opportunity has been structured, in the liberal model, in terms of the opportunity for members of different groups to be treated *as if they were the same*. Yet the emphasis is actually on the provision of an equal opportunity to be *unequal*. This entails an implicit recognition that people are not all the same. Nevertheless, the differences so recognised are seen as largely individual in character and origin and reflect the supposed random distribution of talent in the population.

Despite this, the persistence of gender and ethnic stereotypes among line personnel and human resources managers has been well documented (Jenkins, 1986; Jewson and Mason, 1995; Iganski et al., 1998). This suggests that the rhetorical emphasis on individualism in practice masked widely held beliefs that *group* differences underlay at least some variations in the abilities of individuals. The more positive side of this has been a growing, but by no means universal, recognition that groups' structural positions are potential sources of the differential distribution of individual skills and characteristics. This in turn has led to attempts to address these aspects of disadvantage by positive action measures – such as targeted advertising and training.

Sometimes the development of more pro-active equal opportunities policies embracing positive action can be traced to organizational exigencies. This is particularly the case in respect of those initiatives that have been a response to difficult labour supply or retention conditions. The concern with retaining trained women staff in the financial sector at the end of the 1980s may be seen as a case in point (Jewson and Mason, 1994; Jewson et al., 1995). Equally important, however, have been the insistent political demands of women, minority ethnic groups and, more recently, those with disabilities that have forced equal opportunities onto the agenda and ensured that a group-centred focus remains on the agenda. This in turn has led to demands for more effective monitoring and measurement, and bolstered arguments for targeting and other forms of positive action. These features signal the ultimately political character of equal opportunities as an issue for excluded and marginalised groups.

This political dimension, however, has also paradoxically ensured that, despite the individualist and proceduralist assumptions of the liberal model, there has been a tendency for equal opportunities policies to be seen as being designed solely to serve the interests of particular groups – such as women, minority ethnic groups, those with physical impairments (Kandola et al., 1995).

Difference: the fragmentation of interests?

At the end of the 1980s and the beginning of the 1990s, then, the equal opportunities landscape was dominated by a liberal model which had, in its most advanced manifestations, embraced the concept of positive action directed at redressing group-based barriers to fair competition between individuals (Jewson and Mason, 1994). At a government policy level, this willingness to take group disadvantage seriously culminated, in 1991, in the inclusion for the first time of a question on ethnic group membership in the Census. Ironically, however, just as progress appeared to be being made, the conceptions of groups and categories – and the presumptions of shared interest that underlay them – were already under attack. At the same time the radical New Right agenda of the 1980s had transmuted into a widespread acceptance, across the party political spectrum, that the needs of individuals were the right and proper focus of mainstream politics (Jewson and Mason, 1994). It is possible to identify a number of diverse sources of these new challenges.

Perhaps the earliest attack came from feminist assaults, from the early 1980s onwards, on essentialised conceptions of woman (see, for example, the vigorous debate in the pages of *Feminist Review* from 1984 onwards). Some of the most trenchant challenges came from black feminists who attacked what they saw as the dominance of white middle-class perspectives and argued that patriarchal oppression was mediated by racism in ways which made the experience and opportunities of black and white women quite different (see, for example, Amos and Parmar, 1984; Ware, 1991). At the same time, other writers in the feminist tradition have challenged the essentialisation of ethnic difference, arguing that ethnicity is gendered in ways which both differentiate the experience of men and women but which are also constitutive of ethnic differences themselves. Anthias and Yuval-Davis have argued, for example, that women play a vital role not only in the physical and cultural reproduction of ethnicities but also in marking their symbolic boundaries (1992: 113–15. See also Afshar and Maynard, 1994; Bradley, 1996: 107–12; Brah, 1996).

A further challenge came from Tariq Modood who, in a celebrated article, challenged the use of the political category 'black' as a generic label for all who were seen as victims of white exclusionary practices. Such a practice, he argued, failed to capture the specificity of either Asian experiences or identities and, in so doing, substituted an illusion of political unity for a genuine attempt to address the realities of diverse day-to-day experiences of racism (Modood, 1988, 1992. See also the discussion in Mason, 1990a, 1992). A related critique by Ballard (1992) challenged the simplistic victimology of much of the literature on 'race relations'. He argued that, by defining such relations solely in relation to the consequences of white exclusionary practices, such work often failed to be sufficiently alert to the differences in the experiences of different groups and still less to the details of variations in culture and identity between different groups.

These critiques have been given further impetus by the emergence of evidence that suggests that the labour market experiences of different minority ethnic groups in Britain are increasingly diverging (Jones, 1993; Modood et al., 1997). Recent data appear to show an increasing similarity of experience between white people and *some* minority ethnic groups. They suggest that members of some groups are experiencing significant upward mobility[3] (Iganski and Payne, 1996, 1999; Modood, 1997; Owen, 1993). The growth of a middle class of professional and managerial workers in some ethnic communities has led some to suggest that there is underway a convergence in the class structures of minority ethnic groups towards that of the white population.[4] These data have begun to call into question some of the grosser taken-for-granted categories hitherto used in researching ethnic stratification (see Modood's attack on 'racial dualism', 1992). They also provide further evidence to support the arguments, alluded to above, that it is necessary to pay careful attention to the way ethnicity and gender interact. Many of the discussions of the labour market placement of minority ethnic groups read as if such groups comprise only men. Yet the most recent evidence, in this and other aspects of social life such as education, provides support for those who have long argued that the experiences of women and men of all groups diverge in significant and complex ways (see, for example, Mirza, 1992).

There is also evidence that, like minority ethnic groups, women as a category have also experienced upward occupational mobility in recent years. Certainly, they appear better represented than hitherto in managerial positions. Having said this, it is important to note that some of this apparent change may be accounted for by changes in occupational designation such that a wider range of (often formerly supervisory) positions now attracts the appellation 'manager'. The evidence also suggests that women continue to experience difficulty in moving beyond the glass ceiling into the most senior managerial positions (Wajcman, 1998). Moreover, it remains the case that the vast majority of employed women, of all ethnic groups, continue to be concentrated in junior and intermediate non-manual occupations, leading Modood to conclude that 'gender divisions in the labour market may be stronger and more deeply rooted than differences due to race and ethnicity' (Modood et al., 1997: 104. See also Iganski and Payne, 1996).

A more fundamental challenge to conventional conceptions of groups and categories has come from developments in social theory associated with the rise of postmodernist and poststructuralist thought. According to this view, the pace of change in the (post)modern world, together with an ever-expanding array of choices and possibilities, creates conditions in which individuals are increasingly free to make multiple identity choices which match the purposes (or even the whims) of the moment. In other words, old-style, modernist explanations of the social world in terms of large-scale and relatively stable social categories do violence to the complexity of the everyday experiences of individuals in the postmodern world. (For a useful discussion of these issues, see Bradley, 1996: 21–7. See also Rattansi and Westwood, 1994.)

By emphasising difference, diversity and identity, such theorisations make it much easier to recognise the conditional and situational character of people's identities. They also allow us to take cognisance of the ways in which ethnicity, gender, class and age (to name but a few key aspects of identity) may interact in complex and changing ways to structure people's images of themselves and others.

Abandoning faith in old certainties, postmodernism frequently represents a celebration of difference, choice and, in its extreme forms, the triumph of style. It identifies, in the diverse identity options open to individuals, the opportunity to challenge the stereotyping and categorisation all too often characteristic of the behaviour of 'ethnic majorities' (see the discussion in Jenkins, 1977: 29–30). At the same time it challenges the essentialisation of the ethnic, gender and other categories that have been central to the process of constructing, but also of measuring and tracking, conventionally defined social inequalities.

Finally, we should note the extent to which these developments have taken place in parallel with a reframing of mainstream political debate which has potential implications for the established equal opportunities agenda. From the beginning of the 1990s, it has been possible to discern the emergence of a new conception of citizenship, embraced with minor variations by all the main political parties (see the discussion in Jewson and Mason, 1994). The emphasis has been increasingly upon citizenship as an expression of a contract between an enabling state and individuals who are free to choose and direct their own destinies. This model entails a revised view of the role of the state in Britain and has been expressed in a number of policy developments including new measures to promote affordable child care and the emphasis on supporting those in work. It is a model which seeks to embrace much of the refocused policy agenda of the 1980s – notably the prioritisation of individual over collective interests – while providing it with a more human and caring public face. From this point of view, the renewed commitment of the British state in the 1990s to equal opportunities (including the publication of the DfEE's Ten-Point plan in 1990, the Disability Discrimination Act 1995 and the Race Relations (Amendment) Act 2000[5] can be seen as a reformulation of the equality agenda in terms of the empowering role of the enabling state. Whatever its apparent commitment to redressing collectively based inequalities, however, it is clear that the major objective of policy remains the protection and enhancement of the opportunities of *individuals* to pursue their chosen purposes under the protective mantle of state policy. (For a discussion of the emergence of this agenda and its individualist assumptions, see Jewson and Mason, 1994: 605–6.)

Diversity: converging solutions?

These challenges to the conceptions of groups and categories conventionally underpinning the equal opportunities agenda have coincided with the emergence of the concept of diversity in management thought and rhetoric. This development can, in turn, be seen to be congruent with various changes in the organisation and structure both of business and new management practices. It thus appears as a solution to a range of business problems while presenting itself as a potential resolution of earlier dilemmas in the equal opportunities field (see, for example, Herriot and Pemberton, 1995; Jackson and Associates, 1992; Kandola and Fullerton, 1998; Kandola, Fullerton and Ahmed, 1995; Kossek and Lobel, 1996; Liff 1996; Thomas, 1991; Wheatley and Griffiths, 1997).

The concept of diversity came to Britain from the United States, where it had become extensively popularised in the equal employment opportunities literature in the late 1980s and early 1990s (notably in an influential book by Thomas, 1991). It seems first to have appeared in a UK context in organisations which had either US parent companies or extensive US operations (see, for example, the discussion of Mineralco in Jewson et al., 1995). Diversity, it is claimed, entails a radical reconceptualisation of the equal opportunities agenda. In this model people are valued because of their differences. Because it is committed to using fully the talents of all members of the workforce, allowing them to rise to the limit of their abilities, the diversity model is said simultaneously to address the needs of every individual in the organisation. Because it no longer focuses exclusively on those groups deemed in some way to be disadvantaged or under-represented, it offers advantages to all employees, including white men, and thus engages their commitment rather than promoting their resentment (Kandola, Fullerton and Ahmed, 1995).

In the United States, a burgeoning concern with the promotion of diverse workforces was driven partly by a well-established climate of federal contract compliance requirements and relatively robust anti-discrimination legislation. It was, however, given a further boost by the publication of *Workforce 2000* (US Department of Labor, 1987), which predicted that white males would constitute a minority of those entering the labour force by the beginning of the new century (Jackson and Associates, 1992). To these labour supply concerns was added a recognition that the US domestic market was becoming equally diverse while the pace of globalisation was apparently quickening. A diverse workforce thus had marketing advantages by incorporating a range of skills and cultural sensitivities which allowed the organisation more accurately to identify changing patterns of demand while presenting itself as attuned to diverse customer needs (Thomas, 1991: 3–7).

Similar labour supply concerns emerged in Britain at the end of the 1980s, associated with a so-called 'demographic time bomb', although, with a few exceptions (Jewson et al., 1992: 85), they were less strongly linked to marketing concerns. Moreover, these concerns were generally less well underpinned with evidence, appear to have appealed only to employers in limited sectors such as finance (Jewson et al., 1992) and seem not to have survived the onset of recession at the beginning of the 1990s (Jewson and Mason, 1994).

While a small number of globally-oriented British companies perceived similar market led pressures to their US counterparts (Jewson et al.,

1995: chapter 8), a more powerful driver appears to have been that the changes in management rhetoric and style required by the diversity model were in tune with a wider set of developments in the organisation and structure of companies in the late 1980s and early 1990s. As we shall see, this gives a particular focus to the concept which may have decisive effects on its implications for equal opportunities.

Research by Jewson et al. (1995) indicated that some of the earliest British companies to embrace the diversity concept were those which had also taken on board radically new modes of work, organisation and personnel. In such companies, diversity was perceived as a central feature of every business decision and every aspect of commercial activity (Herriot and Pemberton, 1995). It entailed questioning and restructuring the way in which virtually every task was undertaken and every decision made. It was thus closely linked to a range of other developments such as the growth of concern with multi-skilling and flexibility – and the assault on traditional job demarcation. In addition, it was not infrequently tied to such fashionable concepts as 'business process re-engineering', 'downsizing' and 'rightsizing' – all of which involved seizing the opportunity to problematise all aspects of taken-for-granted ways of doing business and, particularly, of organising labour. In some organisations, this meant cutting the workforce by as much as half. In the public sector, increasing pressure on the revenue base and political changes to the scope of operations, rights and duties had similar effects (see the discussion in Jewson and Mason, 1994; Jewson et al., 1995).

Alongside this process of 'rightsizing' has gone that of delayering (or the flattening of managerial hierarchies) with an attendant devolution of responsibility for operational matters. This has involved stripping out layers of middle management and reassigning their functions to lower-level teams and their leaders. This process has itself been closely associated with an increasing emphasis on team working, which involves focusing the work of a number of functional specialities around the achievement of a defined production task. Teams are typically required to develop their own distinctive work processes and social relations in order to achieve specified output or production targets, with obvious implications for traditional organizational hierarchies and divisions (Jewson and Mason, 1994; Jewson et al., 1995). These developments are often associated with the modern management rhetoric of empowerment. However, it is easier to discern how such aims can be realised in the context of teams involving professionally qualified or highly skilled personnel than those entailing more routine kinds of work.

Nevertheless, it is not difficult to see how a concern with diversity driven by these kinds of management concerns could have implications for the pursuit of the equal opportunities agenda. As we have seen, for those promoting it diversity offers the opportunity simultaneously of enhancing the business case for taking equity issues seriously while undermining traditional sources of opposition within workforces (Kandola and Fullerton, 1998; Kandola, Fullerton and Ahmed, 1995; Thomas, 1991). Diversity, then, is said to represent the central organising concept in the emergence of a new receptiveness to equal opportunities within the business community.

Yet whether such optimistic prognoses can be realised depends on a range of complex factors. These include the degree to which commitment to the diversity paradigm is real rather than merely rhetorical (a new name for old actions or inactions). Like old-style equal opportunities policies, it also depends on the effectiveness of the organisational arrangements for delivering on policy commitments. More fundamentally, it depends on the outcome of some unresolved uncertainties about the precise meaning and implications of diversity. (For a rather different analysis of the range of approaches embraced by the term, see Liff, 1996.)

The concept of diversity, as it is typically encountered in private sector business settings in both Britain and the United States, has in fact two distinct resonances which may be encountered separately or in combination and with varying emphases. On the one hand, it has a specifically *individual* focus. In this conceptualisation (which is the dominant one in Britain) modern business operates most effectively when it harnesses the diverse talents of all the *individuals* who make up the team. This involves not merely drawing on a diverse range of technical skills. It also entails valuing and harnessing the distinctive personal characteristics, and potentially maverick thinking, which different individuals may bring to the deliberations of the team. The aim is to generate the new and creative solutions to familiar problems that may be expected to arise from the clash of views and styles.

On the other hand, the term diversity may also have a distinctly collective resonance. Thus it is often argued that women, *as women*, bring distinctive values, skills of interaction and ways of thinking to the team. As a result, more effective team-building and innovative ways of problem-solving may emerge. Similarly, it is sometimes claimed that people from diverse cultural backgrounds can also contribute new and valued inputs to the process of team deliberation. They do so because, as individuals, they bring personal characteristics, ways of thinking and modes of interaction that are *collective* in origin. Once again the argument is that out of the mélange of different cultural styles will emerge new and innovative solutions. In other words, then, what is being argued is that characteristics that were once seen as problematic because they embodied *difference* from the 'normal' and familiar, are now to be valued for the same reason.

There is little doubt that the individualist version of diversity is the dominant one in Britain (see, Kandola, Fullerton and Ahmed, 1995: 31). In this guise, equal opportunities policy focuses on the empowerment of individuals rather than being directed to the problems of specific minorities. It is a conceptualisation which potentially leaves little room for the recognition of the collective sources of disadvantage which have been of concern to the conventional equal opportunities agenda. This relative dominance of the individualist version of diversity in Britain reflects the different historical, demographic and political situations of the US and the UK (Mason, 1990b: 84–5). In the US the collective resonance of diversity is more strongly underpinned by demographic realities, arguments associated with marketing and by the group-centredness of US coalition politics.[6] There the key to progress, however halting and conditional, has been power – political and economic.[7]

Conclusion: equal opportunities *are* politics

It is important not to underestimate the importance of the intellectual and political challenges to essentialised categories described above. They remind us that the dangers are not confined to explicitly exclusionary political projects (such as those associated with racism or sexism). Instead, they show how all category systems have the potential, if vigilance is not exercised, to reduce the complexities of individual and collective identities and experiences to unidimensional formulae. Indeed, these dangers may be all the more serious when they arise from the pursuit of otherwise well-intentioned analyses of disadvantage, or from ameliorative policies or strategies. In the context of the concerns of this chapter, then, we need to recognise both the variations in experience between different minority ethnic groups and the way these intersect with, and are conditioned by, gender, disability, class and other sources of individual and collective identity. Similarly, we must remember that the category 'women' in practice encompasses a wide range of identities that similarly interact with gender, class, age and disability. As black feminists have forcefully reminded us, not all women experience oppression in the same ways, to the same degrees or by the same men (Amos and Parmar, 1984).

This does not mean, however, that we should too readily accept the more extreme versions of the postmodernist account which appear to suggest that identities in the (post)modern world are simply a matter of choice and style. We know, for example, that ethnicity is a matter both of self-identity ('we' statements) and of categorisation ('they' statements). The same is, in principle, true of gender. In other words, identity and categorisation do not proceed entirely independently of one another. In most societies some groups and individuals have a greater capacity than others to define the terms under which categorisations are made. As a consequence, self-identification takes place in contexts where others' categorisations to some extent constrain the choices that can realistically be made. If others do not accept one's identity choices, it may be difficult, if not impossible, to act out the implications of those choices.

For example, evidence from the Fourth PSI survey shows that Britain's minority ethnic citizens call on a wide variety of cultural and other characteristics in defining their ethnic identities (Modood et al., 1997: 290–338). Nevertheless, there is also considerable evidence that those identifications are made in the context of a recognition of others' categorisations. Thus, a number of respondents of Asian descent indicated that they were inclined to think of themselves as 'black' in situations where they were in contact with white people because of a belief that this was how they were defined by whites. In other words, their identity choices were constrained by the categorisations of others (Modood et al., 1997: 295–6). Nevertheless, there is evidence that Britain's young minority ethnic citizens do perceive a wider range of identity options than some older and more rigid characterisations of ethnic difference may suggest (Modood et al., 1997: 290–338).

However, this poses a serious problem for policy formulation, particularly if a recognition of the collective origins of some patterns of disadvantage is not to be lost. Implementing any policy designed to effect change entails having the means to monitor and measure results. The problem is, if identities in the modern world are as multifaceted as some accounts suggest, how many characteristics can realistically be measured and how should they be weighted in arriving at an assessment of the effectiveness of policy? If 'the only thing we all have in common is that we're all different' (as a respondent at Mineralco told Jewson et al., 1995), how can we compare outcomes – other than between individuals? Where does that leave an equality agenda which wishes still to take seriously collective disadvantage and exclusion as well as individual difference?

Tariq Modood has recently made an eloquent plea for more sensitivity to ethnic difference within a wider conception of citizenship in a multi-ethnic Britain:

> Equality and social cohesion cannot be built upon emphasising 'difference' in a one-sided way ... The emphasis needs to be on common rights and responsibilities. Membership of a specific ethnic community has to be accorded a greater political importance than it has had hitherto, but should be complemented with an equally meaningful membership that brings all citizens together regardless of their ethnic group ... We need to reform and renew conceptions of Britishness so that the new multiculturalism has a place within them. (Modood et al., 1997: 359)

As Jan Webb reminds us, however, this simultaneous sensitivity to difference and common values must be one that retains a hold on the real structural sources of inequality:

> We need to recover a model of equality based not on abstract identical treatment, but on the right of each person to be treated as a respected, responsible participant, including acceptance of substantive differences ... This is not the same as advocating universalism and conformity to a unitary individualistic standard which privileges white men ... feminism continues to need a politics of interest, based on the material disadvantages experienced by many women, as well as acceptance of our evident differences. (Webb, 1997: 168)

These points are very important and well made. I suggest that they remind us of the need explicitly to recognise that ultimately equality and opportunity are political issues. This has important implications. Policy-makers and campaigners alike are constrained to make judgements about what patterns of inequality are sufficiently important to merit action. This means making choices and it means identifying categories of people whose situation merits redress. Such a process should be guided by the voices of the disadvantaged and excluded. However, ultimately neither political activists nor policy makers can avoid making choices which involve the setting of priorities.

This does not mean that we ignore the multiple sources of identity which characterise all our lives. It certainly does not mean seeking to impose our definitions on others. It means being willing constantly to revise and review. However, without some continuity of categorisation and measurement we can have no means of knowing whether, and what, progress is being made. The dilemma is, as it always has been, that the policy process can itself help to ossify and reproduce the categories that are the stuff of which exclusion is made. Diversity as a slogan will not change that. Indeed, in its most evangelical forms, diversity management entails an explicit rejection of the group as the object of policy. Echoing the postmodernist critique, its proponents frequently argue that the increasing diversity of the labour force (in terms of gender, age, ethnic background, nationality, to name but a few dimensions) means that only an individually focused strategy can hope to accommodate the needs of all its members (Kandola and Fullerton, 1998: 21–31; 125–43). This position ignores the group origins of much inequity (whether located in structurally reproduced disadvantage or in collectively focused acts of exclusion). Moreover, it treats all such inequity as equivalent, both in form and scale. Because diversity management is, in the end, primarily an approach to managing employees, it presents itself as having depoliticised the equal opportunities project. In reality, its focus on individuals' needs is not an alternative to making difficult political choices but represents an explicit decision to submerge the moral case for equal opportunities in the business case. This *is* a political choice, but it is the choice to prioritize the needs of the organisation over the claims to equity of the excluded and disadvantaged.

The individualisation of the concept of diversity within British managerial rhetoric stands in stark contrast with uses of the concept in the United States. There, it seems, the management of diversity remains more sensitive to collective, as well as individual, sources of difference. Diversity management more commonly coexists with group-based initiatives reflecting a recognition of the political significance of the diversity of American society. In principle, such a conception makes it possible to be sensitive to the significance of the conditional and situational character of identities, while providing the means to ensure that the equal opportunities project is not submerged in an unrestrained individualism. Whether this is possible within the highly individualistic political and corporate climate of Britain is at best doubtful.

This brings me to my final and crucial point. It is an illusion to believe that the struggle for equal opportunities can be depoliticised. Politics is about power, and it is important to note that this means conflicts between different interests. The apparent resolution provided by diversity management is, in the end, the substitution of a political project focused on the management of employees for one that seeks equity for the disadvantaged and excluded. However, that latter project is one that also implies political choices between the claims and interests of a variety of groups. Diversity management claims to have squared one circle by transforming the struggle for equal opportunities into a managerial technology that does not threaten the interests of the currently dominant – white males. As I have argued above, this is true only to the extent that the claims of the disadvantaged have been subordinated to purported organisational needs which are said to serve the interests of all. As soon, however, as we recognise that differences of interests between groups persist, we encounter a new dilemma. It is not only the dominant and the subordinate whose interests may differ. Within each of these categories, there may also be persistent differences of interest which also compete for the attention of policy-makers. I noted at the outset that conventional equal opportunities policies frequently encounter the problem that measures designed to address the needs of one group may run counter to the needs of another. Moreover, we have seen that the Fourth PSI study concluded that gender divisions in the labour market may be stronger and more persistent than those associated with race and ethnicity. It is not only white males, then, whose interests may be threatened by any particular policy measure. This means that difficult choices and persistent, more or less effective, lobbying will remain central to the equal opportunities terrain. The heart of the equal opportunities project remains the struggle for power. Perhaps this is where we came in. Even the most sensitive and realistic embracing of a group-based concept of diversity cannot provide a way round these dilemmas. This leaves us with the uncomfortable question of whether excluded and marginalised groups are destined always to be locked as much in struggle with one another as with the excluders.

Notes

1. Much of the work I have undertaken during this period has been conducted jointly with Nick Jewson and many of our key ideas have been developed together. Nick therefore shares the credit for any merit the arguments in this chapter may have. Needless to say, I alone am responsible for their deficiencies. It should also be noted that much of our work has concentrated upon ethnic disadvantage and equality issues and that I approach this chapter from the experience of research in these areas.

2. I place the first appearance of the term 'disadvantaged' in inverted commas to signal its problematic character. All too often the term can convey the impression that disadvantage arises in some sense naturally – that no one is responsible. In this context it is often distinguished from discrimination which is seen as involving deliberate acts of exclusion. It thus glosses over some difficult questions, such as those surrounding the notion of institutional racism (or sexism). It may also all too easily imply that the blame lies with the excluded themselves (see the famous Moynihan Report, Rainwater and Yancy, 1967). Alternatively it may invoke images of a helpless passivity in which the 'victims' of disadvantage are represented as powerless to help themselves (see Gilroy, 1990; Carmichael and Hamilton, 1968).
3. Indeed, Iganski and Payne (1996, 1999) have argued that there is evidence that, while remaining significantly disadvantaged and despite continuing discrimination, all minority ethnic groups have made significant progress since first settlement.
4. However, the patterns are complex and need to be approached with caution. We should be wary of concluding, as have some on the political right, that the success of members of some groups gives the lie to the claim that discrimination lies at the root of differences in achievement and opportunity between groups (Honeyford, 1993).
5. The amendment strengthens existing legislation and notably introduces a positive duty for public bodies to promote good race relations and equality of opportunity. It also imposes a duty to assess the impact on racial equality of policies and services, and introduces monitoring of the ethnic compositions of the public sector workforce.
6. We should, however, note that even the group-centred version of diversity can be disadvantaging in so far as it may provide the context for the reproduction of stereotypes, such as those associated with women's domesticity or the exoticness of non-European cultures.
7. I am aware of the growth of challenges to traditional programmes of affirmative action in the United States. However, interviews with US corporate personnel have indicated that the perceived business advantages of the continued pursuit of diversity is likely to maintain their commitment even were such challenges to reach an intensity and degree of success that has yet to be witnessed. (For a discussion of the debate around affirmative action, see Bowen and Bok, 1998.)

References

Afshar, H. and Maynard, M. (eds) (1994), *The Dynamics of 'Race' and Gender*, London: Taylor and Francis.

Amos, V. and Parmar, P. (1984), 'Challenging Imperial Feminism', *Feminist Review*, Vol. 17, pp. 3–19.

Anthias, F. and Yuval-Davis, N. (1992), *Racialized Boundaries: Race, Nation, Gender, Colour and Class and the Anti-racist Struggle*, London: Routledge.

Ballard, R. (1992), 'New Clothes for the Emperor? The Conceptual Nakedness of the Race Relations Industry in Britain', *New Community*, Vol. 18, No. 3, pp. 481–92.

Bourne, C. and Whitmore, J. (1996), *Anti-Discrimination Law in Britain*, 3rd edn., London: Sweet and Maxwell.

Bowen, W. and Bok, D. (1998), *The Shape of the River: Long-Term Consequences of Considering Race in College and University Admissions*, Princeton: Princeton University Press.

Bradley, H. (1996), *Fractured Identities: Changing Patterns of Inequality*, Cambridge: Polity Press.

Brah, A. (1996), *Cartographies of Diaspora*, London: Routledge.

Brooks, D. (1975), *Race and Labour in London Transport*, London: Oxford University Press.

Carmichael, S. and Hamilton, C.V. (1968), *Black Power: the Politics of Liberation in America*, London: Jonathan Cape.

Edwards, J. (1995), *When Race Counts: The Morality of Racial Preference in Britain and America*, London: Routledge.

Employment Department (1991), *Equal Opportunities Ten Point Plan for Employers*, London: ED.

Gilroy, P. (1990), 'The End of Anti-racism', *New Community*, Vol. 17, No. 1, pp. 71–83.

Herriot, P. and Pemberton, C. (1995), *Competitive Advantage through Diversity*, London: Sage Publications.

Honeyford, R. (1993), 'Why Are We Still Fed the Myth that Britain is a Racist Society?', *Daily Mail*, 14 April.

Iganski, P., Mason, D., Humphreys, A. and Watkins, M. (1998), *Recruiting Minority Ethnic Groups into Nursing, Midwifery and Health Visiting*, ENB.

Iganski, P. and Payne, G. (1996), 'Declining Racial Disadvantage in the British Labour Market', *Ethnic and Racial Studies*, Vol. 19, No. 1, pp. 113–34.

Iganski, P. and Payne, G. (1999), 'Socio-economic Re-structuring and Employment: The Case of Minority Ethnic Groups', *British Journal of Sociology*, Vol. 50, No. 2, pp. 195–216.

Jackson, S.E. and Associates (eds) (1992), *Diversity in the Workplace: Human Resource Initiatives*, New York: The Guildford Press

Jenkins, R. (1986), *Racism and Recruitment*, Cambridge: Cambridge University Press.

Jenkins, R. (1997), *Rethinking Ethnicity*, London: Sage Publications.

Jewson, N. and Mason, D. (1986), 'The Theory and Practice of Equal Opportunities Policies: Liberal and Radical Perspectives', *Sociological Review*, Vol. 34, No. 2, pp. 307–34.

Jewson, N. and Mason, D. (1994), '"Race", Employment and Equal Opportunities: towards a Political Economy and an Agenda for the 1990s', *Sociological Review*, Vol. 42, No. 4, pp. 591–617.

Jewson, N., Mason, D., Waters, S. and Harvey, J. (1990), *Ethnic Minorities and Employment Practice, a Study of Six Employers*, Department of Employment Research Paper No. 76, London: DE.

Jewson, N., Mason, D., Lambkin, C. and Taylor, F. (1992), *Ethnic Monitoring Policy and Practice: A Study of Employers' Experiences*, Employment Department Research Paper No. 89, London: ED.

Jewson, N., Mason D., Drewett, A. and Rossiter, W. (1995), *Formal Equal Opportunities Policies and Employment Best Practice*, Department for Education and Employment, Research Series No. 69, London: DfEE.

Jones, T. (1993), *Britain's Ethnic Minorities*, London: PSI.

Kandola, R. and Fullerton, J. (1998), *Diversity in Action: Managing the Mosaic*, London: Institute of Personnel and Development.

Kandola, R., Fullerton, J. and Ahmed, Y. (1995), 'Managing Diversity: Succeeding where Equal Opportunities have Failed', *Equal Opportunities Review*, No. 59, January/February, pp. 31–6.

Kossek, E.E. and Lobel, S.A. (eds) (1996), *Managing Diversity: Human Resource Strategies for Transforming the Workplace*, Oxford: Blackwell Business.

Liff, S. (1996), *Managing Diversity: New Opportunities for Women*? University of Warwick Papers in Industrial Relations No. 57, Coventry: University of Warwick Industrial Relations Research Unit.

Mason, D. (1990a), 'A Rose by Any Other Name ...? Categorisation, Identity and Social Science', *New Community*, Vol. 17, No. 1, pp. 123–33.

Mason, D. (1990b), 'Competing Conceptions of "Fairness" and the Formulation and Implementation of Equal Opportunities Policies', in Wendy Ball and John Solomos (eds), *Race and Local Politics*, London: Macmillan.

Mason, D. (1992), 'Categories, Identities and Change: Ethnic Monitoring and the Social Scientist', *European Journal of Intercultural Studies*, Vol. 2, No. 2, pp. 41–52.

Mirza, H. S. (1992), *Young, Female and Black*, London: Routledge.

Modood, T. (1988), 'Black, Racial Equality and Asian Identity', *New Community*, Vol. 14, No. 3 pp. 397–404.

Modood, T. (1992), *Not Easy Being British*, Stoke-on-Trent: Trentham Books.

Modood, T. et al. (1997), *Ethnic Minorities in Britain*, London: PSI.

Owen, D. (1993), *Ethnic Minorities in Britain: Economic Characteristics*, University of Warwick, Centre for Research in Ethnic Relations, National Ethnic Minority Data Archive, 1991 Census Statistical Paper No. 3.

Rainwater L. and Yancy, W. L. (eds) (1967), *The Moynihan Report and the Politics of Controversy*, Cambridge, Mass.: MIT Press.

Rattansi, A. and Westwood, S. (1994), *Racism, Modernity and Identity on the Western Front*, Oxford: Polity Press.

Rees, T. (1992), *Women and the Labour Market*, London: Routledge.

Thomas, R. Roosevelt, Jr. (1991), *Beyond Race and Gender: Unleashing the Power of Your Total Workforce by Managing Diversity*, New York: AMACOM, American Management Association.

US Department of Labor (1987), *Workforce 2000*, Washington DC: US Government Printing Office.

Wajcman, J. (1998), *Managing Like a Man: Women and Men in Corporate Management*, Cambridge: Polity Press.

Ware, V. (1991), *Beyond the Pale: White Women, Racism and History*, London: Verso.

Webb, J. (1997), 'The Politics of Equal Opportunity', *Gender, Work and Organization*, Vol. 4, pp. 159–69.

Webb, J. and Liff, S. (1988), 'Play the White Man: The Social Construction of Fairness and Competition in Equal Opportunities Policies', *Sociological Review*, Vol. 36, No. 3, pp. 532–51

Wheatley, R. and Griffiths, A. (1997), *The Management of Diversity*, Corby: The Institute of Management Foundation.

6
Managerialism, Modernisation and Marginalisation: Equal Opportunities and Institutional Change

Janet Newman

Equal opportunities in the public sector exists in the uncertain and shifting boundaries between 'politics', 'administration' and 'management'. It is suffused with values and cross-cut by differing ideologies while at the same time being subject to the rationalities of management practice. It is a set of ideas around which deeply embedded forms of conflict are played out and at the same time is a set of laws to be administered. It is an essential precept of 'good management practice' while at the same time being a policy whose status in the new managerial agenda is deeply ambiguous. It is something to which everyone will agree in principle but which few deliver in practice.

To unravel some of these tensions, this chapter explores local government equality policies and initiatives in the UK from an institutional perspective. My aim is to analyse the specific impact – or lack of impact – of equality policies and practices by drawing on some of the insights offered by 'new institutional' theory. This body of theory – which operates at a 'meso' level of analysis – can be used to explore linkages between 'macro' explanations of inequality (which operate at the level of patriarchal or class theory, labour market theory or state policy) and 'micro' explanations (which focus on the role of individual or group action). Institutional theory draws on different disciplines, from economics through political science to organisational studies (see summaries by diMaggio and Powell, 1991; Lowndes, 1996; Scott, 1994). Using this body of theory to explore equality issues presents some difficulties: institutional theory has emerged from predominantly male-dominated academic traditions and does not lend itself easily to the task of exploring issues of diversity, identity and contestation.

Research based on institutional theory has been criticised by feminist analysts for not taking sufficient account of women's voices, and so ignoring the gendered nature of social institutions (Calas and Smircich, 1992).

However, this body of theory has value for exploring the way in which equality policies and initiatives are promoted, resisted, complied with, accommodated and adapted within the institutional context of a specific local authority. It can be used to illuminate the way in which public sector organisations adopt, comply with or challenge the 'rules of the game' embedded in their political, economic or social environments. Compliance with such rules and norms – or at least the appearance of compliance – is likely to affect the legitimacy of these organisations in the eyes of key stakeholders, and thus their survival and success (such as access to new sources of funding). This approach highlights the informal norms which pervade the internal culture of the organisation. Equal opportunity is often conceptualised in terms of formal rules and procedures. These are cross-cut by informal norms which influence the ways in which rules are interpreted, the degree to which the organisation takes its own rules seriously, and conventions about what is likely to happen to those who infringe them. The institutional framework of equality sets the parameters within which organisational conflict around equality issues can be expressed and through which it is contained or displaced. It legitimates a focus on the rule-making and rule-breaking roles of social actors themselves – on elected members and managers, on equality activists and equality units, and on the staff, users and communities who are interpellated by equality policies. An institutional focus, then, can be used to explore the complex and dynamic processes through which informal rules and norms concerning equality issues are contested, resisted, appropriated or mobilised by social actors. At the same time it suggests ways in which equal opportunity policies and programmes serve to institutionalise political agency.

The rules, norms and 'logics of appropriateness' (Meyer and Rowan, 1991) embedded in the institutions of equal opportunities operate in different arenas: in the response of a public sector organisation to political institutions in the wider environment; in the management institutions which set the rules of the game for organisational action; and in the rules and norms through which the political agency of equalities staff and other actors is institutionalised. These are considered in turn in the following sections, focusing primarily on local government. The chapter goes on to develop a framework for understanding the institutional context of equality in an individual local authority, and to suggest some implications of New Labour's modernisation agenda. It ends by returning to institutional theory and suggests some limits to the form of analysis it offers.

Responding to the political environment: equal opportunities as ritual and ceremony

Equal opportunities can be viewed as an aspect of organisational legitimisation: the way a local authority presents itself to its stakeholders through its policies and strategies, and through the words and actions of senior members and managers. The informal norms that lead local authorities to adopt equality policies do not originate with a single local authority but form part of a dominant 'logic of appropriateness' within local government as a whole. To be without such a policy is viewed as unacceptable; to have one which is perceived as too radical is equally problematic, especially for local authorities that are embracing the informal rules of the emerging 'modernisation' agenda. diMaggio and Powell use the term 'isomorphism' to signify the processes through which an organisation adopts features from its institutional environment:

> Organisations compete not just for resources and customers but for political power and institutional legitimacy, for social as well as economic fitness. The concept of institutional isomorphism is a useful tool for understanding the politics and ceremony that pervade much modern organisational life. (1991: 66)

Isomorphic processes may take place as a result of coercion: for example, local authorities being required to adopt a piece of equality legislation. They may be mimetic: for example, local authorities setting up equality units or adopting equality policies based on models initiated by others. They may be normative: the spread of dominant templates of what constitutes good practice. For example, Cunningham (1998) notes the emergence of a new framework for equality across the NHS and Civil Service with a common shift towards the pursuit of a 'business case' on equality policy sustained by thinking across the policy community of Whitehall and the NHS.

From this perspective changes in equal opportunity policies and programmes can be viewed in terms of local authority's response to its institutional environment. That environment is shaped from above (legislation and formal rules set by government, regulators, auditors and inspectors) and through the norms developed through interaction with peer organisations and within professions. Such policies and programmes may be largely ceremonial, their function being to secure organisational legitimacy through appropriate signs and symbols. A delicate balance has to be struck between being seen to do the right thing while not disrupting other, potentially conflicting, aspects of legitimating behaviour. So, for example, it may be viewed as important, in equality terms, to have a job-sharing policy. At the same time this must not be allowed to undercut the important symbolic roles which senior managers are expected to play in relation to members, partner organisations, local business, etc. So while there is no formal cut-off point based on seniority in a job-share policy, informal norms may develop which effectively bar job sharing above a particular level.

To suggest that a local authority has adopted a policy or initiative in order to keep pace with ideas of good practice does not mean that it does not take it seriously. However, the relationship between policy and implementation may be loosely coupled: 'because attempts to control and co-ordinate activities in institutionalised organisations leads to conflicts and loss of legitimacy, elements of structure are de-coupled from activities and from each other' (Meyer and Rowan, 1991: 41). Loosely coupled systems allow multiple goals to be pursued in different parts of the system independently of each other. For example, personnel goals, financial goals and equality goals may be uncoordinated. So within a local authority the corporate centre may develop policies on social exclusion, but these may have little impact on service planning or operational management. A loose coupling between policy and implementation also allows goals to be ambiguous: 'we care about our staff' as a goal may have little impact on day-to-day decision-making processes. Tighter coupling brings a closer alignment between policies and outcomes. Conformity is enforced through inspection, outputs are monitored and outcomes evaluated. One government initiative in the UK, labelled 'Opportunity 2000', encouraged organisations to set their own goals and targets for changing the numbers of women at senior levels of management, and to monitor the outcomes. This appeared to signal a shift towards tighter coupling – a closer alignment of policy and delivery. The effects, however, were limited. Attempts to align policies with each other, and to achieve tighter coupling between policy and implementation, are often resisted. In UK local government there has been a particularly strong resistance to tighter links between equality policies and other policy areas, or to a more tightly coupled policy implementation process.

The ceremonial or symbolic role of equality policies, and their lack of purchase on the material and cultural structures of oppression or discrimination, can be easily criticised. A local authority can look good while doing little. However, there are two important qualifications to be made to this line of argument. The first concerns resources. Whatever the positive intentions of a local authority the context in which local government has operated in the UK during the Thatcher and Major administrations means that their capacity to redress material inequalities has been severely limited. The second qualification concerns the positive symbolic role of equality policies, and the activities which flow from them, for staff. Bradley notes changes in the pattern of job segregation which she attributes in part to a 'climate of equality' stemming from equality policies and programmes:

> Such a climate enables women to pursue claims for equality more easily and allows progressive managers to open up opportunities for female employees; while men who resist such changes do so with some uneasiness and feel the need to justify their resistance. (1999: 87)

Symbols may be weak in terms of their capacity to bring about material change. However, symbols in the form of language, myths, ceremonies and other cultural signs – including written policies – play important roles in constituting the informal rules of social action.

This section has suggested some of the issues arising from the way in which a local authority adopts institutions from its political environment, and the formal and informal rules of the equality game which flow from their response. The institutional legitimacy of public bodies has been seriously challenged by the Macpherson Report on the Stephen Lawrence Inquiry (see Introduction) which has led to a higher profile for equality issues. It remains to be seen whether serious attempts to challenge deeply embedded patterns of racism will be made. More pessimistically, it may lead to a reconfiguration of equal opportunities as a form of 'risk management'; that is a set of ritualised and procedurally based defensive strategies. What is clear, however, is that public bodies are becoming more vulnerable to challenges from citizens and communities.

Reconciling conflicting rules of the game: administrative rules and managerial incentives

A second level of analysis in developing an institutional perspective focuses on the internal institutions of local authorities. One of the key shifts during the 1980s and early 1990s was the erosion of the dominance of administrative institutions and their partial displacement by the rules and norms of business and management. This has had a major impact on how equality agendas are played out in local government. The late 1990s witnessed a further shift as the discourse of modernisation undercut old 'welfarist' institutions, and as the new Labour administration promulgated the elaboration of new rules and norms concerning how a local authority might respond to a range of policy agendas. In earlier work (Newman, 1994, 1995) I traced the changing articulations between the equality agendas of political movements and the professional and managerial agendas of the public sector. Equality policies were formulated in the context of bureaucratic administration and based on the values of probity and impartiality. Their roots in liberal ideology focused activity on fair access to employment for individuals, at the expense of activity to redress more structured form of group inequalities. Liberal notions of fairness and equality were institutionalised and codified in policies, procedures, guidelines and other formal rules flowing ultimately from the equality legislation of the 1960s, and were regulated through specific functions or positions – equality officers, personnel officers – within the bureaucracy.

The liberal model of equality is cross-cut by models drawn from social welfare ideology. These developed out of the expansion of professionalised state welfare services in the 1960s which aimed to ameliorate residual social problems. Within organisations this underpinned a range of initiatives designed to overcome disadvantage result ing from 'deficits', for example positive action training for specific groups of 'minorities' to enable them to compete on equal terms. This model acknowledged structured forms of inequality but tended to treat gender as a universal category linked to disadvantage. Many women – especially those who successfully played the game according to the norms of liberal equality policies – rejected such stigmatising practices. Race, gender and disability became the basis for categorising people and problems rather than complex and contested lines of identity and practice. The institutional forms of both liberal and welfarist equality ideologies live on in aspects of New Labour's social welfare reforms of housing, health, education and welfare benefits. Lister argues that the Prime Minister and Chancellor 'have increasingly distanced themselves from traditional left notions of equality in favour of those of equality of opportunity' (Lister, 1998: 217). The reform agenda is underpinned by the discourse of social exclusion/inclusion rather than that of equality, and paid work and education are viewed as the prime mechanisms for overcoming social exclusion. New forms of stigmatising practice are emerging around divisions between those who take advantage of opportunities for paid work and education/training and those who do not, underpinned by a discourse of individual responsibility/duty (Dwyer, 1998).

The new managerial ideology which suffused public services through the 1980s and into the 1990s (Clarke and Newman, 1997) had contradictory consequences for equality issues. The development of 'human resource management' led to an emphasis on maximising the potential of every member of the workforce and on overcoming any barriers to this rooted in discriminatory practice. This was often accompanied by rhetoric about the positive contribution which a diverse workforce could bring to an organisation, though the individualist and impoverished basis of 'diversity management' has been much criticised (see Mason, chapter 5 this volume). At the same time, HRM, linked to severe funding crises in local government, led to the introduction of new employment practices (short-term contracts, local pay bargaining, and so on) which tended to disadvantage low-paid and 'expendable' groups of the workforce. Managerialism also shaped the restructuring of local authorities around business units, each with their own budget and targets, with delegated authority and responsibility for line managers. The strengthening of managerial autonomy has been a double-edged process. Those managers who wish to pursue equality agenda have more control over resources and staffing decisions; but those who are unsympathetic are also empowered. The pressures of the new managerial climate led many managers to marginalise equality issues in order to pursue their business goals, despite the rhetoric of the benefits to be gained from 'mainstreaming' equality issues by integrating it with line management practices. Often this was a case of the generalised shift to a more macho climate which has accompanied competition and the focus on business results. However, the tensions experienced by middle managers can also be located in a clash between new and old rules of the game: between the institutions of bureaucratic rationality ('follow the procedures') and those of managerialism ('achieve your targets', 'take risks', 'be entrepreneurial', 'achieve efficiency savings'). Managerialism has not entirely displaced bureaucratic administration but sits alongside it in an uncomfortable – and often destructive – conjuncture of conflicting institutional norms.

The formalised administrative basis of equality policies has continued despite the shift to managerial modes of coordination and control.

Indeed, aspects of the new agenda have been deployed in attempts to strengthen equality initiatives, for example in articulating a 'business case' for equality; in linking issues of diversity to quality management; or in using managerial techniques – goals, targets, monitoring, and so on – to link policies to outcomes. It offers a new language which can be appropriated to support equality issues. However, as Cunningham notes:

> The ability of equality managers to undertake this task is contingent upon the extent to which equal opportunity was developed and legitimised prior to organisational reform. In addition an acknowledgement by equality managers of the new issues thrown by the shift to a new paradigm should not lose sight of the issues that remained unresolved in the old. (1998: unnumbered)

The business rationale has been used with some success to redress the imbalance of men and women at senior levels. There have also been inadvertent consequences of restructuring. A decade or more of 'downsizing' has provided new opportunities for women, black and minority ethnic staff to be promoted to middle (and sometimes senior) management posts as a result of early retirement and redundancy policies. The disappearance of much of the 'old guard' in authorities has provided an opportunity for new models of leadership to emerge. However, one consequence of successive waves of downsizing has been to increase the pressure on professional grades and middle and senior managers. It is perhaps no accident that just as previously marginalised groups have attained some foothold in management ranks the managerial task has become much more pressurised and stressful. The long-hours culture of many local authorities has major implications for men as well as women, significantly affecting the balance between work and home, between family or caring responsibilities and the job. There remain real tensions between equality policies and the performance demands of the managerial task in local government and elsewhere. This means that equality goals are likely to remain loosely coupled to other sets of goals; more the focus of ceremonial compliance than a force for change.

Making and changing the rules of the game: political agency

Equality policies and programmes, however much they appear to be bureaucratic and rule-based, did not arrive full blown as an integral part of local authority practice. They are the product of struggle: of political agency both at national level (the political struggles which eventually resulted in the passing the 1960s and 1970s equality legislation) and at local level (the struggles within trades unions and local communities to get particular issues on the agenda). Local authorities themselves have played a key role in advancing ideas about good employment practice, and some served as a site of resistance to the negative climate on equality issues during the Thatcher years. Political agency by staff, equalities officers, councillors, trades unions and activists in local political parties continues to be a vital means of developing equality initiatives and defending existing policies from further erosion. A local authority's norms and practices may also be challenged by the communities of interest and of identity amongst whom local authority members need to build electoral support.

Local authorities are a site in which political agency becomes channelled, institutionalised and potentially deradicalised. Equality policies and practices can be viewed as a means of containing political agency by setting out the rules of the game for its expression. Activism on equality issues has traditionally been accommodated through the functional specialism of the equalities officer and equality unit. Such units have served as an organisational base and source of legitimacy for many activists struggling for change. Such activism has often been contained as equality officers learned to tread the delicate tightrope between responding to the interest of their internal and external constituencies. They have had to conform to the new managerial ethos while maintaining links with key constituencies. They have had to adopt the language and perspectives of women's groups, trades unions and other social movements while also being able to present arguments in a form acceptable to senior managers and members. They have had to conform to the existing rules for channelling conflict (writing reports, addressing committee meetings) while simultaneously attempting to change the rules to allow other voices to be expressed. Despite these tensions many have become highly effective in deploying the new language and ethos in order to build legitimacy for fairly radical equality agendas (see Scott, Wright and Kelly, chapters 9, 10 and 11 this volume).

The shift to managerial regimes has had a significant impact on the way in which political agency is accommodated, absorbed and managed. Informal rules and norms prescribe which struggles are allowed to surface and how far political agency is to be expressed. In most cases there is a hierarchy of legitimacy for different equality struggles, with disability being accorded high legitimacy and sexuality low, with race and gender somewhere in between. This is reflected in symbolic hierarchies (e.g. what groups can be 'named' in official documents), in the hierarchy of equality officers (what posts exist and in what relationships to each other) and in patterns of advantage and disadvantage in access to resources such as training and development opportunities. The increasing dominance of the 'new public management' means that the radical potential of action focused on specific forms of oppression and discrimination is being weakened. The shift is one towards a general equality culture rather than one in which different group interests can be articulated and identities acknowledged. Dedicated officers dealing with race, gender or other forms of discrimination are disappearing in favour of generic equality units. Equality is becoming defined as simply a matter of good management practice and personnel procedures. The language of equality is becoming depoliticised, with the result that conflict is viewed as illegitimate. The new ethos is one of partnership and the goal is the establishment of consensus-based cultures in which everyone can contribute fully by 'getting on board' or 'signing up' to the new values. The raising of equality issues cuts across the grain of the new managerial order; those who break the informal rules of the emerging culture may be labelled as 'difficult'. The role of the equality unit as the channel for institutionalised conflict thus takes on a new significance.

The process of change in equality management has brought us to an uncomfortable juncture between the individualising ideology of managing diversity and the universalising rubrics of equality as good management practice. When equality simply becomes part of good practice, the opportunity to challenge the existing rules, norms and conventions become limited. However, the shift to managerial regimes has not been smooth or unproblematic, in part because of the political character of local government and its relationship to the wider political environment. Local authorities are not uniform, and respond to tensions in their institutional environments in different ways. They struggle to retain legitimacy with groups in the wider community – black constituencies, women's groups, trades unions – while meeting the requirements of neutral and impartial (i.e. gender-, colour- and class-blind) decision-making structures. They do not simply adopt the rules of the game in their environment but engage in a mix of rule-adopting, rule-making and sometimes rule-breaking behaviours as they respond to external political shifts. For example, some London boroughs 'broke the rules' by retaining high-profile equality initiatives long after the new climate had deemed them illegitimate, getting labelled as 'loony left' in the process (a term used by right-wing politicians and media in the UK to stigmatise some Labour-controlled councils in the early 1980s). Understanding the specific form of equality institutions in a particular authority is therefore important.

Institutional diversity: analysing your local authority

Local government is diverse: history, geography, culture and politics all influence the trajectories through which the institutions of equality have been shaped and reshaped within a specific local authority. Logics of appropriate action in a London borough may be different from those in a rural county. Constitutional change may lead to increasingly divergent approaches to equality in England, Scotland and Wales. It is important, then, to develop frameworks which might help unpack the equality institutions within a specific local authority. Figure 6.1 suggests a framework for exploring the character and complexion of a particular local authority's approach to equal opportunities.

The effectiveness of equality policies and initiatives will depend on complex interactions between different elements. Getting one bit right will not mean success if other variables cut across it. For example, there may be very positive leadership, but without political backing it may be ineffective. A good set of policies can be undermined by managers or professionals pursuing their interests. Equality units can have a high status and the backing of members, but if a fear-based culture limits political agency within the organisation, little real change may ensue. Formal equality rules can be undercut by informal rules of the game kept in place by powerful actors unsympathetic to equality issues.

The different variables outlined in Figure 6.1 suggest a number of dimensions on which local authority orientation and practice can be mapped. For example, one typology, based on the interaction between 'responses to the institutional environment' and 'political agency' is suggested in Figure 6.2. The vertical axis represents the extent to which equality is viewed as an integral part of the modernisation agenda, or how far a high profile on equality is viewed as likely to damage the legitimacy of the local authority in the eyes of government and other stakeholders. The horizontal axis represents the extent of political agency (activism) within the local authority, and its connection to other forms of agency through networks with communities, trades unions and other sources of potential influence. Mapping these together produces a typology of likely outcomes for the equality

Response to the institutional environment
- What is the impact of the history and culture of your local authority on the legitimacy accorded to equality agendas?
- How is your local authority positioning itself in the modernisation agenda and what are the implications of that for equality internally and externally?
- How is modernisation changing the way in which equality agendas might be legitimately pursued – what new languages and practices are emerging within the organisation?

Political institutions
- What are the rules of the game among members about how equality issues should be regarded?
- What forms of inequality are viewed as legitimate topics for discussion in council or committee? Is there an informal hierarchy of equality agendas?
- What is the nature of the links between members and particular constituencies of political support (e.g. trades unions, black and ethnic minority groups)?
- How are women members, gay and lesbian members, black and ethnic minority members, members with disabilities regarded and treated by other members?
- Are lines of inequality and discrimination among the member group viewed as a legitimate concern?
- How is the move to cabinet structures likely to change patterns of inequality within the member group?

Managerial institutions
- What signals about equality issues are embedded in the leadership style of the organisation?
- Are equality issues incorporated into management standards?
- How are the actions of line or unit managers in relation to equality issues monitored?
- Do equality policies focus on how results or outcomes are to be achieved, or do they just specify principles and procedures?
- Are equality issues viewed as part of the strategic agenda?
- How far is the culture of the organisation, and the way it is experienced by different groups, part of the equality agenda?
- How far does the local authority link internal and external equality agendas?

Political agency
- What is the role and status of the equality unit/equality officer within your authority?
- What are the informal rules about how conflict or dissent arising from equality issues can be expressed?
- What is the role of trades unions in ensuring equality issues are on the agenda?
- What opportunities exist for communities of interest or identity to meet and shape policies from within the organisation?
- What opportunities exist for communities of interest or identity within the area served by the local authority to influence local authority policy and priorities?

Figure 6.1   Local authority approaches to equal opportunities

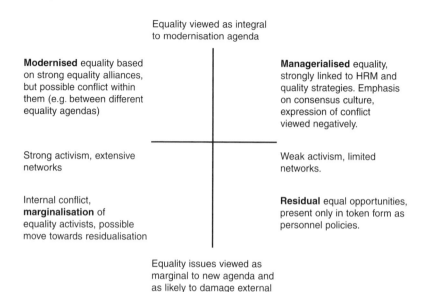

Figure 6.2   Typology of outcomes for equality agenda

agenda, broadly stereotyped under the labels 'modernised', 'managerialised', 'marginalised' and 'residualised'.

The implications of the national context are significant. The tendency to centralise power at Westminster means that there is less capacity for local authorities to determine their own policies on major social issues, or to set their own agenda on equality issues. The continued squeeze on resources means that equality units and equality programmes will continue to be high when lists of potential cuts are drawn up. The new climate has introduced more competition between local authorities as some seek to achieve 'beacon status' while others focus on avoiding the squeeze on resources or loss of autonomy likely to result from being defined as a 'failing' local authority (and the threat of central government intervention which follows). Such competition increases the pressure on local authorities to engage in action likely to strengthen their legitimacy in the eyes of government, the Audit Commission and other major stakeholders, so reducing their willingness to engage in radical initiatives. Institutional isomorphism coupled with strong central controls is likely to be a continuing influence on the process of marginalising equal opportunities.

The dynamics of change

This chapter has been concerned with equal opportunities and the dynamics of institutional change. The value of such a perspective lies in highlighting continuities in the old 'rules of the game' despite other forms of structural or cultural change. So the logics flowing from patriarchal power may continue despite the disappearance through retirement or redundancy of many senior men who embodied its more blatant forms. The appointment of more women at senior levels will not necessarily eradicate the old rules of the game which served to marginalise women and other groups. Attempts to change the rules to introduce more 'women-friendly' practices are difficult: new rules will interact uncomfortably with, rather than displace, existing norms and practices. Equality activists operate in the uncomfortable conjunction of old and new institutions. They may be squeezed by the contradictions between old and new rules of the game; but they may also exploit such contradictions to pursue old agendas in new clothes. But whatever the potent possibilities of the new, it is important to defend old institutions from the tyranny of change in a local authority. Equality policies provide an important framework of formal rules which less powerful actors within the organization can use to address the most blatant excesses of hostile managers or members. More importantly, they provide a source of legitimacy for those pursuing more positive outcomes.

There are, however, some limitations of an institutional perspective. The first concerns the conceptualisation of agency. Institutional theory recognises the role of social actors in shaping the rules of the game, but it is more difficult to accommodate the impact of political agency. The impetus and drive for equality originated, and is partly sustained, through political agency outside the frameworks of formalised institutions. The struggles around gender, race, sexuality and disability tend, with some exceptions, to be non-institutionalised: indeed, they flourish precisely through the challenges they present to mainstream institutions.

The problems of conceptualising political agency within institutional theory are linked to a more fundamental difficulty: the conception of power. Economic and political strands of the theory tend to conceptualise power in terms of utility maximising individuals pursuing their interests. This may be helpful in understanding some ways in which equality initiatives fail; for example, the financial incentives placed on business unit managers may lead them to make decisions which prioritise economic considerations over equality policies. However, the new institutionalism is less helpful in offering ways of analysing other dimensions of power, including the structural power of one social group over others. Nor is it possible to conceptualise the shifting and fluid nature of power linked to more complex conceptions of social identity. New institutionalism conceives of social actors as discrete individuals who come with neatly packaged sets of social interests. An understanding of the dynamics of change requires a more complex approach to the dynamics of power and it relationship to complex and shifting social identities. Fiona Williams' model of the multifaceted and interrelated nature of these forms of identity and social division offers a way of seeing 'diversity' as a series of interrelationships rather than as a group of separate categories (Williams, 1992). Identities artic- ulated through gender, race, disability, sexuality and class should not be seen as permanent, essential or uniform, but as shifting, various and interrelated (see, for example, Lewis, chapter 8 this volume). Different patterns of identity are defined by the subjects themselves as well as shaped by the social, cultural and material conditions around them. This form of analysis is helpful in illuminating two important issues in the dynamics of change surrounding equality policies and initiatives. First, it provides a framework for moving beyond the 'category politics' which has sometimes dogged equal opportunity policies, where groups are constituted as discrete and sometimes competing entities (Newman and Williams, 1995: 120). Second, the development of ideas of diver- sity has implications for political and social action: power becomes more fragmented and fluid, and lines of struggle more complex and multiple. The old simplicities of class conflict or gender politics are displaced by myriad forms of engagement and activism. Creating the space in which different groups can come together, share experience and develop new forms of social and political action becomes an important element of equality practice.

A third difficulty in using institutional theory lies in the concept of isomorphism itself. Local authorities do not all take on similar charac- teristics as they respond to a common external agenda. Similarly, local authority departments do necessarily replicate the institutions of the centre, nor copy each other through some form of evolutionary isomorphism. Davina Cooper's work stresses the contested nature of governance, and the conflicts played out between different tiers of government (Cooper, 1998). She studies a series of attempts to breach established rules of the game – institutionalised in political boundaries, legal authority and formal rules of governance. Her work highlights the importance of studying the strategies deployed in struggles to win institutional legitimacy, rather than viewing legitimacy as the product of an adaptive process of change. Institutional theory tends to view change as linear and based on the emergence of distinctive pathways in which new norms and logics of appropriateness are elaborated. An alternative conception of change – broadly Gramscian – would view it as a more unstable, uneven and contested process. Such a model high-lights the significance of tensions and instabilities as points around which new alliances might be shaped and new forms of action emerge. This form of analysis underpins the final section of this chapter on possibilities and prospects for change.

Modernising equality: possibilities and prospects for change

The ideological and institutional context of local government shifted markedly after the election of the first Labour administration in 1997. There are, of course, significant continuities with the previous Conservative administrations (in the continued search for the contain-ment of welfare expenditure; the search for organisational efficiencies; the focus on performance; and the search for business or market-based solutions to social and policy problems). However, it is also possible to identify some core themes in the 'new agenda' of public policy and management. The emerging discourses of Best Value, partnership, cross-cutting issues, public consultation and democratic renewal appear to offer an expanded concept of equality in a number of ways, yet contain a number of internal ambiguities or tensions.

The introduction of 'Best Value' embodies continuities with the performance and competition focus of Thatcherism alongside the new agenda of public participation (for fuller discussion see Kelly, chapter 11 this volume). Although Best Value offers a softer imagery of per-formance improvement than the CCT[1] regime, the squeeze on local government finances together with continued ratcheting up of per-formance demands is likely to have significant implications for already disadvantaged groups of the workforce. The selection of services for market testing or outsourcing may well replicate the pattern of CCT in which low-paid, black and female employees were most disadvantaged. The 're-engineering' of services using IT – for example, the introduc-tion of call centres – often has profound implications for patterns of female employment (not least in the geographical relocation of 'back-room' services). Best Value strengthens the managerial agenda; the tighter focus on performance is likely to influence the perceptions of managers and professionals in complex ways. On the one hand, there will be more incentives for managers to engage with frontline staff in bringing about performance improvements. On the other, the increasingly important business focus is likely to strengthen the informal norms that equality agendas are somehow passé and not to be taken seriously, especially where they might limit the achievement of efficiency targets and other business goals. It may also lead to a further spread of the rather macho culture that has accompanied the use of competition in public services.

The wider but more subtle impact of Best Value on equalities agendas arises from the more conscious assessment of labour as a cost – a cost which has to be driven down in order to enable a service to compete effectively. The primary effect will be a further squeeze on the wages of the most vulnerable groups of staff (those in services regarded as most peripheral, and therefore most likely to be subject to competitive market testing or outsourcing to private sector contractors). Driving down labour costs will transfer costs to other state agencies (those administering social security, family credit, etc.). It will also result in the exacerbation of other social problems (health, family failure, social exclusion etc.) that the government wishes to overcome.

This leads directly to a second theme in the modernisation agenda: the focus on 'joined up government' in order to address cross-cutting issues (health, social exclusion, crime and disorder, regeneration and so on – see Wilkinson and Appelbee, 1999). The focus is on working through partnership to deliver policy outcomes in key areas of social and public policy that cut across traditional boundaries. This offers great potential for the development of policies intended to redress areas of inequality in the communities served by a local authority and its partners. There have been some significant successes: for example, community safety policies have sometimes been drawn up in consultation with women's groups in order to address women's safety concerns. However, the outcomes have been constrained by the limited power and role of local government to deliver on its policy goals. Few authorities, even working in partnership, can command the resources to address longstanding structures of inequality: the poverty of lone mothers, the low pay of women in the flexible labour force, the mobility problems faced by women with disabilities, the isolation of many older women, the health problems of young women engaged in prostitution, etc. As a result, new policies – however broad in concept – often result in a series of relatively small-scale projects based in different agencies. While each has value in its own terms, these tend to suffer from a lack of integration (each partner shapes initiatives in a way which matches its own agenda) and a lack of continuity (projects are often based on short-term funding arrangements).

More fundamentally, many of the cross-cutting issues focus on the needs of particular groups – the old, the young unemployed, the socially excluded, lone mothers. These tend to be based on a residual definition of inequality which assumes that the main lines of structural inequality around gender, race and class have been resolved, leaving isolated pockets who continue to experience 'social problems'. Such groups are constituted as 'outside' mainstream society, represented as modern, affluent, active and, above all, employed citizens. Concerns around social exclusion puts poverty back on the agenda while sharpening perceived links between youth, ethnicity and criminality. The focus on lone mothers raises important links between gender, poverty and employment, while threatening an authoritarian set of conditions for accessing state benefits. Each of these groups is constituted as the object, rather than the subject, of social action. They are outside the body of active, responsible citizens to whom exercises in public participation are addressed (see Bagilhole, chapter 4 this volume).

Public participation constitutes a third major theme in the 'new agenda' (see also Scott, chapter 9 this volume). This has the potential to give greater voice to groups traditionally excluded from policy-making processes: the elderly, people with disabilities, young people, people from different minority ethnic groups, and so on. It has given greater legitimacy to existing groups of staff working with service users and communities to involve them more closely in decision-making, and has led to a raft of innovations in public participation and involvement, from citizens juries through to focus groups and citizen panels. Such techniques present potential challenges to the traditional patriarchal and paternalistic relationships between local authorities, users and citizens. They open up new spaces which can be captured by user groups, voluntary organisations and community bodies seeking to claim a stronger role in decision-making. As a consequence, they have often elicited deep resistance on the part of professionals, managers and members, many of whom have rediscovered the tenets of liberalism in order to challenge the legitimacy of new voices on the basis that they are 'unrepresentative'.

Consultation may be loosely coupled to other activities. It may be little more than a form of ritual that the corporate centre engages in to establish its legitimacy, or which services conduct in order to go through one of the steps in a Best Value review, with few real outcomes arising from the findings. Even where there are genuine attempts to engage in deeper forms of dialogue with the public and a willingness to act on the results, such exercises are limited in their capacity to deal with issues of diversity and inequality. Notions of public dialogue and community involvement typically rest on ungendered and unracialised conceptions of 'the public' and naive and non-antagonistic images of 'community' (Hughes and Mooney, 1998). Differences of interest, of identity and of social or economic position are dissolved in a general orientation towards inclusiveness. The cross-cutting of multiple lines of interest and identity, of overlapping and competing 'publics' are rendered invisible.

Each of these themes reflects a more general ideological shift away from the conceptions of equality enshrined in the institutions of the welfare state and public administration, however limited these were in their effectiveness. The new agenda is organised around a residual conception of equality: it operates from an assumption that the needs and interests of the majority will be met through the process of modernisation of employment, of welfare and of the state itself. The 'Third Way' is based on a conception of an expanded, meritocratic middle class. The role of government is viewed as providing 'voters and their families' with the opportunities to fulfil their potential (Tony Blair, quoted in *The Guardian*, 15 January 1999: 3). The needs of those outside the new consensus are to be met by targeted provision: it is claimed to be no longer possible to provide the formal equality of access to universal state benefits and other forms of social provision. Two-tier systems are rapidly emerging in health, education, pension provision and other services. The focus on 'joined up government' is unlikely to succeed in overcoming the lack of attention to structural forms of inequality.

These processes are shaped within a set of deeper contradictions in the modernisation agenda. The fracturing of the postwar welfare settlement has resulted in new and complex lines of identity and the emergence of new forms of social division. The emphasis in New Labour on community, on consensus and on the importance of the family as the building block of society hark back to a very traditional set of images at the same time that it is seeking to transform the economy of the UK around notions of modernisation. As we noted in *The Managerial State:*

> There is a peculiar oscillation between 'modernisation' and 'tradition' at the point where the economy and social meet. It is as if the

modernisation of the economy, organisations, working patterns and employment conditions must be countered by the preservation of the 'traditional way of life' – despite the social and cultural diversity that has undercut that tradition. Just as there is 'no going back' on the centrality of markets to economic life, so there is 'no going forward' beyond the conventionalising imagery of communities, traditions and families within the nation ... Despite the symbolic attractions of the old ... attempts to resolve the crisis of the social by restoring 'authority', 'responsibility' and the patriarchal family form that embodies them will sustain the crisis rather than make it go away. 'The people' – in all their unequal and complex diversity – cannot be reunited as such a public. (Clarke and Newman, 1997: 139)

The future prospects and possibilities for equalities agendas depend on the working through of such contradictions between traditionalism and modernisation. They also depend on the shaping of new alliances between established political formations – trades unions, anti-racist and women's movements, 'old' Labourites, and so on – with those seeking to shape a new political agenda. The role of voluntary and community-based organisations, public managers and professionals, and local government itself in shaping alternative conceptions of what it means to be 'modem' should not be underestimated.

The political, economic and social settlement which New Labour is seeking to build contains inherent tensions and instabilities. For example, there are tensions between the continuance of the economic transformations introduced by Thatcher and the inclusive social goals of New Labour. There are tensions between the discourse of justice and fairness which underpins political rhetoric and the inherent injustices arising from the transformation of social welfare. There are tensions between the project of modernisation and the traditional images of family, community and society on which it is based. Such tensions allow space in which political agency can be expressed, new voices heard and new agendas emerge. It might be suggested that local authorities have a key role in fostering debate and in building the capacity of communities to develop and pursue their own agendas. How far they are able to do so in the context of the arguments put forward in this chapter is unclear. Managerialisation and modernisation may, in their different ways, lead to a positive reworking of the old, bureaucracy-based institutions of equal opportunities to produce a greater focus on outcomes, a stronger climate of openness and accountability, and a more sophisticated understanding of the need for institutional legitimacy in the eyes of diverse communities of interest and identity. They may, however, produce little more than a continued marginalisation of equalities along with the old social welfare agenda, old Labour and old patterns of trades unionism. Which combination of these futures will be realised depends on how far new forms of political agency emerge out of the tensions and contradictions within the unstable settlement of new Labour.

Note

1. CCT – Compulsory Competitive Tendering: a process whereby certain designated local authority services were compulsorily put out to tender to private
   sector companies, as well as in-house local government contractors. This
   tended to result in contracts going to the lowest bidder, with the effect that
   labour costs were cut and that working conditions for staff in these services
   worsened.
   Best Value – Best Value was introduced by the Labour government to replace
   CCT. The Best Value regime links performance monitoring, service review,
   consultation, and the use of contractors to deliver services, with the intention of ensuring quality, efficiency, and effectiveness in the business of local
   government.

References

Bradley, H. (1999), *Gender and Power in the Workplace: Analysing the Impact of Economic Change*, London: Macmillan.

Calas, M. and Smircich, L. (1992), 'Re-writing Gender into Organisational Theorising: Directions from Feminist Perspectives', in M. Reed and M. Hughes (eds), *Re-thinking Organisations: New Directions in Organisational Theory and Analysis*, London: Sage.

Clarke, J. and Newman, J. (1997), *The Managerial State: Power, Politics and Ideology in the Remaking of Social Welfare*, London: Sage.

Cockburn, C. (1991), *In the Way of Women: Men's Resistance to Sex Equality in Organisations*, London: Macmillan.

Cooper, D. (1998), *Governing out of Order; Space, Time and the Politics of Belonging*, London: Rivers Oram Press.

Cunningham, R. (1998), 'Managing Equality in the Context of the New Public Management; Conflicts and Contradictions in a "Post-bureaucratic" Paradigm', conference paper for the 13th Annual Employment Research Unit Conference, September, Cardiff: Cardiff Business School.

diMaggio, P. J. and Powell, D. (1991), 'Introduction', in Powell and diMaggio, *The New Institutionalism in Organisational Analysis*, Chicago: University of Chicago Press.

Dwyer, P. (1998), 'Conditional Citizens? Welfare Rights and Responsibilities in the Late 1990s', *Critical Social Policy*, Vol. 18, No. 4.

Hughes, G. and Mooney, G. (1998), 'Community', in G. Hughes (ed.) *Imagining Welfare Futures*, London: Routledge.

Lister, R. (1998), 'From Equality to Social Inclusion: New Labour and the Welfare State', *Critical Social Policy*, Vol. 18, No. 2, May.

Lowndes, V. (1996), 'Varieties of New Institutionalism: A Critical Appraisal', *Public Administration*, Vol. 74, No. 2.

Meyer, J. and Rowan, B. (1991), 'Institutional Organisations: Formal Structure as Myth and Ceremony', in W. Powell and P. d'Maggio (eds), *The New Institutionalism in Organisational Analysis*, Chicago: University of Chicago Press.

Newman, J. (1994), 'The Limits of Management: Gender and the Politics of Change', in J. Clarke, A. Cochrane and E. McLaughlin (eds) *Managing Social Policy*, London: Sage.

Newman, J. (1995), 'Gender and Cultural Change', in C. Itzin and J. Newman (eds) *Gender, Culture and Organisational Change*, London: Routledge.

Newman, J. and Williams, F. (1995), 'Diversity and Change: Gender, Welfare and Organisational Relations', in C. Itzin and J. Newman (eds) *Gender, Culture and Organisational Change*, London: Routledge.

Scott, R. (1994), 'Institutions and Organisations', in R. Scott and J. Meyer, *Institutional Environments and Organisations*, London: Sage.

Wilkinson, D. and Appelbee, E. (1999), *Implementing Holistic Government*, Bristol: The Policy Press.

Williams, F. (1992), 'Somewhere over the Rainbow: Universality and Diversity in Social Policy', in N. Manning and P. Page, *Social Policy Review 4*, Canterbury: Social Policy Association.

7
Gender Politics in the 'New' NHS
Angela Coyle

In this chapter I am concerned with examining gender equality in the context of the reform and restructuring of health care in the UK and, in particular, in the reconfiguration of community and primary health services into Primary Care Groups (PCGs). The introduction of these new structures for the management and delivery of primary health care have been hailed as the biggest 'shake-up' in the UK National Health Service (NHS) for fifty years (*Guardian*, 1 July 1998). So far massive upheaval is not much in evidence but certainly PCGs are regarded as a crucial element in the Labour government's agenda for a 'new' and 'modernised' NHS. Locally determined and managed health care is to be achieved through new and extended forms of professional collaboration between health care workers, such as doctors and nurses, and across health and social care agencies in a given locality. As a policy agenda committed to social inclusion, user participation and equality in health care standards, there is much here that is potentially very attractive to those working for gender and 'race' equality in the organisation of health care.

Primary Care Groups are required to work at grass-roots level and to foster new community and user involvement in the development of local services. They offer nurses opportunities for an enhanced role with new responsibilities and a more egalitarian professional collaboration with doctors. Although it is anticipated that PCGs will be doctor-led, women who work at the 'care face' of primary health care, as community nurses, health visitors and midwives, are in principle well placed to provide PCGs with the knowledge and networks necessary for managing and delivering local health services in socially inclusive ways. There is the potential for alliances between women as health care workers and users, and for women, including black and ethnic minority women, to have a far greater influence and voice in the content and delivery of health services. But just how is this potential for increased equality and social inclusion to be realised? Are doctors going to become more interested in nurses' views? Will managers take more notice of front-line staff? Is anyone listening to the patient?

I argue here that overcoming inequality and social exclusion will require nothing less than the transformation of the gendered and racialised professional hierarchies that have underpinned health care for decades. Professional relations which variously subordinate, exclude and marginalise women have been reproduced within successive models of organisation, management and public policy, even when they are to the detriment of service delivery. Unless there are new challenges to such inequality, there is little to suggest that the 'new NHS' agenda and PCGs will be any different from previous regimes. This chapter, which draws on my case study research on the introduction of PCGs, questions how established relations of inequality might be disrupted. Both the managerial restructuring of the 1980s and 1990s and the various equal opportunities initiatives developed over the same period have had great implications for women, but neither of these forces for change has significantly dismantled the gendered organisation of health care. Meanwhile a feminist challenge has been variously absent, fragmented or becalmed.

Patterns of gender and inequality in the organisation of health care

The NHS has over one million employees, approximately three-quarters of whom are women. It is the biggest employer of women in Europe, but a predominantly female workforce does not in itself make for an egalitarian workplace. The Equal Opportunities Commission (EOC) survey of the NHS in 1990, concludes that 'discrimination against women in the NHS is deeply engrained' (EOC, 1991: 17) and that 'racial discrimination not only restricted black people's recruitment to the service but also took the form of profound inequalities of opportunity and status between black and white employees' (EOC, 1991: 38).

Employment for women has been concentrated in just four occupational areas. These are nursing, which is 90 per cent female, professions allied to medicine (PAMs) such as physiotherapy and speech therapy, which are 88 per cent female, clerical work and administration, which is 85 per cent female, and ancillary work such as catering and cleaning where women make up 75 per cent of the occupational category.

Women are still under-represented in senior levels, where they make up 22 per cent of general management and 19 per cent of senior medical (consultants) posts (Department of Health, 1998).

Black and ethnic minority women have been excluded, subordinated and subject to racial harassment in all occupational categories (EOC, 1991), but poor monitoring hinders a proper analysis of their position. It is nursing that accounts for the bulk of black and ethnic minority women's employment in the NHS. Here they make up just over 5 per cent of all nurses and tend to be clustered in lower-paid and lower-graded nursing jobs, and in low-status NHS work such as mental health and geriatric medicine with limited opportunities for training, career development and promotion (Beishon et al., 1995). Black and ethnic minority women are severely under-represented and marginalised in NHS management (Bhavnani and Coyle, 2000). In 1990 the King's Fund Equal Opportunities Task Force noted that applications from black groups for nursing training and posts were declining rapidly (EOC, 1991: 39). Since then black and ethnic minority women have continue to reject nursing as a career, once one of the few avenues of professional work open to black women (Hine, 1989).

The connection between such patterns of inequality, segregation and the bureaucratic organisation of health services is very well rehearsed (see, for example, Davies, 1992, 1995; Halford et al., 1997; Homans, 1989; Savage and Witz, 1992; Witz, 1992). Women have not necessarily been excluded from areas of work in which men are dominant, such as medicine, but they have been concentrated in junior roles and lower-status specialisms (Allen, 1994). In management, women have tended not to be considered of managerial potential, except at lower levels, despite having been the indispensable backbone of NHS administration for decades (Rosser and Davies, 1987). Elsewhere in the NHS women's professional work has been clearly constructed according to deeply patriarchal demarcations. Gamarnikov (1978) has argued that there is familial division of labour between doctors and nurses in which she likens doctors to the 'father', nurses 'the mother' and the patient 'the child'. The caring role of nurses can only proceed after it has been defined and authorised by doctors' clinical diagnosis. Despite their numerical dominance, nurses have never successfully challenged the authority and power of doctors to control and limit nursing practice. Celia Davies questions whether nursing is a profession at all. She suggests that nursing has been constructed as an adjunct occupation, supportive of men but not equal to them and which actually contributes to a definition of medicine as powerful and masculine (Davies, 1995: 61).

Gender and organisational change

As in other public services in the UK and elsewhere, the 1980s and 1990s were decades of extensive restructuring and organisational change for the NHS, with significant implications for women's work. Clarke and Newman (1997) suggest that the development of public sector managerialism over this period helped dismantle traditional bureaucratic hierarchies and created new opportunities for groups of staff previously excluded in the old arrangements.

Unquestionably women have gained a bigger role in the new NHS managerial culture, sharing in management job creation. However, managerialism was a response to crisis, not a strategy for gender equality, and as the now extensive 'new public management' literature makes plain, its focus has been cost control, targeted rather than universal welfare and the extension of managerial discipline through market mechanisms (Clarke and Newman 1997; Flynn, 1993; Pollitt, 1993; Walsh, 1995). The impact on women's work has been highly contradictory.

Nursing: The borderlands of gender, career and profession

The early 1990s saw the introduction of devolved NHS 'Trust' structures created to enable health care to be run on a more competitive and 'business like' basis (Flynn, 1993). These locally managed Trusts cut brutally into the organisation of nursing. Large bureaucratic nursing hierarchies which had previously managed both community and acute hospital nursing services across a designated Health District gave way to much smaller, flatter nurse structures located in individual Trusts and with the organisation of community and acute nursing newly separated. Under these new arrangements old nursing 'empires' were lost, senior nursing posts disappeared, nursing career paths were severely truncated and nurses' professional sphere of influence diminished (Coyle, 1995; Davies, 1995; Halford et al., 1997). Although new nurse manager roles were created along with NHS Trusts, senior nursing positions became more limited in number, career paths shorter and career progression more complex. For example, nurses who wish to progress from ward sister into management now have a wide gulf to bridge and need to adopt a reflexive and risk-taking career strategy (sometimes moving out of the NHS for a period) to acquire necessary managerial skills and experience. It is male nurses who seem to find it easier to comply with this career model. Even though they make up just 10 per cent of the nursing profession, men make up a third of nurse management posts.

Debates about the changing work and responsibilities of nurses and nurse practitioners have been in the public domain for some time. The chronic shortage and turnover of doctors in the NHS, combined with the ever-rising demand for their services, has led to some innovative thinking on the role of nurses. Higher-level training and specialisation for nurse practitioners mean that nurses can both act as doctors' gate keepers and assume some of the tasks previously undertaken by doctors. These developments do not necessarily represent an enhanced status for nurses. As far as the medical profession is concerned the extension of the nursing role seems more to do with the shedding of tedious work: 'We may never get thousands of new doctors, but the least we could do is spend some money to take away from doctors some of the trivial things they should not be doing in the first place' (Vice-president of the Royal College of Physicians, quoted in *The Observer*, 9 July 1998: 21).

Nurses may be much in demand but their role in the new managerial ethos of the NHS has been, and continues to be, highly circumscribed. Davies (1995) and Halford et al. (1997) argue that nurses have been actively excluded from the managerial agenda whilst the medical profession has been strengthened by it. Doctors have used their enhanced managerial capacity to reinforce their view that nurses cannot and should not manage, or at best have a limited management contribution to make, focused on quality and the delivery of care. It is with some justification that nurses might perceive managerialism as detrimental, but their occupational strategies tend to reinforce the view that they are resistant to change. They continue to stress their caring professional role (in opposition to 'uncaring' management) and the pursuit of specialist clinical skills and degree level qualifications as a the route to higher professional status (Halford et al., 1997: 103). It is not an approach that has served them particularly well. It has divided and polarised the profession into graduate and non graduate nurses (many of whom are long serving black nurses) and has done nothing to arrest the substitution of nurses by unqualified nursing assistants.

Medicine: the institutionalisation of gender and power

On the face of it, women doctors have fared better. Between 1986 and 1996 the proportion of women doctors working in NHS Trusts has increased from 25 per cent to 31 per cent. As women now make up nearly half of medical school entrants, this trend looks set to continue. Although the majority of women doctors are still concentrated in junior grades, there are now more women consultants and registrars in some of the growing specialisms, such as paediatrics. Over the last decade, the percentage of women consultants across all specialisms increased from 14 per cent to 19 per cent (Department of Health, 1997b). This increase in women doctors has occurred over the same period in which increasing numbers of male doctors have been leaving the NHS and medicine has become a less attractive career choice for men (*Guardian*, 29 July 1998). With a projected crisis in doctor recruitment there is clearly scope for the continuing feminisation of medicine. However, whether this signals greater gender equality is unclear. Men still continue to dominate the profession, especially through their occupancy of high status specialisms. In surgery, for example, men make up 96 per cent of all consultants (Department of Health, 1997b: 15). Their adherence to training and working arrangements based on long working hours has profoundly exclusionary effects and is illustrative of the institutionalised means by which men can still maintain gender divisions.

Management: masculinity and control

The introduction of new management structures created new management jobs and women have shared in this occupational growth. Given the levels of feminisation in the NHS, however, it would be very strange for women not to have some kind of presence in health management. Women make up 51 per cent of NHS 'administrative managers' but this umbrella occupational category conceals the diversity within it. Women are concentrated in relatively junior grades with limited opportunities for any strategic input as this manager I interviewed noted:

> When I first came into the NHS from the private sector, I realised that I didn't need to fight to get women into management. Access wasn't the problem. I realised why. The majority of managers are actually administrators. They have been given the title of manager because that is the pay grade they're on but in actual fact many in this disparate group is not operating at a managerial level. (Health Authority Management Development Adviser)

By 1998 women made up 22.3 per cent of chief executives (a 10 per cent increase between 1989 and 1994) and 47.5 per cent of senior management posts (a 16.4 per cent increase between 1989 and 1994).

But most of this growth occurred between 1989 and 1994 along with the creation of NHS Trusts. This reorganisation broke up large NHS structures into smaller units and in doing so created more chief executive and general management jobs but with a sexual division of labour between chief executives much in evidence. The increase in the number of women chief executives is almost entirely attributable to the establishment of Community Trusts and Family Health Services Authorities (FHSAs) in the early and mid-1990s. It is still mostly men who run the large acute hospital trusts. Subsequent restructuring has seen the amalgamation of Trusts and the abolition of FHSAs which, according to the former head of the NHS Women's Unit, has resulted in 'a significant cull in women top managers' (Langridge, 1999). Between 1994 and 1998 the proportion of women in chief executive positions has remained almost static, increasing from 21 per cent to just 22.3 per cent (Langridge, 1999).

Rather than leading to a significant shift in power relations between women and men, organisational change has altered the ways and forms in which gender relations are expressed. Clarke and Newman (1997) argue that women are no longer excluded from management but are kept 'in place' and out of powerful and influential positions by more complex discursive processes that question their competences to manage. Men have actively sustained a competitive 'macho' management culture which associates managerial competences with the qualities of masculinity. Celia Davies has suggested that successive health reforms have actually been concerned with the reform of the relations of men and, in particular, the extension of managerial control over the medical profession, with remarkably little regard given to the reform of women's work. Women are more affected by the fall-out from the 'clash of masculinities' that reform has entailed (Davies, 1995: 166).

Equal opportunities policies in the NHS

Unlike local government, the NHS has not been the focus of grass roots feminist and 'race' equality activism or cultural challenge. Although there has been a variety of local, voluntary and *ad hoc* equality policies in existence in the NHS since the 1980s, a corporate response to equalities policies did not get underway until the early 1990s. Equalities initiatives in the NHS seem marked by the gap between high-level corporate commitment and local inactivity. When the EOC found Southern Derbyshire District Health Authority unlawfully discriminating against women with children, it noted that although the Health

Authority Personnel Services had produced written equal opportunities guidelines, managers were unaware of their existence (EOC, 1990).

The link between inequality and discrimination and staff shortages, high turnover and recruitment difficulties in the NHS has long been established (EOC, 1991). As a large employer subject to public scrutiny, the EOC findings were issues of corporate concern, and in 1991 the NHS became a member of Opportunity 2000. This nationwide campaign, targeted at employers, promoted the business case for providing equal opportunities for women. A women's unit was set up within the then NHS Management Executive, with strong backing from the then Secretary of State for Health. The NHS set a series of corporate goals aimed at increasing the proportion of women in strategic and decision-making roles. The women's unit funded a raft of positive action schemes, including training and mentoring. After five years the women's unit was disbanded. It is difficult to assess its achievements because it is hard to know exactly what is being measured. A study carried out with women's unit support drew the conclusion that two years on from the launch of Opportunity 2000 in the NHS, its equalities policies were more extensive than other health service employers in Europe (Hegewisch et al., 1993), but this finding does need qualification. First, it has been trades unions rather than NHS management that have pushed for equalities measures to be written into national and local bargaining agreements. Second, many of the measures designated as equality measures in the NHS were found by this study to be provided by European employers as established and statutory provision rather than special measures for women. Third, although no other European health service employer had such a range of policies, the report indicated that the NHS was less likely to monitor its workforce than any other employer and therefore lost the opportunity to assess the effectiveness of its policies. The women's unit might have claimed the increased proportion of women in senior management and clinical posts as one of its significant achievements (Jarrold, 1995), but there was in fact no mechanism for attributing such change to policy. The women's unit needed to demonstrate its achievements, but in doing so it paradoxically contributed to the perception that the gender equality battle had been won, almost.

In 1996 NHS equality structures were reconfigured. The women's unit was replaced with a new equal opportunity unit, responsible for all aspects of policies covering gender, race and disability. The creation of this new unit was in line with the noted preference amongst employers for a unitary approach to equality policies (Jewson et al., 1995) and with the tendency for women's equality agenda to give way to a mainstreamed and gender neutral HRM approach based on diversity (Bacchi, 1996). It also made more explicit connections between employment policy and service delivery:

> The Government is committed to tackling discrimination and inequality in the Health Service. The quality of services provided depends upon having a workforce which draws from all section of the community and is capable of providing for the needs of a diverse population. We want to see a Health Service where employers recruit people from all backgrounds, where family friendly working practices encourage them to stay, where the working environment is free from harassment and hostility and where progress is monitored and achievement celebrated. (NHS Equal Opportunities Unit, September 1997)

The equalities unit has a much strengthened focus on 'race' equality and a now familiar performance-related managerial agenda which includes 'mainstreaming' equality issues by linking equality targets to managers' performance appraisal, setting new standards for benchmarking equality in employment and service delivery and placing an increased emphasis on monitoring and auditing, as well as piloting specific positive action initiatives.

The most recent survey of equal opportunity policies in the NHS, commissioned by the NHS equalities unit (IRRS, 1998), indicated that almost all Trusts (98 per cent) now have some kind of policy statement covering issues of gender, ethnicity and disability. The majority (80 per cent or more) have specific policies on well-established employment procedures such as maternity and parental leave, job sharing, recruitment and selection. However, just a third of Trusts set themselves specific gender equality goals and only a quarter set 'race' equality goals. Although the majority of Trusts now undertake workforce monitoring of some kind, little use is made of these data and it is generally not used to identify equal opportunities priorities. Few trusts monitor those procedures – such as access to training and promotion outcomes – which could serve as key performance indicators. In general Trusts are interested in a local equality agenda rather than a national or corporate one and with those measures such as flexible working which help address local staff recruitment and retention problems (IRRS, 1998).

A decade of equalities work has not touched many of the wider processes of inequality, subordination and exclusion that are discussed in this chapter: the erosion of women's professional career structures and professional development; the diminishment of women through masculine discourses and the institutionalisation of male power; and the marginalisation and harassment of women, especially black and ethnic minority women. The flow of women out of the NHS has not been stemmed (from nursing in particular), nor have significant numbers of new recruits been persuaded to enter it. At a corporate level the NHS is well aware of these tensions, and as the NHS embarks on yet another wave of restructuring and reform there is a renewed imperative to develop equalities strategies that will deliver a version of equality in keeping with a health agenda based on social inclusion.

The 'new' NHS and primary care

The government White Paper 'The New NHS' (1997) set out the incoming Labour government's reform agenda. Since then the structures of the internal market have been dismantled, new frameworks for partnership and collaboration across health and social care agencies such as Health Action Zones (HAZs) and Health Improvement Programmes (HIMPs) have been introduced, along with Primary Care Groups (PCGs). The 'new' health agenda clearly links poor health with poverty and social exclusion, and hence health improvement, with the provision of socially inclusive health services. So far these reforms have generated a lot of goodwill amongst even the most change-weary as they offer a vision of health services based on social justice and stress a social change agent role for health care professionals.

But many doubt the capacity of the NHS to transform itself. In his analysis of earlier waves of health care reform, Pollitt (1993) argued that the potential for creating a more transformative culture was limited by an 'impoverished management' narrowly focused on efficiency and cost control rather than innovation and empowerment. Although the NHS does contain pockets of flexible organisation based on team working, devolved management decision-making and a customer orientation, it remains very wedded to hierarchy, professionalism, specialised divisions of labour and centralised forms of control (Clarke and Newman, 1997; NHS Confederation, 1998a; Walby et al., 1994). Moreover, there is much in the 'new' agenda which represents a continuation with the former 'new' public management: targeted rather than universal services, performance indicators which have increased rather than diminished social exclusion and purchaser or 'commissioning' structures which have excluded lower level staff (mostly women) from the identification and management of need (Mackintosh, 1997).

Primary Care Groups

General practitioners (GPs) are doctors contracted to work for the NHS on a self-employed basis to provide non-hospital-based health care to the local communities in which their practices are located. Some practices are single-handed (one-doctor practices) whilst many are partnership practices varying from two to up to seven partners. Most GPs, especially in the larger partnership practices, employ a small staff, usually comprising one or two practice nurses, a practice manager and reception staff. Although community nurses work from GPs' practices, they have until now been employed not by GPs but by the NHS Community Trust that organises community nursing services for an area.

The reorganisation of GP practices into locality-based group structures – Primary Care Groups in England, Local Health Groups in Wales and Local Health Care Cooperatives in Scotland – has been one of the most widely debated reforms in the 'new' NHS. From April 1999, all GP practices have been required to be part of a formally constituted local primary care group, serving populations of up to 100,000 and working in partnership with the local Health Authority and other local health and welfare agencies on the strategic development and delivery of locally determined health and social care. In many respects PCGs build on previous GP organisation. Approximately 50 per cent of all GPs have been working already within some kind of devolved financial 'fund holder' arrangement (Department of Health, 1997a) with experience of controlling budgets and purchasing health services directly. Some suggest that the only real difference that PCGs make is that all GPs are fund holders now (*The Economist*, 31 July–6 August 1999: 22). For all those groups not previously involved in commissioning health services – most of whom are women – such as nurses, professions allied to medicine and community health managers, and many GPs in non-fund-holding practices, the new PCGs represent considerable change, especially in the longer term. There is no ready made blueprint for Primary Care Groups, rather they are envisaged as a phased development over ten years with much scope for diversity of local structures and working arrangements. Some PCGs hope for minimum changes whilst others are already aspiring to become independent, free-standing health trusts, or even health care businesses in their own right.

Reorganisation into primary care groups raises many questions as to how these changes will affect women. What will happen to the terms and conditions of employment of nurses, midwives, health visitors and professions allied to medicine who are currently employed and managed by Community Trusts under the umbrella of NHS terms and conditions of employment? Will GPs agree to take on existing NHS pay structures and employment policies such as flexible working and extended maternity and family care leave? What will happen to those managers, predominantly women, who currently run the Community Trusts? Will they find places in the new structures and working arrangements or will PCGs represent a continuation of the 'cull' in women managers? What, indeed, is the future role of the Community Trusts? Some anticipate that Community Trusts will be disbanded, whilst others envisage they will develop to provide corporate management services for the PCGS.

An inclusive approach to PCG organisation is not much in evidence (Marks and Hunter, 1998). Many GPs are concerned that their real purpose is to exert greater control and financial discipline over GPs by involving them in financial decision-making and health care rationing (previously GPs could overspend on their budgets and still escape real penalties). Moreover, whilst the government is clearly keen to substitute nurses for doctors in a wide variety of roles, GPs have resisted government attempts to create PCG boards more representative of nurses and user groups and have only agreed to cooperate since the government agreed to PCG boards which give GPs an in built majority and the right of veto. Whilst GPs may be asserting their control over the new structures in order to resist government reforms which they believe will draw them increasingly into health care rationing, the form of their resistance is having the effect also of excluding women from decision-making and influence.

The ability of doctors to control the new PCGs does not bode well for an enhanced role for nurses and professional collaboration. The Royal College of Nursing has initiated leadership programmes for 'nurse commissioners'. Nurses and managers I interviewed doubted the effectiveness of this national focus on nurse leadership when the problems nurses face are more immediate and local:

> Nurses talk of skills for commissioning – health assessment profiling and that sort of thing. It's premature; first we need someone to listen to us. Doctors don't listen to nurses. Managers don't listen to nurses. Only nurses listen to nurses. I want to see nurses flourishing, acting with fluency and confidence and not phased by large meetings. (Health Authority Nurse Adviser)

Powerful nurses may not be what GPs want:

> They've been told that they have to have a community nurse on board, to give a nurse's view. I would bet my bottom dollar that

what will happen is the group will have a favourite, either a health visitor or nurse who they see as compliant with their wishes and my guess is that they will try to select that individual. Someone they can control rather than someone that will challenge. Now I may be doing a grave disservice to GPs but I don't think I am. They will go for the tame view and I think that's really sad. (Health Authority Management Development Adviser)

In her research on home and social care services for the elderly, Maureen Mackintosh (1997) has shown how 'front-line' nurses and other care workers (usually women) have been distanced from management decision-making, often to detriment of the service. Not only has women professionals' local knowledge not been taken into account, but any such input has often been regarded as a threat to the managers' prerogative. As PCGs have become established so too have new gender borderlands:

There is an opportunity there for nurses. GPs are in the majority (on PCG boards) because they bear the financial risks. We're saying 'we're forming a new club, how do you want to be involved?' The term I use is democratic hierarchy. (GP Chair of PCG)

Thus nurses and other para professionals have been largely marginalised in the debates and preparations for the new PCG structures:

'Did you see that poor nurse beside you? She was absolutely brainstormed, "How long has this been going on? We don't know any of it? Nobody's told us any of this."' (Coordinator of Local Nurses' Forum)

Primary care management

Although Primary Care Groups are not expected to become highly managed structures, they are developing new management systems and creating new Chief Executive posts. The business of managing primary care and community health services has always been women's domain and many women managers in Community Health Trusts and GP practices, whose jobs are at risk in the new configuration, have an eye on these new jobs, but whether primary care will create new opportunities for them is far from clear.

The job of practice manager evolved along with GP fund holding throughout the 1980s and 1990s and quickly became a feminised role. The job and status of practice managers varies considerably with the size and complexity of the GP practice and the attitude of GPs themselves, who, I was told, often regard their practice manager as a 'glorified receptionist'. In some of the larger fund holding GP practices, the job of practice manager has been a demanding management role, with responsibility for budgets, staff, patients and surgeries, information technology and the management of the complex professional teams based in the practice. In these kind of practices men make up a third of practice managers, whereas women practice managers make up almost 90 per cent of managers in smaller non-fund-holding practices (Audit Commission, 1996).

Like nurses, practice managers also feel highly marginalised from current developments:

> We see it as an opportunity to use the expertise that we have if somebody allows us to. There is a view that GPs will not need prac-tice managers because a group manager/chief executive will take over our role. We don't get much feedback on what's happening. What's starting to happen is those GPs who do have some business acumen are able to see the possibilities and will do the planning on behalf of everyone else. You know, 'don't worry lads, we've got it in hand.' It may not be what others want. It's very difficult to be a player if you don't share the arena – if you're not allowed into the arena. (Practice Manager)

Community Trust health managers, currently responsible for the organisation and delivery of a wide range of primary nursing and health care services, not only feel marginalised but also are well aware of the dangers that the new structures present:

> We've been told that we should be working ourselves out of a job. There will be massive issues. Some things will go backwards, things like part time working and flexibility. There won't be the staffing to meet the standards we currently have. There's bound to be changes in working conditions. There will be a pressure over hours, split shifts and things like that. We don't know how much nurses will be able to negotiate. They will be more scattered. Nurses will be a scarce commodity but they are not organised enough. (Senior Manager Community Trust)

They can see the potential for nurses but doubt whether it will happen:

> Community nurses are now identified as key. But nurses themselves are not on the same level and GPs are not always welcoming. One of the largest PCGs here has already said there is no place for nurses in

it! The training and development issues are vast. Nurses have got to be developed to make a useful input. There are very great differences that are not being spoken about. Differences in salaries, in historical power bases. Until that is acknowledged I can't see how it will even start to work. What I don't know is who is thinking about any of this at the moment. (Executive Director of Nursing, Community Trust)

Gender equality in postmodern organisations

In this chapter I have discussed how a 'new' health service is being constructed on some very 'old' gendered assumptions which will certainly get in the way of any transformative agenda for socially inclusive health care unless hierarchical power relations are challenged. There are few indications as to where this challenge might come from. Equalities policies have helped 'feminise' employment policies and regulate sexual and racial discrimination in the workplace. But equalities policies help employers manage consensus and risk, rather than causing disruption. Nevertheless, equality policies have been a source of much learning for those involved, and have renewed the focus on organisations as a key site for the production and reproduction of gendered power relations, identified by Walby (1997) as 'public patriarchy'.

Contemporary perspectives see organisations as pluralistic structures and as sites of difference, conflict, flux, fragmentation, dislocation and power contestation where different agendas and vested interests are constantly in play (Clegg, 1990; Hatch, 1997; Leonard, 1997; Morgan, 1986). Feminist critiques of organisations share this perspective and indicate how the daily enactment and expression of these different interests is never gender neutral (Acker, 1990; Cockburn, 1991; Savage and Witz, 1992). This new representation of organisations as sites of contestation is incredibly helpful in explaining why planned change is so difficult:

> Implementation is never predictable or certain ... [organisations] are composed of individual and groups with interests that colour the interpretation and implementation of any proposals for change. These individuals and groups have their own agenda for change – organisationally and/or professionally. (Halford et al., 1997: 94)

The difficulty, however, is that when there is no perceived basis for consensus or collectivity, there appears to be no obvious framework for action. There can be no blueprint for equalities practice. Whereas we might have once regarded gender equality work to be the pursuit of incremental, progressive reform over time, challenging injustices affecting all women, it is now clear that gender equality is not linear, progressive nor undifferentiated. There are gains and losses, advances and retreats. The gains of one group may be detrimental to another. No gain can be assumed to be everlasting. Some women can be privileged in relation to other categories of women and indeed some men.

According to Foucault, this process of identifying and questioning power relations and the status quo is crucial. It is in itself a key and ongoing 'political task' (cited in Hatch 1997: 367). In their study on gender relations in public services in London, Abrar et al. (1998) identified the absence of feminist advocacy in the reorganisation of London health services. Despite being such a feminised organisation, women in the NHS, and nurses in particular, are rarely able to bring a gendered analysis to their experience and it is clearly difficult to do so. Halford et al. (1997) indicate that when nurses do challenge male doctors' authority, they experience such a level of harassment that most opt for a mode of exaggerated femininity in their dealings with doctors.

Women nurses and managers do talk of the need 'to have clout' in the new structures of primary health care, but primarily this seems to mean ensuring that women have a place in the new hierarchies, rather than challenging them. What the NHS has not seen is a strategic alliance of women constructed around a common purpose. In recent years women managers have developed a critique of 'macho' management styles, posing in contrast a women's leadership and transformational management 'style' which is constructed as different and implicitly better (the most cited exposition of this discourse is in Rosener, 1990). This rather essentialist view of women's leadership has some currency amongst NHS women managers but seems to be confined to trying to model different kinds of individual behaviour: 'Leaving work at reasonable times; holding board meetings within normal working hours; ensuring that all staff took their full entitlement of annual leave; and viewing maternity leave as an opportunity to develop other staff via secondment' (Carol Pearson, Chief Executive Bournewood Community and Mental Health NHS Trust, cited in NHS Confederation Update: 3).

Some insights into a more challenging form of feminist leadership are provided by Cynthia Cockburn's (1998) account of how disparate groups of women have worked together across conflicting national and ethnic identities. She argues that inequalities between women based on class and ethnic difference need to be acknowledged and affirmed, not ignored. Women's collectivity cannot be assumed but has to be constructed, based on strategic alliances which recognize both commonality and difference. To date women in the NHS have not been able to overcome their own professional, social and cultural boundaries; white women's professional strategies have not been inclusive of black and ethnic minority women. Within the new primary health care structures there is scope for an alliance of women, as health care workers and as users, to secure the health services that they need. It won't be easy. It is not the intention of the 'new' NHS to foster such agency nor to become what Macintosh (1997: 4) has described as the 'public stage' on which the challenge from the excluded takes place. So where to begin?

> Until nurses stop seeking affirmation and approval, they're not ever going to feel strong. They're always looking to see whether or not it is OK. Well you don't look, you say to the chief executive 'I don't agree.' (Nursing Officer)

References

Abrar, S., Lovenduski, J. and Margetts, H. (1998), 'Sexing London: The Gender Mix of Urban Policy Actors', *International Political Science Review*, Vol. 19, No. 2, pp. 147–71.

Acker, J. (1990), 'Hierarchies, Jobs, Bodies: A Theory of Gendered Organisations', *Gender and Society*, No. 5, pp. 390–407.

Allen, I. (1994), *Doctors and their Careers a New Generation*, London: Policy Studies Institute.

Audit Commission (1996), *Fund Holding Facts*, London: HMSO.

Bacchi, C. (1996), *The Politics of Affirmative Action*, London: Sage.

Beishon, S., Virdu, S. and Hagall, A. (1995), *Nursing in a Multi-ethnic NHS*, London: Policy Studies Institute.

Bhavnani, R. and Coyle, A. (2000), 'Black and Ethnic Minority Women Managers in the UK', in M. Davidson and R. Burke, *Women in Management: Current Research Issues*, Vol. 2, London: Paul Chapman.

Clarke, J. and Newman, J. (1997), *The Managerial State*, London: Sage.

Clegg, S. (1990), *Frameworks of Power*, London: Sage.

Cockburn, C. (1991), *In the Way of Women*, Basingstoke: Macmillan.

Cockburn, C. (1998), *The Space between Us*, London and New York: Zed Books.

Coyle, A. (1995), *Women and Organisational Change*, Discussion Series No. 14, Manchester: Equal Opportunities Commission.

Crompton, R. and Sanderson, K. (1990), *Gendered Jobs and Social Change*, London: Allen and Unwin.

Davies, C. (1992), 'Gender, History and Management Style in Nursing: Towards a Theoretical Synthesis', in M. Savage and A. Witz (eds) *Gender and Bureaucracy*, Oxford: Blackwell.

Davies, C. (1995), *Gender and the Professional Predicament of Nursing*, Buckingham: Open University Press.

Department of Health (1997a), 'Statistics of General Medical Practitioners in England: 1986–1996', *Statistical Bulletin*, May.

Department of Health (1997b), 'Hospital, Public Health Medicine and Community Health Service Medical and Dental Staff in England 1986 to 1996', *Statistical Bulletin*, July.

Department of Health (1998), NHS Hospital and Community Health Services Non-Medical Staff in England: 1987–97, *Statistical Bulletin*, May.

Doyal, L. (ed.) (1998), *Women and Health Services*, Buckingham: Open University Press.

The Economist, 31 July–6 August 1999, p. 13.

Equal Opportunities Commission (1990), *Formal Investigation Report: Southern Derbyshire Health Authority*, Manchester: Equal Opportunities Commission.

Equal Opportunities Commission (1991), *Equality Management: Women's Employment in the NHS*, Manchester: Equal Opportunities Commission.

Flynn, N. (1993), *Public Sector Management*, second edition, London: Harvester Wheatsheaf.

Gamarnikov, E. (1978), 'Sexual Division of Labour: The Case of Nursing', in H. Kuhn and A. Wolpe. (eds) *Feminism and Materialism*, London: Routledge and Kegan Paul.

Guardian Society Special Issue, 'Best Foot Forward: The Next 50 years for the NHS', 1 July 1998.

Guardian Society, 15 July 1998, p. 21.

Guardian Society, 29 July 1998, pp. 8–9.

Halford, S., Savage, M. and Witz, A. (1997), *Gender, Careers and Organisations*, Basingstoke: Macmillan.

Hatch, M. J. (1997), *Organisation Theory: Modern, Symbolic and Postmodern Perspectives*, Oxford and New York: Oxford University Press.

Hegewisch, A., Brewster, C. and Sirnes, C. (1993), *Equal Opportunities Policies in Europe: How the Health Service Compares*, Cranfield School of Management.

Hine, D. C. (1989), *Black Women in White*, Bloomington. Indiana University Press.

Homans, H. (1989), *Women in the NHS: Report of a Case Study into Equal Opportunities in Clinical Chemistry Laboratories*, London: HMSO.

Industrial Relations Services Research (IRRS) (1998), *Survey of Equal Opportunities and Monitoring in the NHS Trusts*, NHS Executive.

Jarrold, K. (1995), *Opportunity 2000 – Women in the NHS, Progress Report Letter*, EL (95) 126, NHS Executive, 3 November.

Jewson, N., Mason, D., Drewett, A. and Rossiter, W. (1995), *Formal Equal Opportunities Policies and Employment Best Practice*, Research Series No. 69, Department for Education and Employment.

Langridge, C. (1999), 'Leaving the Laurels Behind', *Health Service Journal*, 10 June.

Leonard, P. (1997), *Post-modern Welfare*, London: Sage.

Mackintosh, M. (1997), 'Public Management for Social Inclusion', paper presented to Conference on Public Management for the Next Century, Manchester, 29 June–3 July.

Marks, L. and Hunter, D. J. (1998), *The Development of Primary Care Groups: Policy into Practice*, Birmingham: The NHS Confederation.

Morgan, G. (1986), *Images of Organisation*, London: Sage.

NHS Confederation (1998a), *Update*, No. 3, February.

NHS Confederation (1998b), *Briefing*, No. 9, February.

NHS Equal Opportunities Unit (1997), *The NHS Equal Opportunities Unit*, information circular, NHSE.

Observer, 19 July 1998, p. 21.

Pollitt, C. (1993), *Managerialism and the Public Services*, second edition, Oxford: Blackwell.

Rosener, J. (1990), 'Ways Women Lead', *Harvard Business Review*, November–December, pp. 119–25.

Rosser, J. and Davies, C. (1987), 'What Would We Do Without Her? Invisible Women in NHS Administration', in A. Spencer and D. Podmore (eds) *In a Man's World*, London: Tavistock.

Savage, M. and Witz, A. (eds) (1992), *Gender and Bureaucracy*, Oxford: Blackwell.

Walby, S. (1997), *Gender Transformations*, London: Routledge.

Walby, S. and Greenwell, J., with Mackay, L. and Soothill, K. (1994), *Medicine and Nursing: Professions in a Changing Health Service*, London: Sage.

Walsh, K. (1995), *Public Services and Market Mechanisms*, London: Macmillan.

Witz, A. (1992), *Professions and Patriarchy*, London: Routledge.

8

Categories of Exclusion: 'Race', Gender and the Micro-social in Social Services Departments

Gail Lewis

In the two to three decades since the political activism of 'new social movements' put the question of equality onto organisational agenda, a profoundly deepened understanding of the potential gains of, and constraints upon, equalities policies has developed. Equalities policies and strategies have been examined to reveal distinctions as to their scope and the political visions which underwrite them, as in, for example, Jewson and Mason's (1986) early attempt to categorise equality policies and distinguish between their 'liberal' and 'radical' variants. Similarly, a more finely tuned distinction between the objectives or targets of equality policies has occurred, as between equality of opportunity, equality of treatment and equality of outcome. Blakemore and Drake (1996) have amalgamated these two strands and divided equalities policies into minimalist and maximalist forms. In practice the attempt to construct typologies by distinguishing between the political philosophies underpinning equal opportunities policies, their scope and objectives can lead to some problematic blind alleys. It can lead to an overstated divide among approaches, whilst obscuring their degrees of convergence (Forbes, 1991). Similarly, it can lead to simplistic characterisations of conservative and progressive forms of equal opportunities (Cockburn, 1989). It can also lead to a formalistic and prescriptive focus on the procedural mechanisms designed to achieve greater equality within an organisation (whether this be reviewing procedures for bias, or targeting a certain percentage of posts at under-represented groups within the limits of the law). Clearly reform of organisational procedure has an important role to play in the pursuit of greater equality. However, the fetishisation of procedure can easily result in failure to recognise the impact of *process* on the pursuit of equality within an organisation. This in turn can result in a failure to examine the dynamic of micro-social relations among groups and individuals within the organisation, a dynamic that can pose knotty and difficult questions as to the scope and potential of equalities strategies. More recently the notion of equal opportunity has been joined, or replaced, by the idea of managing diversity. This has carried with it a shift from a focus on policy and procedures to one concerned with valorising, supporting and freeing the creative potential of diverse categories of staff within the organisation.

This latter development has emerged in the context of the new managerialism and has carried with it a recognition of, and concentration upon, the importance of organisational culture in inhibiting or promoting equalities objectives. In some ways the distinctions and tension between 'equal opportunities' and 'managing diversity' have reflected new managerialism's rhetorical challenge to what it defined as excessive professional power and bureaucratic inertia (Clarke and Newman, 1997). In doing so it highlighted that equal opportunities has tended to be concerned with the development of policies and procedures aimed at creating equality of opportunity for marginalised groups. In this way equal opportunities has operated within bureaucratic categories and rules which have aimed at establishing conformity with the behavioural norms the policy prescribes. Moreover, this relates to the distinction between equality of treatment and equality of outcomes, for, as Gibbon has suggested:

> On the whole EOP development seems plausibly linked to bureaucratization, and possibly appeals to bureaucratic organizations or branches of organizations because of its *formalizing* qualities. Moreover, the more bureaucratic an organization is, the more it is arguably likely to pursue implementation seriously. The promotion of equality of outcome, *by contrast*, requires the *suspension* or sidelining of bureaucratic norms and procedures within an organisation ...
> (1990: 19; emphasis in original)

Bagilhole has described the assimilation of equalities agenda into the bureaucratic machinery of organisations as 'sanitisation' (1997: 58) – a process that subverts the political origins and focus of equal opportunities. Moreover, despite any pretensions to the contrary, the more recent managing diversity approach is characterised as equally depoliticising by Bagilhole. For her the 'managing diversity' approach both 'harness[es] "equal opportunities" strategies to business competitiveness' (1997: 57), and disconnects equal opportunities from its roots, since 'while equality *and* group justice was the concern of the political left in the 1980s, the emphasis is now on quality' (1997: 58), thereby knocking the 'e' off equality (Gilroy, 1993). In this way 'equal opportunities' as equal treatment can coexist with the idea of individualistic competition (1997: 59).

Thus, the development of a more complex understanding of equalities agenda has involved greater discernment of the types of equality which might be pursued together with contextual analysis of the articulation of equality agenda and hegemonic organisational forms within the public sector. This has been accompanied by a key development in critical understandings of equality agenda, that is the concern to place the distribution and operation of *power* at the centre of analysis. As Thompson states, 'power is ... a central feature of the struggle to promote equality' (1998: 43). In this view the important point is made that power is a dynamic structuring a range of social relations and not just class or employee/employer relations as is often commonly assumed. Thus, power is 'a structural property in the broader sense relating to the various ways in which society is structured – rather than simply a question of class dominance' (1998: 47) and is, therefore, central to the pursuit of equality within organisations.

By insisting that power itself become a central subject of equalities strategies, Thompson draws directly on the political critiques and knowledges that emerged from the new social movements. These new political constituencies had pushed and reconfigured the boundaries of traditional, trade union-based worker protection and representation within organisations. Cynthia Cockburn, in her insightful and stimulating article on the complexities of equalities, had already signalled some of these issues when she wrote:

> There are aspects of the post-Fordist, post-Modernist moment with its emphasis on new subjects, on multiplicity, flexibility and choice, that can be seized to advantage not only by employers but also by people at work. Equal opportunities is readier to step into that new world than the unions. (1989: 223–4)

Equal opportunities in this sense has the potential to provide the parameters and contents of a new employee politics. Her immediate interlocutors at this point were trade unions, arguing that these working-class organisations should seize the time and help foster 'alliances between the multiple, divided subjects of disadvantage' (1989: 223). In pointing to the complexities of equal opportunities, Cockburn sought to distinguish between 'the short and the long agenda' of equal opportunities policies (EOP) in order that strategies aiming at profound organisational restructuring in the interests of diverse constituencies of staff be devised and implemented. Importantly, she illustrated both that there may be no easy correspondence between the various constituencies that might benefit from equal opportunities, and that the gains of equal opportunities are vulnerable to destabilisation and marginalisation by organisational change and individual tactics. The webs of factional power, together with the dynamics within and between these factions are, therefore, central to the shape, success or failure of equal opportunities strategies.

Within feminist writing on equality issues there has been increasing recognition of their complexity and a concern to explore the implications of this deepened understanding for how we might conceptualise equal opportunity, positive or affirmative action, to use some of the many names used to reference the domain of inquiry. As Bagilhole has put it:

> When we look at the relationships between gender, 'race' and disability, we must see them as dynamic and interactive. It is not enough to add mixed categories such as ethnic minority women or disabled women into existing frameworks. (1997: 40)

This raises the central issue of the categories in both the deployment and analysis of equalities strategies. Indeed, in analysing the 'politics of affirmative action' Bacchi has distinguished between conceptual and identity categories in equality or positive action policies:

> I distinguish between conceptual categories which are to do with ideas like 'equal opportunity', 'preferential hiring/promoting', 'reverse discrimination', and identity categories such as 'women', 'Aborigines', 'men', and so on. (1996: xi)

The collective impetus of recent work on equal opportunities has drawn attention to the need for a more complex theorisation of the role of the organisation itself in facilitating or constraining the pursuit of equality. This means more than just to reiterate the by now well-accepted view that policy and procedural change is not enough to deliver equality of either opportunity or outcomes. Nor is it simply to say that as aspects of society, organisations will inevitably be arena that reflect wider societal inequalities. As Thompson states:

> Organisations are dangerous places. They are major sites of power and conflicts of interest, and so considerable harm can result from the complex and potentially destructive processes that go on between individuals, between groups, and between organisations and their employees. (1998: 174)

Organisations as sites of power are also, therefore, productive (to invoke Foucault, 1978). That is to say that in the complex dynamic of interaction between the wider society and the organisation, the organisation becomes a space in which inequalities are *constituted* or brought into being. This is so not just in terms of the formal hierarchies of status, authority and chains of command, but also as arena in which the 'big' axes of differentiation and inequality are themselves constituted. Of course, the movement of what we might, for the sake of analytic procedure, call social subjects (i.e. people already positioned within axes of inequality and differentiation outside the organisation) across the boundaries demarcating the organisation from its wider social context ensures that already formed social positions and identities enter the organisation from outside. However, it is my argument that organisations should be seen not just as *reflecting* inequalities generated outside its boundaries, but as places where inequalities, and the categories and identities constituted through these differentiations, are brought into being, constituted and 'performed'.

In this sense the complexity of equalities agenda needs to be understood in a double sense. Complex in the sense of strategies aimed at responding to the organisational effects of complex social phenomena articulating various dimensions of power and identity, known as gender, 'race', class, sexuality or disability. Second, complex in the sense that these agenda are internally complex, contested and contradictory responses to the attempt to resignify and reconfigure these articulations of power inside the organisation.

Two implications flow from this way of conceptualising complexity. The first is that it impels us towards a yet more complex understanding of the categories through which equalities agenda are both formulated and implemented. In other words, we need to take Bacchi's distinction between category as conceptual and category as identity and explore how organisational subjects constitute themselves as gendered, 'raced' or sexualised *selves*. Second is the related step of analysing how these processes of constitution of selves intersect with the conceptualisation of equalities categories such as gender and 'race'. The focus is, then, on organisational culture, understood as the values, norms, assumptions and practices that circulate within the organisation, but in a way that draws analytic attention to the micro-social relations that produce the organisation as a 'lived' entity. In this 'lived' entity, organisational subjects will be positioned within and across multiple axes of differentiation and hierarchy. Moreover, this multiple positioning implies that many subjects will simultaneously inhabit both subordinate and *dominant* locations and identities. Given this, 'complexity' must be viewed as not just the condensation of several subordinate locations within an individual, as is implied in some attempts to think through the complexity of equal opportunities, as the following illustrates:

> If we take the oppressions of racism, sexism and disablism, a person can be pictured as a sponge floating on a societal pool of social divisions ... At certain times the sponge will encounter and soak up various disadvantages, and in different combinations and proportions ... An ethnic minority woman might need to fight racism at one point and sexism at another time, and at other times the sexism she is fighting is tainted and influenced by racism. Her allies may change in these different fights and so might her strategy. The dynamic mix of sexism, racism and disablism demands different reactions at different times and in different contexts. (Bagilhole, 1997: 41)

In contrast to this approach, I want to refocus attention on the interweaving of subordinate and dominant sides of binary divisions and the inter-group relations and identities they structure. Thus, greater theoretical sophistication requires attention to the articulation of power by and across people positioned as at once subordinate and dominant. This requires, for example, that we think of the white woman (as well as the 'ethnic minority' woman, the white man and the 'ethnic minority' man) as formed at the intersection of gender and 'race', along with other axes of differentiation. It requires understanding that the micro-social of organisation will be textured by processes of constitution of whiteness, as well as blackness or Asianness, masculinity as well as femininity; able-bodiedness as well as disabledness, etc. Thus, equalities agenda need to pay attention to the dynamics of production of dominance by individuals and groups who may also be positioned as subordinate. This approach requires recognition of the agency of multiply positioned subjects. It suggests that in part organisations are constituted as spaces of greater or lesser degrees of inequality by the practices of self deployed by those who work in them.

This approach invokes Butler's (1993 and 1997) notion of performativity and sees gender and 'race' as iterative and citational practices performed by all social and organisational subjects. The iterative or citational quality of gender and 'race' suggests that the constitution of selves as gendered and 'raced' is achieved through the repetition of norms even as this historicised repetition is concealed.

> Performativity is thus not a singular 'act', for it is always a reiteration of a norm or set of norms, and to the extent that it acquires an act-like status in the present, it conceals or dissimulates the conventions of which it is a repetition. (Butler, 1993: 12)

For equal opportunities, then, the issue is not just to what extent the organisation's policies and procedures promote or constrain equality of opportunity or outcome. Nor is it even only about the ways that the organisational culture promotes or constrains the effects of gendered and 'raced' practices. It is both these, *plus* the ways in which gender and 'race' are 'performed' by organisational selves and how these 'performances' facilitate or constrain the pursuit, implementation and achievement of equalities agenda. The organisation as a gendered and 'raced' entity will then be structured by the citational practices of gender and 'race', just as the organisational norms of gender and 'race' will be embedded in yet concealed by these performative practices.

I hope to explore further this understanding of the complexity of the micro-social relations that are central to the pursuit of organisational equality by analysing a particular moment in a specific organisational context. The chapter is structured around a discussion of two sequences of accounts collected during research I conducted into two Social Services Departments in England. The first is taken from an interview with a white, English area manager; the second from a black, African-English team manager. In using interview material to illustrate my argument about the connections between equalities strategies and processes of constitution of gendered and 'raced' selves, I am treating speech, or language, as a social practice that carries a double temporality. It is a social practice that occurs in the present, but its constitutive power is achieved by drawing on (invisible) historical meanings and norms. Language is seen as facilitating the constitution of social locations and identities through processes of interpellation (Althusser, 1971), not simply reflective of them. Gendered and 'raced' selves are made recognisable by the iterative quality of language and speech. In the accounts that follow, the woman speaking uses 'her self' to illustrate some specific aspect of the 'livedness' of her working life in a social services department. In the course of these accounts the women carve out a speaking position within which they construct categories of 'gender' and 'race'. Their 'self' becomes the terrain upon which these categories are constructed and, moreover, they construct their 'selves' in ways that reproduce binary thinking and reinscribes them within mutually exclusive categories. However, their enunciatory positions do not construct a single binary in which only sexual or 'racial' difference is signified, but rather both at once. Thus, they provide us with useful material through which to consider the extent to which 'the self' offers fertile soil for the development of critical analysis of the organisational formation in which relations of inequality are constituted. They alert us to the complex gender and racial economies that comprise and articulate the 'everyday' of organisational life. Moreover, they show the limitations of equalities strategies that understand the complexity of organisational inequality in terms of multiple subordinations rather than the complex interaction of dominance and subordination.

Equal opportunity and sexual and 'racial' difference

The discussion so far shows that the pursuit of organisational equality poses difficult theoretical questions about the points of connection between the categories 'race' and 'gender'. This, in its turn, raises difficult political questions about how feminists can develop forms of theoretical and strategic intervention into the organisational world in ways that expose and undermine the reproduction of 'difference' as so many discrete forms of inequality. These are the issues I want to think about through an examination of the two accounts that follow. In this we need to think about two questions. On the one hand, the ways we have constructed the domains of gender and 'race' (and by extension the social relations of inequality they reference). On the other hand, how we might reconstruct these domains/categories in ways that begin to undermine the assumption about their mutually exclusive character, in both empirical and methodological terms.

What I want to argue is that the political and analytical place that those concerned with organisational inequality need to move towards is one where the categories of 'race' and gender are understood as *always* mutually constitutive, even when the language of one (or the other) is foregrounded. In other words, that in racially structured capitalist patriarchal societies, *each* of us is always constituted as a racial and a gendered (and classed, etc.) subject and that the analytical categories used to explore organisational practice have to be able to hold and reflect that. The ways in which this process of mutual constitution occurs will, of course, be context-specific – and in this case this is the organisational context of the social services department. However, if 'gender' and 'race' are mutually constitutive categories and processes of becoming, their operation must also be implicated in the production of relations of inequality *within* their referential constituencies as well as between these constituencies. In this sense I also want to consider to what extent the enunciatory positions adopted by differentiated categories of women (understood here as empirical subjects) also involve them in the *constitution* of relations of 'difference' and inequality among women.

Speaking women

Let me begin to elaborate these points by considering the two accounts. I have given them the names Annie and Shirley. Annie was an area office manager and so was at the third tier of management within the organisation. She was responsible for three teams of social workers. Shirley was manager of one of these teams, placing her in the fourth tier of management, with Annie as her line manager. Most of Shirley's work involved the direction and supervision of her team's case load, with her own case load being restricted to those cases defined as particularly difficult or sensitive. Both the extracts are taken from sequences that occurred well into the interview, when both of us had relaxed and gained a flow of interaction.

Annie: White woman area manager

G.L.: *How do you think differences of 'race' and gender reflect themselves in this area office?*
Annie: Well, I have not been here very long, but I think there are issues around gender, certainly, in that there are two female (team) managers, Bianca and Shirley, who are both black, and a white male, team manager, and he is acting up into the deputy post, and I certainly would say I like Bianca and Shirley a lot. It is not that I don't like Richard, but I feel more comfortable with women any way and I am conscious that as a group of three women, we combine together to somewhat undermine and get at Richard. [*laughs*] I don't know why I am laughing, and it is not funny and not good. Shocking really. It's no better, so if you can do that to one person you can do that to another.

Yes, it's not good, but we do it, and within that both those two women are very competent, very good workers, and there is something about this that is very good for me and although this isn't my permanent job, I am able to swan around and be area manager with team managers, um, and although I haven't thought about it until just now, but there is this sense of it is like having a better possession, a better car [*pause*] and part of that is of course not about the fact that they are good workers, but it is that added dimension of good workers who are women and are also black, it is like you have got the icing on the cake.

Shirley: Black woman team manager

G.L.: *So tell me then, how do 'race' and gender work here?*
Shirley: I was just thinking when I was talking about the qualities in women, it seems what I perceive is that largely speaking women have the ability to pick up very minute details which sometimes are overlooked by male workers, who might look at something from the way, [*pause*] from a very factual point of view, rather than from an insightful, experiential point of view. A woman might well, say, describe how a mother and child had interacted with her, and the details of the description might be to do with eye contact, voice level, you know, I might not necessarily hear that from a male worker, so in terms of overall perception the perspectives are quite different [because] of our experience as carers. Um [*pause*]. What I find men are very good at is the dialogue with other professionals and presenting us in court, and with that kind of confidence of working with outside agencies.
The other amazing thing is that in my team there is a social worker who is probably nearing fifty, and he has long, grey hair and he wears jeans and denim jacket and he goes to court like this, no black worker, whether woman or man, could go to court like this and not be criticized. However, this white worker has this particular style of his that says this is me and I am not going to change, and he is a very good social worker, but he doesn't feel the need to conform.
G.L.: *So you are saying that all this refers to women (as carers, as nurturers etc.)*
Shirley: 'No I was particularly thinking about black women.'
G.L.: *But don't white women tell us that they are also brought up to do all those kind of nurturing things, so where does 'race' come in?*
Shirley: I was going to say that it is that thing that is missing with them, that added layer to black women's lives that enables us to be much more insightful, I feel, I feel that if anything the one thing we do have in common is the experience of racism, and it is something that affects every aspect of our life, child rearing to professional and somehow

there is this common belief amongst us that is not necessarily explicit in talking and I suppose that is a problem, that we can recognise and be familiar with, and that we can actually be quite undermining [to each other] so that even that I'm a team manager, that my status might well be more powerful than say a social worker, and that is very difficult for them to accept. We have this thing in common, because there is this connecting umbilical cord, we should all be on the same level.

If we deconstruct these accounts I think they suggest some interesting points about the intersection of gender and 'race' as categories of 'difference' through which experience and identity are constructed and, indeed, deployed. Let us take these in turn.

Annie begins her response by establishing the organisational positions and the gender and 'race' of the people she directly manages – i.e. her team leaders. Having done this she immediately moves on to construct a totalising gender divide, in which the three women stand on one side, and the man stands on the other. In doing so she erases the differences of grade and 'race' between herself and the other two women. She is acutely aware that as a *management* practice the marginalisation she refers to is, at the very least, dubious – but her narrative does this in a way that establishes a kind of unity among the women. However, in the next paragraph she immediately begins to undermine this unity within 'the gendered same' and she does it, first, by re-establishing the women's respective locations within the organisational structure – thereby establishing the black women's hierarchically subordinate position. This allows her to invoke a sense of 'ownership' of these women, which, in discourse analytic mode we can suggest is highly racialised in that it constructs a chain of association back to slavery. In this she performs 'racial' 'difference' and constitutes her whiteness without ever explicitly mentioning it. Therefore, we can deconstruct her account in terms of its constitutive effects and how she performs notions of gender and 'race' which speak to and enact 'difference' which (re)constitutes unequal social and organisational relations. She constructs herself as both a woman and importantly, though more implicitly, white.

Let us now turn our attention to Shirley. This speaker does not begin her account by foregrounding structural locations within the organisation, but rather puts the issue of gender at the front of her opening remarks. She uses the notion of gender as a category through which to 'explain' differences in the style of working amongst men and women in her social work team. However, she quickly moves on to the issue of 'race' and suggests that this has a twofold relevance for our discussion.

First, in the context of the work of social work, gender differences are of a secondary order, and with whiteness (at least), or white maleness, having an inter- and intra-organisational effect which expresses itself as a kind of 'freedom' denied any black people. The ambiguity about whether it is 'whiteness' *per se*, or more specifically 'white maleness', which is the determining factor raises unresolved questions about how she sees the relative importance of 'gender' as a structuring principle for white people's subjectivity and experiences in comparison to those of black people. Nevertheless, having pushed 'race' to the foreground she holds on to it in two ways: first, she specifies that it is *black women* who, for her, have specific qualities that are important for social work – qualities which derive from the experience of racism; second, she talks about the effects of the construction of black experience as singular and homogeneous. This second point, she says, often leads to the expectation on the part of black colleagues that black people in more senior positions within the organisation will not, and should not, impose the hierarchies of authority that accompany differential locations within the organisational hierarchy.

I would argue that these extracts are interesting and revealing because they exemplify two things. On the one hand, they illustrate the complex interweaving, of 'race' and gender as categories of 'difference' which mediate experience and shape how individuals interpret their experience and how they construct the organisation as a racialised and gendered space. On the other hand, they are demonstrations of the way that people often speak *as if* they are just talking about one set of unequal relations – one axis of 'difference' – at the very same moment as they invoke and perform several such relations. Gender and 'race' then can be thought of as 'metalanguages' (Brooks-Higginbotham, 1992) – languages that carry, yet mask, the embeddedness of these categories in a variety of axes of differentiation and power. This has implications for those concerned to enhance the potential of equalities strategies to deliver their objectives. The task, therefore, is to find ways that facilitate an alertness to the complex interweaving of gender and 'race', dominance and subordination. In its turn this would enable avoidance of analyses that reproduce the idea that gender and 'race' are discrete, or additive categories, and strategies that position any one axis of 'difference' as *the* primary one.

Thinking through mutual constitution in the micro-social

The first thing we need to establish is that 'gender' and 'race' are constituted categories which are always in process – that is, they are always in the act of becoming. Again feminist work provides a good starting point. In particular two theorists from the US have provided the conceptual tools with which to begin disrupting this process of analytical separation and/or primacy.

One, Joan Scott, addresses the definition of gender; while the other, Evelyn Brooks-Higginbotham, addresses the issue of 'race' as a metalanguage. In their distinct ways these writers are concerned with the meaning of terms which lie at the very heart of questions of 'difference', meanings that have provided the nodal points for the articulation of new political subjects and collectivities whose claims and challenges helped foster the development of EOPs. Together they provide useful starting points for my own analysis because they help us to understand 'gender' and 'race' as processes by which fields of intersecting 'difference' and inequality are constituted.

Let us look at how they frame the issues. Joan Scott writes of 'gender' in the following terms:

> The core [of my] definition [of 'gender'] rests on an integral connection between two propositions: gender is a constitutive element of social relations based on perceived differences between the sexes, and gender is a primary way of signifying relationships of power ... [This second part might be] rephrase[d] as gender is a Primary field within which or by means of which power is articulated ... Established as an objective set of references, concepts of gender structure perception and the concrete and symbolic organisation of all social life. To the extent that these references establish distributions of power (differential control over and access to material and symbolic resources), gender becomes implicated in the conception and construction of power itself. (Scott, 1988: 42–5)

Whilst Evelyn Brooks-Higginbotham writes of 'race' in this way:

> Like gender and class, then, race must be seen as a social construction predicated upon the recognition of difference and signifying, the simultaneous distinguishing and positioning of groups vis-à-vis one another ... Race serves as a 'global sign', a 'metalanguage', since it speaks about and lends meaning to a host of terms and expressions, to myriad aspects of life that would otherwise fall outside the referential domain of race ... Race not only tends to subsume other sets of social relations, namely, gender and class, but it blurs and disguises, suppresses and negates its own complex interplay with the

very social relations it envelops. It precludes unity within the same gender group but often appears to solidify people of opposing economic classes. Whether race is textually omitted or textually privileged, its totalizing effect in obscuring class and gender remain. (Brooks-Higginbotham 1992: 253–5)

It is immediately clear that there is some variation in how these two women construct their arguments. Scott tends to reproduce the analytical and methodological separation of gender and 'race', whereas Brooks-Higginbotham, wants to show how 'race' as a language of the 'everyday' masks yet *contains* other axes of 'difference'. Yet I think they both begin to provide us with some of the tools feminist academics, policy-makers and others need to enhance our ability to think simultaneously through these categories as we try to explicate the processes by which 'difference', and the inequalities and subjectivities it constitutes, is reproduced. In similar ways these authors offer an opportunity for a deepened understanding of the 'play' of both gender and 'race' and in so doing make these categories more conceptually complex. They challenge us to try to hold the complex interplay among diverse axes of differentiation and subordination by suggesting that as categories of analysis 'gender' and 'race' must be understood as vectors through which complex webs of power relations are articulated and indeed resisted.

They achieve this precisely because they attribute a multi-dimensionality to these categories. Thus, for Scott and Brooks-Higginbotham, 'gender' and 'race' are *constitutive* of difference, rather than just reflective of it. As such, these categories are *implicated* within and *expressive* of power: they mask other social relations in the very same moment as they carry and reinflect these other relations. Therefore, in understanding these social and analytical categories as relational we must see this relationality as multifaceted rather than simply binary. This is an approach to sexual and 'racial' 'difference' that captures more of the 'lived' complexity expressed in the accounts of Annie and Shirley. Indeed, a review of these accounts illustrates the utility that a more complex understanding of the articulation of 'race' and gender, and other axes of identity, differentiation and subordination, has for the organisational pursuit of equalities strategies. It is perhaps within variants of black feminism and black feminist informed analyses of the complex operations of intersecting relations of subordination and power that a way of thinking has developed that has the potential to capture the approach indicated by Scott and Brooks-Higginbotham.

This is summed up in the idea of 'Simultaneity of Oppression' (Hull, Bell-Scott and Smith, 1982).

In an overview article of black feminist analyses, Rose Brewer (1993) identified the idea of simultaneity of oppression as being at the core of what she calls black feminist theorising. This she distils into the following propositions:

1   Critiquing dichotomous oppositional thinking by employing both/and rather than either/or categorisations;
2   Allowing for the simultaneity of oppression and struggle; thus
3   Eschewing additive analyses ... race + class + gender;
4   Which leads to an understanding, of the embeddedness and relationality of race, class and gender and the multiplicative nature of these relationships: race × class × gender;
5   Reconstructing the lived experiences, historical positioning, cultural perceptions and social construction of black women who are enmeshed in and whose ideas emerge out of that experience; and
6   Developing a feminism whose organizing principle is the interaction of class, culture, gender and race.
    (1993: 16)

This distillation of the key principles of a particular feminist perspective is helpful in that it begins to provide the schematic shape for analysis of unequal social relations. Moreover, it does so in a way that allows us to hold in view the various modalities through which these inequalities manifest themselves: as social position, as discursive constitution, as lived experience.

However, where it is more limited is in its suggestion that this approach is and *can only be* limited to a particular group of women, the single defining feature being that of occupying *a subordinate racial* position, albeit one enmeshed with these other axes of subordination. This is similar to the approach adopted by Bagilhole criticised earlier. Such approaches suggest that it is only where women are the *targets* of racism and sexism that the notion of simultaneity is appropriate and as a consequence they reproduce their own Manichean visions.

In contrast to this I want to argue that an approach rooted in the idea of *'simultaneity'* is one which can, and should, be applied to the analysis of all (in)equalities issues and that indeed this is the position to be derived from the accounts by Annie and Shirley. That is, where white women are the subjects of analysis, issues of 'race' need to be centred as a key category of analysis, alongside those of gender, class, etc. Similarly, where black women are centred, issues of gender need to be foregrounded alongside those of 'race', class, etc. The same is true for white men and black and other racialised men of colour, and indeed any of the other categories of people who are usually the subject of equal opportunities.

This, in turn, requires an approach in which 'dominance' as well as subordination is seen as part of the complex web of social and organisational relations in which we are all entangled. That is, as policy analysts and practitioners we need to see the subjects of oppression/subordination, at least potentially, as also and simultaneously constituted in positions of dominance/power. This is especially true in relation to public sector organisations where the, albeit limited, effects of two decades of EOP have resulted in some shifts in the organisational location of previously under-represented groups.

Thus, a multiplicatory approach to the intersection of 'race', gender, class, etc. will be understood as meaning that a person or group can, within specific contexts, at one and the same moment occupy positions of both *subordination and domination*. Indeed, it seems to me that it is precisely this type of complexity suggested, but not elaborated, by Cockburn (1989) when she argued that there may be no easy commensurability of view or objective among the different constituencies that form the subjects of an equality strategy. It was precisely the tensions generated by such incommensurability that made the pursuit and implementation of equalities agenda a complex matter. We see examples of these kinds of complexity in the accounts from both Annie and Shirley.

Annie was in a position of dominance as an area manager and as a white person; indeed she actively constructed a position of racial dominance for herself. She was also in a position of structural subordination as a manager at the third tier of the organisational hierarchy, and as a woman within the gender economy of the department.

Shirley was in a position of some dominance in structural terms within the organisation as a team manager (and perhaps in the wider world this would translate into a position of relative dominance in class terms), but she was in a position of subordinance in organisational, gender and 'race' terms.

It was this complex interplay of simultaneous *subordinance and dominance* that was both evoked and deployed as the means by which these women gave meaning to and negotiated their organisational life. Moreover, their accounts suggested that it was in the dynamics of the everyday interactions within the organisation that these contradictory positions were constituted.

It has been my argument that an understanding of this process of mutual and simultaneous constitution of gender and 'race' needs to be incorporated into the development of equalities strategies. In saying this I am not advocating an organisational restructuring in which the specificities of particular forms of differentiation and difference are occluded and merged into one homogeneous and marginalised cluster. I am arguing, however, for a perspective which moves beyond binary thinking (and the closures this leads to) and enables us to hold the idea that constitution of organisational selves is performative and intimately connected to processes of differentiation. Therefore, where we see subordination we must also look for dominance and this latter may reside in the 'changing same' as well as the 'other'. To succeed in developing this kind of theoretical starting point, the focus of our analytical gaze must be the culture of the organisation. For as Janet Newman has reminded us:

> The informal organisation may continue to transmit cultural messages about the 'proper place' for women: and a gendered hierarchy ... may be sustained and reproduced through cultural messages ... Other informal hierarchies are held in place alongside those of gender. Culture is the site where, for example, the wider ideologies of racism and homophobia become lived out in organisational discourses and practices. Interventions which stop at the level of the formal organisation (for example, the production of new policies and procedures) are, as a result, likely to be limited in their effectiveness. (1995: 11)

Newman is right to point to the ways in which the culture of an organisation may produce and sustain a range of inequalities. As stated earlier, I would argue that 'culture' in this context should be understood as the array of policies, practices, representations, structures, values, norms and assumptions that shape interaction between individuals and units within the organisation. Thus, I would want to agree with Newman and argue for an expanded notion of culture operating here so as to encompass the informal as well as the formal dynamics. In this context the organisation as lived entity is seen as being moulded from a series of performative practices that produce and reproduce the networks of micro-social interaction. This means that to suggest that we think of multiple systems of social hierarchy being reproduced *alongside* each other limits our capacity to grasp the mutual imbrication of forms of social or organisational inequality and dominance. Instead we should conceive them as being reproduced in and

through each other in mutually constituting ways. It is the articulation
of different axes of inequality which collectively make up the organisational formation and structure, the 'everyday' of organisational interaction. We are impelled towards this form of conceptualisation by the
data considered here. The accounts of Annie and Shirley illustrate how
gender and 'race' are mutually constitutive categories that provide
channels for the constitution of self and positions from which to
speak, even while, as metalanguages, this mutual imbrication is
obscured. In this vein, 'race' and 'gender' as both performance and
metalanguage have circulated within and across the professional and
organisational structures of social services departments and acted to
destabilise or undermine the emergence of an equalities culture within
the organisation.

These points suggest that in thinking through equal opportunities
policy, strategy and practice, we retain the idea of the specificity of
diverse forms of organisational inequality, but do so in new ways.
Thus, the centrality of specificity should be taken to mean that it is
imperative to attend to the specific forms of articulation of gender and
'race' for specific groups and individuals in particular contexts at particular times. This will include those constructed as being in some way
dominant within gender and 'racial' binaries. It means remembering
that the construction of 'racial' or ethnic minorities depends upon the
construction of 'racial' or ethnic *majorities*, and similarly with gendered
subjects. The 'difference' and organisational inequality equal opportunities seeks to disturb is not conceived as signalling only the boundaries *between* gendered and 'raced' beings, but also, the differences
within the group positioned on one side of the binary. The constitution
of difference is, then, multiple not just in the range of experiences and
relations it signals (gender, 'race', sexuality, disability, age), but also in
the sites, processes and performative practices which produce it.

The accounts considered here illustrate well the mutual constitution
of gender and 'race' through performative practice. The social services
context that structured and mediated these practices of gender and
'race' point to the relevance for the pursuit of organisational equality
of the approach outlined here. At the very least it suggests that we
abandon the discursive orthodoxies that underpin most variants of
equal opportunities, since these construct stable and fixed boundaries
around the categories gender and 'race'. At present, the frameworks of
understanding that inform most equalities thinking preclude reworking of the discursive categories through which 'race' and gender are
conceptualised and constituted. As such these frameworks limit the

extent to which equalities strategies can speak to the specific ways that gender and 'race' articulate and constitute one another. To move beyond these constraints requires that attention be paid to the performative practices that structure the micro-social of organisational life.

In making this argument I am not proposing that there is no place for the development and implementation of formal policies and procedures aimed at promoting greater equality within organisations. Equally, the focus on recognising and valorising diversity associated with managerialist approaches to organisational equality have an important role to play in advancing equalities agenda. However, by sidestepping interpersonal dynamics and the processes by which organisational identities are brought into being, deployed and negotiated, these approaches speak to only part of the problem.

The focus on the micro-social and the performative suggests that pursuit of greater organisational equality will have to focus on at least two factors missed by the prevailing orthodoxies. First, it suggests that the shape, implementation and practice of equal opportunities will always be contingent – i.e. require attention to be paid to the specific history, character and structure of the organisation. For example, how greater equality in the content of everyday practice might be pursued in social services departments, NHS hospitals, or an institution of higher education is likely to vary despite the reorganisation each of these has been subject to during the last decade or so. Second, it requires recognition of the multiplicity of identities and the dynamics of the lived experience of organisational life. For while Bacchi is right to suggest that 'it is indeed the case that identity involves differentiation, just as categorizing necessarily involves inclusion and exclusion ... not all of us are placed equally in these processes. Categorizing is the preserve of those who dominate our academies, legislatures, media, unions and boardrooms, and these are predominantly white middle-class males' (1996: 161), attention to the micro-social draws attention downwards to the dynamic within these institutions. The micro-social shows that the formation of multiple identities in specific organisational contexts enables individuals to inhabit identities of domination in ways that both entrench and cut across the always already existing categories of orthodox EOPs. The process of categorising that has become the substantive content of much equal opportunities may have become disconnected from the politics of equality and incorporated into the agenda of those that dominate private and public sector organisations. However, attention to the performative in the micro-social enables recognition that those positioned within categories of differentiation can reproduce organisational inequalities by the constitution and deployment of differentiated identities.

The logic of my argument is that pursuit of organisational cultures that facilitate a progressive move to greater equality requires a policy environment that pays attention to the performative practices through which organisational selves and interpersonal dynamics are constituted. It means thinking beyond either a focus on the removal of biased or discriminatory procedures that characterise the earlier generation of EOPs or the recognition of diversity germane to some forms of managerialism. Rather it means both these and an eye to the ways in which patterns, practices and identities of dominance are brought into being in the process of negotiating organisational life. It means recognising that 'whiteness' and 'maleness', for example, are positions and identities achieved through performative practices and that those who achieve them might also be positioned in categories and identities equated with organisational subordinance. How such a policy environment might be achieved can only be discerned collectively, as part of a series of conversations, like that represented by this volume, within and across institutions and as part of the personal practices undertaken in the course of organisational life. What I want to suggest is that the first step towards it is recognition that how we constitute our organisational selves is as important a part of the equalities agenda as the contexts and procedures structuring organisational life. In short, I want to inject a politics of personal practice into the debate about equalities strategy.

References

Althusser, L. (1971), 'Ideology and Ideological State Apparatuses', in *Lenin and Philosophy and Other Essays*, trans. Ben Brewster, London: New Left Books.

Bacchi, C. L. (1996), *The Politics of Affirmative Action: 'Women', Equality and Category Politics*, London: Sage.

Bagilhole, B. (1997), *Equal Opportunities and Social Policy: Issues of Gender, Race and Disability*, London: Longman.

Blakemore, K. and Drake, R.F. (1996), *Understanding Equal Opportunity Policies*, London: Prentice Hall/Harvester Wheatsheaf.

Brewer, R.M. (1993), 'Theorizing Race, Class and Gender: The New Scholarship of Black Feminist Intellectuals and Black Women's Labor', in S.M. James and A.P.A. Busia (eds) *Theorizing Black Feminisms: the Visionary Pragmatism of Black Women*, London and New York: Routledge.

Brooks-Higginbotham, E. (1992), 'African-American Women's History and the Metalanguage of Race', *Signs*, Vol. 17, No. 2.

Butler, J. (1993), *Bodies That Matter*, New York and London: Routledge.

Butler, J. (1997), *Excitable Speech: A Politics of the Performative*, New York and London: Routledge.

Clarke, J. and Newman, J. (1997), *The Managerial State: Power, Politics and Ideology in the Remaking of Social Welfare*, London: Sage.

Cockburn, C. (1989), 'Equal Opportunities: The Short and the Long Agenda', *Industrial Relations Journal*, Vol. 20, No. 3, pp. 213–25.

Forbes, I. (1991), 'Equal Opportunity: Radical, Liberal and Conservative Critiques', in E. Meehan and S. Sevenhuijsen (eds) *Equality Politics and Gender*, London: Sage.

Foucault, M. (1978), *The History of Sexuality*, Vol. 1, New York: Random House.

Gibbon, P. (1990), 'Equal Opportunities Policy and Race Equality', *Critical Social Policy*, Vol. 28, summer, pp. 5–24.

Gilroy, R. (1993), *Good Practices in Equal Opportunities*, Aldershot: Avebury.

Hull, G.T., Bell-Scott, P. and Smith, B. (eds) (1982), *All the Women are White, All the Blacks are Men, But Some of Us are Brave*, Old Westbury, New York: The Feminist Press.

Jewson, N. and Mason, D. (1986), 'The Theory and Practice of Equal Opportunities Policies: Liberal and Radical Approaches', *Sociological Review*, Vol. 34, No. 2, March.

Newman, J. (1995), 'Gender and Cultural Change', in C. Itzin and J. Newman (eds) *Gender, Culture and Organisational Change: Putting Theory into Practice*, London and New York: Routledge.

Scott, J. (1988), 'Gender', in *Gender and the Politics of History*, New York: Columbia University Press.

Thompson, N. (1998), *Promoting Equality: Challenging Discrimination and Oppression in the Human Services*, Basingstoke: Macmillan.

9
Women and Local Government – Dialogue, Deliberation and Diversity

Marion Scott

My work in Islington was both the best and the worst of my professional life – a thoroughly consuming experience. I headed the Women's Equality Unit at the London Borough of Islington from 1988 to late 1997. The unit was located in the strategic centre of the authority throughout this period. The experience changed me as a feminist. My understandings were enlarged by working with other women on their issues – lesbians and black and ethnic minority women, older women, disabled women and others, including refugees. I learned more about women – became prouder but also angrier, more passionate. I became more cynical about the possibilities of effecting change in a large institution. Cynical because expertise and organisational awareness were not enough to effect change. Providing the necessary facts and figures about the need for change did not necessarily result in policy or practice in a climate in which many officers and politicians denied the need for any more 'equality' for women. I developed my understanding of power and the political nature of women's equality work. Like other equality professionals, I experienced isolation, criticism, ridicule and dislike. Women's officers are vulnerable precisely because the work is about power, personal commitment and women. These patterns of opposition and resistance to equalities work were paralleled with the experiences of women in different sorts of organisations (Cockburn, 1991). I learnt to appreciate councillors, particularly those who chaired or sat as members on the women's committee. They worked in challenging and difficult circumstances and encountered resentment and resistance, yet remained pragmatic, principled and committed. Those who work to achieve change through institutions need passionate commitment and the passion of allies both inside and outside the authority. I became convinced that women's activism and democratic engagement at all levels were a vital part of this profoundly political work. This represented a new model of change for me.

In the following chapter I aim to reflect upon my experience on 'the front line' over nearly ten years. I will review aspects of the achievements of women's equality practitioners, showing throughout that much of their work was a precursor to mainstream practice in local government today. I will move on to examine the type of policy discourses with which the equality project engaged and then look in more depth at the ways in which we pioneered and explored creative forms of consultation and democratic participation. From this I will highlight the parallels between the current concerns in local government and the principles and practices which we developed and applied. Finally, I will reflect on the reasons why our experience and expertise is not sufficiently acknowledged in contemporary debates. I will argue that, as women's equality officers and as women, we are not valued or heard.

The Unit's beginnings

The Women's Unit was set up in 1982/3 following the creation of a Women's Committee inspired by the example of the Greater London Council (GLC). It was initially called the 'Women's Committee Support Unit' after the GLC model. The title expressed the more explicit political content at that time. The unit had been championed by women in the local Labour Party and elected councillors rather than town hall officers. Feminist councillors expected they would take a large role in equalities work and that they would need officer support.

Between 1983 and 1988 the unit carried out ground-breaking work, particularly in terms of local authority employment policies. This work was done with the direction of key councillors and input from the unions. The unit also published the first Islington Women's Guide, which became a model elsewhere. A *Borough Plan for Women* (now out of print) was created in the mid-1980s from an extensive piece of research involving focus groups. Officers sought then to integrate the findings into the policy and practice of relevant departments.

I joined in 1988 as Head of Unit when it was transformed from a collective of four to a more traditional structure with three full-time and one half-time officers. We changed the name to 'Women's Equality Unit' in around 1990, aligning ourselves with the names of other policy units and the race equality unit in the centre. This title in part represented a shift towards a more institutional and less councillor-oriented image, and in part reflected the unit's outward-looking work.

By the late 1980s, politicians were keen to refocus the work of the unit. Work continued on some employment-related work with positive results in particular areas such as getting women into non-traditional employment; policies to combat sexual harassment; and policies to promote the safety of employees. However, we became more focused on service delivery issues in terms of creating better and more equitable public services for local women.

The Unit in the 1990s

Our job had always been to see what was not being done, what more needed to be done and what needed to be done differently. Our constituency was largely but not exclusively made up of users of current council services. It was not a deficit model. We did ask what men got that women should have, but we also asked what women might want or need (in a less androcentric world). We were practical and oriented towards everyday services. Despite a background of local government cuts, staffing levels at the unit were increased in 1992 and resisted reductions until 1998/9.

In the 1990s the unit's own work programme took a new shape with four complementary elements:

- a strong and detailed focus on council service delivery within a framework of policy development;
- a community orientation which included consultation (see below);
- a contribution to equal opportunity in employment for women within the council;
- an engagement with the broad legislative, policy and local context in which the local authority was placed.

Our strategy was practical and pragmatic in that we located our work as firmly as possible in the planning processes and policy directions of the council. It was holistic in that we looked at particular services 'in the round' and took into account women's diverse experiences and needs rather than existing services and past practice. These concerns resulted in an emphasis upon partnership working between the unit and service departments; a focus upon 'real lives, whole lives'; and attention to cross-cutting issues. For instance, starting with existing services in leisure and libraries we looked at the diverse population and the specific needs of different groups of women. We suggested that non-traditional services could be offered along with the keep fit classes. We also promoted crèche provision. The result was a substantial increase in provision and take-up of women-only sessions, especially in the swimming pools in many centres. It was economically attractive to the managers and appealed widely to women in the local community. We worked with other departments with greater and lesser impact. The most professionalised and resource-intensive (e.g. Social Services and Education) were the most challenging.

Policy-makers were encouraged to see particular groups of women as a starting point, rather than the existing pattern of local authority service provision. For example, older women are often seen through the frame of the welfare model, in that they are clients or service users when they need aids and adaptations for the home or require day care services and so on. Pressure from groups of older women and co-optees/non-voting advisers on the Women's Committee was a reminder that the majority of older women are active citizens and require a wide range of services.

We were committed to working on the interests of different, diverse groups of women. We did this through targeted projects or by integrating perspectives into more generic pieces of policy or service development. For example, one project researched issues for black and minority ethnic women in relation to domestic violence and the council's provisions. Another involved supporting Age Concern and other voluntary organisations to do outreach work with the community and assess the quality of day care services for Asian elders. This was part of a wider review process. Our committee papers relating to policy or service delivery would explicitly talk about lesbians. We indicated if the proposal or analysis was relevant to them. We also targeted limited work at disabled women. We did not satisfy our own or other women's aspirations for inclusivity, but we were very aware of the challenge.

We took up issues that cut across traditional service and policy boundaries, such as child care, sexual harassment and domestic violence, and employed specialist staff to promote understanding and coherent service response in these areas. The unit as a whole looked at the social, economic and other consequences of a range of issues and worked with service departments to produce models of good practice, training, and guidance from which policy change flowed.

Policy discourses and our discursive strategies

Local government is shaped significantly by different policy discourses, and language is an important and contested element of equalities work. We were intuitively conscious of this from the start, knowing that to make women matter they had to be named. We couched our work in the dominant language of the council and sought to position women in debates and arguments in such as ways as to result in maximum political effect and practical outcome. We never referred to patriarchy or feminism in written papers, justifications or discussions. We used the concepts sexism, racism and discrimination. In general we adopted less contested, more widely appealing arguments, which shifted with time and context.

From the 1980s onwards, in common with women's units in many local authorities, we responded creatively to an evolving local authority agenda. We would map our understandings against the emerging priorities, concepts and explanations that shape mainstream local government policy. We analysed and critiqued new concepts or approaches in local government or equalities strategies to understand and highlight the implications for women. We looked for resonance, equivalence and opportunities so that we could give or keep women a place. We looked for ways the agenda we pursued with and for women might be interpolated into the council's agenda.

We engaged vigorously with new methods, priorities, policies and new categories of identity. These included policy innovations such as Compulsory Competitive Tendering, Performance Indicators, Community Safety, Best Value, Community Planning and Social Inclusion/Exclusion (see Bagilhole, Wright and Kelly, chapters 4, 10 and 11 this volume).

We responded to new trends in policy discourse, for example particular applications of terms such as diversity (also see Mason, this volume) and mainstreaming (also see Rees and Wright, chapters 3 and 10 this volume) because these were part of the developing equal opportunities scene in UK local government in the 1990s. We cautiously welcomed the interest in mainstreaming and felt well qualified to comment, based on our lengthy experience. However, like some race equality activists, we were suspicious that these trends represented moves to make equalities work less political and more comfortable for white, male managers.

We would try to match the needs of women with the profiles of intended beneficiaries of new policies or processes, even where women were not mentioned or other targets were intended. For example, social exclusion is a very generic policy concept which can be appropriated to contain and therefore apply to some/many women (also see Bagilhole, chapter 4 this volume). This was not the original policy intention, which was in effect a movement away from the equality agendas and categories of the 1980s.

In addition to strategically using the 'fashionable' policy frames of local government, we also worked to make our own phrases and questions familiar to the mainstream. We wanted to make common phrases such as: 'women are not a homogeneous group'; 'what are the specific needs of women in relation to this service/policy?'; 'women need a voice'; 'what issues are there for women?'; and 'what issues are there for black and ethnic minority women, lesbians, older women, women with disabilities, carers, young women?'; some of these phrases and questions were taken up, sometimes.

We did not favour the limited term 'equal opportunities'. Its use related better to employment than service delivery and it does not focus on equal outcomes. We adopted the looser umbrella concepts of 'equality' or 'equalities' wherever appropriate. We also tried to avoid the overuse of generic statements about the equality of a broad range of groups – for example, women, black and minority ethnic people, disabled people and so on. Different equality agendas need their own forms of organisation and response and language. We thought it was essential that women and subgroups of women were named as requiring action and were involved in consultation. We wanted to keep a wider range of women visible in terms of any new formulations in policy, strategy and service documents.

It was a challenge to keep a step ahead and stop women being considered only as an afterthought. We experienced resistance and negativity towards women: women were often seen by politicians, council officers and the public as unneedy, undeserving, demanding or undifferentiated from men; or equally misleading, women were presented as a group with a homogeneous, undifferentiated identity. Sometimes women were even described as a minority! These reactions could be unconscious or deliberate. But to be honest, we also experienced the tensions of language in our own formulations when we used the term 'women' to cover all kinds of women in the way that others would talk about users or people.

Always under pressure, we did not have time to unravel the meanings or elaborate our discourse on difference, sameness and 'category politics'. But we were very clear that national and local policy-makers used concepts and categories relating to equality that were not value free but were shaped by political goals and intentions. This represented a 'common-sense' understanding of what has come to be termed 'category politics' (Bacchi, 1996), which involves the struggle between different groups or actors to control the meaning of 'essentially contested concepts' such as equality, positive action and equal opportunities.

We engaged with the discourse and the policy frameworks because our work and proposals had to mainstream, integrate and 'fit in' with the strategic direction of the council. The wider aim was to improve local authority services across the board rather than focus upon short-term or one-off equality projects. We needed to make use of prevailing frameworks because of the relative absence of women in positions of power to influence the shape and direction of policy discourse and the ways in which policy is framed. We engaged in 'discursive strategies' on behalf of women and also used the opportunities to include women's own comments into the process through consultation.

The work described above shows how we were early practitioners of some positive forms of mainstreaming and the sort of cross-departmental, thematic working which has been characterised by the post-1997 UK Labour government as 'joined up thinking'. The role of consultation and the need for women's diverse voices to be heard in the policy process have also been addressed at several points so far. In the second part of the chapter I focus upon the pioneering work of women's committees and women's units in creating responsive and empowering mechanisms for consultation and participation in local democracy (see also Edwards, 1995; Stokes, 1998).

Consultation and democracy – responsive, representative and empowering

The late 1970s, against a backdrop of social movements including the women's movement, saw local activists in the Labour Party, especially in London, opening up democracy and local government. Individuals involved in new social change turned to traditional political arenas to make a difference. They argued that specific sections of the community were losing out – not having a say in their local services, not getting their needs met and not knowing how things were done. The creation of women's committees can be viewed as part of a range of non-mandatory initiatives, including employment, race and policing, introduced by some authorities, largely 'New Urban Left' authorities in the 1970s and 1980s. Not surprisingly, given the specific political base, the first six women's committees were all in the London area (Goss, 1984).

Women's committees were created as an apparently straightforward way to increase the influence of women and to improve services and conditions of employment within the existing democratic mechanism – the committee system. Women's committees were intended to 'bring a women's perspective' to local politics and, as such, one of their main roles was that of policy analyst. Women's committees and women's units, which tended to be staffed by officers who operated as or described themselves as feminists, discussed and highlighted the impact of 'gender-blind' policy and service provision on women. The committees were also created to increase women's voices in decision-making. They had a lot of formal power, but in practice their real power and effectiveness often depended upon the particular alliances, personalities and skills of negotiation of individual members, especially the chair, and also the local political climate and context. However effective, their existence sent a powerful signal that gender was recognized as a legitimate part of local politics and the work of the council. For that reason alone most women's officers and supporters of women's committees wanted to retain them. I suspect the politicians and policy advisers/decision-makers who wanted to abolish them for economic or other political reasons also recognised this symbolic power and focus.

Community involvement was a key feature of 'local socialism' (Boddy and Fudge, 1984). Women's units supported the committees in their drive to make links with and channel resources to local women's groups and to reach and involve local women from diverse backgrounds in the work of the council. We soon recognised that there were many valid forms of involvement that could complement the activities of the committees and the units. Another reason for our emphasis on community consultation was our need to ground our knowledge and analysis. This is an issue for all public policy-makers but we, as women's officers, were in practice more often challenged about the basis for our expertise, mandate and professionalism. Consultative mechanisms also came in time to be justified in terms of more efficient targeting of services. We developed various forms of 'connectedness' that had potential for both efficiency and democracy. These included reactive contact with individual members of the public, and proactive contact with individuals, groups and organisations.

Islington women's unit did not set up or service a separate women's interest forum as existed elsewhere. There was a more *ad hoc* strategy for consultation bringing particular groupings of women together for specific purposes often related to a wider policy framework or timetable, for example, in respect of housing policy. Events, large and small, provided opportunities for women to talk with each other and to the local authority, including councillors. These events were seen as amongst the most diverse organised by any local authority department and were our public face. Our regular newsletter enabled women to keep in contact with each other, connect to the local authority and communicate with voluntary and community organisations. Events were used to gather information and views formally (sometimes attended by hundreds of women and girls). For example, three methods were used to elicit views at a young women's festival and forum: video responses from young women; a question time event with the Leader of the council and other decision-makers; and a written survey. The information gathered was used to inform committee reports. One clear demand which emerged from such feedback exercises was the need for better information about how the council works. A guide to the council was produced by the unit for women and was later adopted by the council for use with the whole community!

In response to the emphasis in the early 1990s upon citizenship, we devised a seminar programme and a handbook – *Women's Voices, Public Voices* – with the aim of empowering women from a variety of backgrounds to participate more effectively in public life, such as standing as school governors. The unit further enabled democratic involvement by providing advice and support, in very difficult times with limited resources, that strengthened women's organisations and created opportunities for them to influence and have a voice through the unit and the committee.

Asking women 'what they want' is not simple. Their answers will be different at different times and in different contexts. Instant response surveys, short-term groups and consultations asking very broad or general questions can be ineffective, as can focus groups which do not take complexity into account. As women, we have ambivalent and gendered perceptions, understandings and explanations of our needs and interests. These arise from different politics, values, ideology and cultures. Other aspects of identity or community bring further complexity. Women must have opportunities to develop a consciousness of what is and what might be and what should be. This is where the capacity of women's voluntary and community groups to create an informed constituency is so important. They should not be dismissed as 'activists' or special interest groups. The unit was thus supporting political participation in its widest sense.

That was then and this is now: new agendas and unfinished business

Women's units were part of a movement initiated in some local authorities in the late 1970s and early 1980s to bring local democracy closer to the people and tackle discriminatory practices in employment and services. As the units evolved they joined the 'mainstream' policy discourse, and expressed their work in terms of efficiency – talking about targeting, take-up and quality of services. But our starting point was always responsiveness to the whole community, with people-focused approaches – something now enshrined in 'community planning' (see also Kelly, chapter 11 this volume). The project is not complete.

Consultation and research with local service users and potential users has become essential for local authorities. Talking to women as women in relation to public policy and service delivery has even become part of the official agenda. Local authorities accept the need for targeted consultation in theory if not in practice. From the 1980s, women's officers in a number of local authorities (often with community-based backgrounds) were pioneering consultative work and providing the expertise and the community links to develop effective strategies. Despite low levels of participation in relation to local government in the UK, our contribution created, and showed how to create, the climate for participation and built the capacity amongst local women to get politically involved.

There are other parallels between the current aspirations of local and central government, think tanks and academics for public service and the principles and practices of women's units over the past twenty or so years. They include a desire for community involvement; a stress upon efficient and responsive public services; the encouragement of innovative and risk-taking organisational cultures; and the need for holistic services and processes often addressing neglected subjects and needs. We were leading-edge for our practices around inclusion. We were 'modernising government' a long time ago.

We introduced new, controversial or neglected subjects onto the political and policy agendas of the local state, backed by women and feminists inside and outside the Labour Party. Issues such as racial equality, child care, domestic violence, gay and lesbian rights and safety are now recognised as part of the wider political agenda.

As well as new foci and community involvement, we developed new methods. Many of the strategies for change long applied or advocated by women's units are now in the mainstream, often at the heart of Best Value, some with and some without a specific gender dimension. Unfortunately, the use of a 'gender lens' for identifying gender dimensions is not routine enough. More commonplace are needs-led, information-based decisions; regular monitoring; targeted and well-focused services; life events/issues (also known as cross-cutting themes) as drivers for planning and review rather than existing services or agencies; project, team and cross-departmental approaches.

Lasting good practice includes multi-agency fora to tackle domestic violence which, along with safety, is now a cross-cutting theme; private–public child care partnerships; and joint work with the voluntary sector. Other significant methodological precursors were outcome-oriented women's action plans; mainstreaming within generic programmes and strategies through gender, race and other analyses (e.g. quality and customer care); gender (and race) audits revealing gaps and problems; and gender equality performance indicators. Women's officers have also been involved in exploring how to devise meaningful indicators to measure progress in complex policy areas like ending domestic violence.

Women's units developed a rich body of experience for delivering 'joined up thinking' and 'joined up' service delivery. There is some evidence that post-1997 Labour ministers and central government departments recognize these contributions better, but they are not drawing on them explicitly or enough. The innovative aims and practices of women's, race, disability and gay and lesbian units/officers have rightly been adopted by the mainstream because the whole community can benefit from what they sought – accessible and accountable services and transparent procedures. However, in the drive to revitalise our locally provided services and the democratic context in which resources are allocated, there are some old mistakes. The new forms of participation and consultation like the citizens' jury model or electronically based approaches have limitations because, ironically, gender, race, disability and sexuality implications are once again neglected. A jury might be representative in numerical terms but, for example, if a women who has experienced domestic violence or a black person is in a minority, they may not be able to say what they think or their views may be ignored. Electronic democracy in the UK is in its infancy, but there is a growing understanding of the issues raised by women's use of and access to information and communication technologies. Each method of consultation needs to be developed, tailored and tested for women.

More radically, a revival of democracy could also start by valuing women's existing organisations, networks and sites of presence and community. A new model of democratic involvement might build on the ways women are able to encourage participation, decision-making and leadership in the organisations and groups in which they are prominent and about which they care. The expertise to do these things exists. Why haven't women's officers or gender equality advisers been more explicitly involved in the formulation of the new agendas and new approaches? One simple answer to the failure to involve is that the officers are no longer working in the field or are overstretched. Women's units have mostly closed, been amalgamated and reduced to single officers in equalities units. Islington's unit survived with at least three posts into the twenty-first century on the strength of its work and political commitment, but it is not clear for how much longer it will survive.

Another reason is that women's units as a whole were never properly and publicly acknowledged in mainstream local government discourse or by key decision makers or opinion formers as *successful*. There was always resistance to their priorities and methods and debate about their impact. Why was this? First, the context was hostile. They came into existence at the very moment central government put the financial squeeze on local authorities. Many local authorities entered crises of management, resources and direction. The context is still one where central government does not place much value upon local government. The equality agenda is still regarded with suspicion and hostility because of its close association with the so-called 'loony left' or 'old Labour'.

Second, there were few quick fixes. It may sound straightforward to address issues of appropriate service delivery for women, but it is demanding of understanding, analysis and resources. Women's units were never allowed the luxury of excuses relating to the constraints of central government or the economic context, unlike local authorities themselves. When local authorities find that there are few quick, easy, cheap solutions, it is simpler to say that the women's unit has failed or is 'outdated'! Chief Officers, senior management and politicians deny their relative indifference but have weak, unrealistic alternative strategies for addressing women's equality and gender issues.

Third, women's officers and women's agendas are challenging on a personal, political and institutional level. You are perceived as oppositional whether that is your style or intention or not. In fact, you do need to be oppositional quite often. When local authority women's officers challenge local authority policy-makers or service planners on the basis of women's views and other sorts of evidence they are sometimes regarded as if they have declared 'gender war'. This does not fit easily with a dominant organisational and managerial culture which dictates that institutions and their parts should all march with the same rational vision.

Fourth, although local authorities were innovative when they created women's units, they never satisfactorily resolved the role and purpose they should serve. In the main, the local authority mainstream had an uncertain relationship to women's units because of their challenges, their commitments and their alliances (with community, with politicians, with feminists). Units disturbed the hierarchy, the traditional structure. Between a local authority and its women's unit, there could have been an attempt at a difficult partnership (using an inter-agency or strategic model) where partners had explicitly shared and different aims but could still work together. The women's unit would then openly have been able to function with feminist values and as more of a 'thresholder' organisation, rather than as a part of the bureaucratic hierarchy. It is necessary because of the nature of the project women's equality. I believe it was partially understood by the originators of the units. Have we come full circle? If the desire to be responsive to local communities and open themselves to enabling and hearing women's many voices is genuine then new policies and structures need to learn the lessons of complexity and to learn to make space for some oppositionality through partnerships with teams, agents and stakeholders like women's units.

Local government is part of a society that still has discrimination and misogyny at its core. Feminist understandings are bitterly and violently contested. It is hugely difficult for a council – even a Labour council under New Labour – to value feminist understandings. The health of a locality and the nation can be measured against the attitude of the mainstream to social change and opposition. A society or organisation that is fearful of an informed constituency or a challenge to the established order cannot grow. What it leaves women with is the need to talk and to contest understandings – especially with each other but also with the state and through 'thresholders' like women's officers. Women's officers are both insiders and outsiders and as such can critically reflect upon issues and act as a bridge between local community and local government. The lesson to the public and social policy-makers – men and women alike – is: enable and hear the deliberations and demands of women in all their diversity, with all their identities.

References

Bacchi, C. L. (1996), *The Politics of Affirmative Action: 'Women', Equality and Category Politics*, London and Thousand Oaks: Sage.
Boddy, M. and Fudge, C. (eds) (1984), *Local Socialism?*, London: Macmillan.
Cockburn, C. (1991), *In the Way of Women: Men's Resistance to Sex Equality in Organisations*, Basingstoke: Macmillan.

Edwards, J. (1995), *Local Government Women's Committees*, Aldershot: Avebury.

Goss, S. (1984), 'Women's Initiatives in Local Government', in M. Boddy and C. Fudge (eds) *Local Socialism?*, London: Macmillan.

Stokes, W. (1998), 'Feminist Democracy: The Case for Women's Committees', *Contemporary Politics*, Vol. 4, No. 1.

10
Life after the GLC: Local Government and the Equalities Agenda in England

Mandy Wright

In the early 1980s, the Greater London Council (GLC) and a number of other London and Metropolitan local authorities introduced and actively promoted equal opportunities policies on women and race. Those were heady days for those of us who got involved. Women were being asked into town halls to comment on and input ideas on how council services and employment could better meet women's needs. My first experience was as a member of two groups – one on women and transport, the other on women's employment in London. Exhilarated by being involved and recognising that here was a concrete way of influencing some of the services which crucially affect women's lives in London, I applied for and got a job as Employment Adviser in the GLC's Women's Committee Support Unit.

The work was exciting. On the agenda was getting better jobs for women in the Council and in the community, as was improving service delivery in areas like transport, planning and the creation of more childcare places. Involving women and women's groups in the community was seen as essential.[1] Differences between women were recognised and, in part, addressed. Anything and everything seemed possible.

Almost twenty years later, it all seems a long time ago. I am older, wiser and still working in local government in a central body. Equalities are still an important part of my work but only part of it. Many aspects of local government work have changed. Key to what has happened is the changing and growing involvement of central government and the imposition of compulsory competitive tendering (and now Best Value), cuts in local authority spending, the introduction of statutory performance indicators and the Labour government's modernisation agenda.

This has been accompanied by decentralisation and devolution; and a growing focus in authorities on becoming more effective and business-like. Over time, management and, some would say, management fashions have become important, replacing the dominance of the professions and good administration. All these changes have affected authorities, and they have affected me and others working on equalities.

The views which follow are my personal reflections after almost twenty years of local government work.[2] It seems to me, reflecting on what has happened, that equalities practitioners have shown an ability to adapt and to manage through all the changes imposed on us. We have had to be particularly adept at the much vaunted local authority ability to take central government or other initiatives and make them work, however difficult they may be to deliver in practice. In taking this approach, equalities practitioners have been pragmatic and used current management and policy fashions in vogue among authorities. While this may have been essential to keep equalities on the agenda in some authorities, it does run the danger of uncritically rejecting as a failure what was done before, without properly evaluating it and without recognising what has been achieved.

Looking back to where we started, we can ask a number of questions about what has actually been achieved. What is (on) the equalities agenda now and where is equalities work going? Most important of all, what have we learnt about what works and what does not – and how do we go forward?

What has been achieved?

In terms of employment, there has been real and steady progress for women in local government between 1983 and 1998 although it still remains true that local government in England and Wales has a pre-dominantly female workforce (71 per cent) managed by predominantly male Chief Officers (90 per cent).[3]

In 1983 women were concentrated in traditional female jobs. Among white-collar staff, 53 per cent of full-time women were in clerical jobs, as opposed to 16 per cent of men who were largely concentrated in administrative, professional, technical and managerial jobs. Segregation was even more extensive in manual jobs with women doing home help and care assistant jobs, domestic assistant jobs and catering and cleaning. Men were caretakers, refuse collectors, gardeners, and so on. Two decades on, segregation has decreased somewhat. Forty-five per cent of white-collar women are in clerical jobs, and just under 40 per cent

are in administrative, managerial, professional, and technical occupations. Segregation has particularly reduced in professional occupations.
However, women still dominate the lowest, white-collar grades (Table
10.1) and segregation remains entrenched in what were the manual
grades. Two-thirds of full-time manual women are still concentrated in
three jobs – cook, care assistant and home help – and most are white,
even in very racially diverse areas.

Many council services have workforces which are predominantly
female, such as education, social services and libraries (Tables 10.2

Table 10.1   Gender distribution of white-collar employees
in local government, England and Wales, 1996

	Women %	Men %
PO range (points 35–49)	34	66
SO range (points 29–34)	52	48
Scales 5 and 6 (points 22–8)	59	41
Scales 3 and 4 (points 14–21)	78	22
Scales 1 and 2 (< point 14)	88	12

Source: Employers' Organisation for Local Government Surveys.

Table 10.2   Gender distribution of local authority by function,
England

	Women %	Men %
Education: teachers	72	28
others	88	12
Construction	7	93
Social services	84	16
Libraries	77	23
Recreation	48	52
Environmental health	40	60
Refuse	12	88
Housing	62	38
Planning	47	53
Engineering	29	71
Finance and computing	58	42
Corp. services – other	63	37
Fire services	13	87
Other services	59	41
Total directly employed	70	30

Source: L42 Survey, June 1998.

and 10.3). District councils which do not have these services tend to be more evenly balanced in the make-up of their workforce as compared to counties, unitaries and Metropolitan and London boroughs. This means that the majority of councils do not have predominantly female staff, although taking local authorities as a whole, women council workers outnumber men by two to one (Table 10.4).

Significant progress has been made in the more senior grades with the numbers of Chief Executives growing from 3 in 1986 to 44

Table 10.3   Gender distribution of local authority by function, Wales

	Women %	Men %
Education: teachers	71	29
others	89	11
Construction	4	96
Social services	87	13
Libraries	75	25
Recreation	48	52
Environmental health	40	60
Refuse	6	94
Housing	53	47
Planning	45	55
Engineering	28	72
Finance and computing	55	45
Corp. services – other	60	40
Fire services	16	84
Other services	67	33
Total directly employed	69	31

Source: L42 Survey, June 1998.

Table 10.4   Gender distribution by authority type, 1998

	Women %	Men %
Districts	49	51
Counties	79	21
Metropolitan Districts	70	30
London Boroughs	70	30
Unitaries, England	70	30
Unitaries, Wales	69	31
All	71	29

Source: L42 Survey, June 1998.

(11 per cent) in 1999 and of Chief Officers from 50 in 1984 to 240 in 1998 (11 per cent) (Table 10.5). A large proportion of women (two-thirds) work part-time compared to the wider economy (Table 10.6), although the proportion falls when teachers are included (Table 10.7).

Women's pay still lags behind that of men (Table 10.8), although the gap has narrowed since 1983, and overall is smaller for local government than for the wider economy. The introduction of single status in 1998, where manual and white-collar workers were assimilated to a single pay spine, has helped to address some potential equal value differences. Differential access to bonus schemes has also contributed to the gap between the pay of manual men and women and this issue is now being

Table 10.5 Percentage of Chief Executives and Chief Officers who are women, 1991–98 (England and Wales)

	1991 %	1992 %	1993 %	1994 %	1995 %	1996 %	1997 %	1998 %
Chief Executives	1	2	3	4	5	8	10	10
Chief Officers*	5	5	6	6	7	9	10	11
Deputies (i.e. 2nd tier)	7	9	10	11	11	13	14	16

* In 1998 the format of the survey was changed so for that year the figure for Chief Officers includes Chief Officers and Directors. For the same reason the figure for Deputies in 1998 includes Deputy Chief Officers, Assistant Directors and Heads of Service.

Source: Employers' Organisation for Local Government Surveys.

Table 10.6 Working patterns, 1996

Percentage of Staff Working	Local Government*		All Employees*	
	Male	Female	Male	Female
Full-time	84	33	92	55
Part-time	16	67	8	45
Permanent contract	91	88	96	92
Temporary contract	9	12	6	8
Flexitime	32	20	9	11
Term-time only	2	26	2	8
Job share	0.4	2.5	0.2	1.5
Annualised hours	4	4	4	4

* Figures *exclude* teachers, police and firefighters.

Source: Labour Force Survey, Spring 1996.

Table 10.7 Working patterns, 1998

Percentage of Staff Working	Local Government*		All Employees*	
	Male	Female	Male	Female
Full-time	88	52	92	56
Part-time	12	48	8	44
Permanent contract	92	87	93	92
Temporary contract	8	13	7	8
Flexitime	26	16	9	12
Term-time only	11	32	1	8
Job share	0.3	3.2	0.1	1.7
Annualised hours	7	7	3	3

* NB: Figures *exclude*, police.

Source: Labour Force Survey, Autumn 1998.

Table 10.8 Average hourly earnings of women compared to men (full-timers only)

	1983 %		1996 %		1998 %	
Local Government (England & Wales)	APT & C	68	APT & C	73	Local Gov't Services*	84
	Manuals	73	Manuals	82	Teachers	90
	Teachers	–	Teachers	89		
Whole Economy (GB)	Non-Manual	62	Non-Manual	70		
	Manual	69	Manual	72	All	81

* With the introduction of Single Status, separate figures can no longer be calculated for Manual and APT & C staff.

Source: New Earnings Survey.

addressed in many authorities. With the wider use of job evaluation and these other changes, the gap should narrow further in the future.

Pay (and terms and conditions) sometimes tends to be the poor relation in equal employment opportunities' initiatives. Some equalities units and policies do not even cover pay, focusing on recruitment, promotion and training, although improving pay would have a significant impact on gender inequality. The Single Status Agreement gives authorities more flexibility locally which can be used to develop patterns of work which better meet both service needs and employees' needs, but there is little evidence of equalities staff and others recognising its potential to improve women's position.[4]

Under the last Conservative government, (1992–97), the ways in which contractors managed pay and other employment matters were explicitly ruled out as issues which councils might take into consideration in reaching a decision on the tendering out of council services. This impacted particularly on manual women workers and the quality of services they provided (Escott and Whitfield, 1995). The current government has recognised the link between quality of service and the quality of employment and has changed the law on tendering to allow authorities to take into account contractors' performance on equalities in employment and other workforce matters (DETR, 2001).

Despite some early and innovative approaches to service delivery and involving customers/users/community groups, particularly in London, the focus of most equalities work in local authorities was predominantly on personnel. Service initiatives tended to be specific initiatives for women rather than changing mainstream services, and often were 'piecemeal' (Collier, 1998). Thus, for example, there were initiatives involving women and sport, women's health and combatting violence against women. There were, and still are, however, innovative examples – for example, training women in the community who might want to become councillors or more effective voices for community groups.

Turning now to issues of political representation: what changes can we note in the proportions of women sitting as councillors? Detailed factual evidence from the past is difficult to find. Statistics were not collected or kept on any systematic basis. Sample surveys and the 1997 census of councillors indicate that women made up 12 per cent of councillors in England and Wales in 1964 and 27 per cent of councillors in 1997, but with significant regional variations – from 20 per cent in Wales to 29 per cent in the South West in 1997 (Table 10.9).

Table 10.9   Women as a percentage of all councillors, England and Wales

	1964	1976	1985	1993	1997
%	12	17	19	25	27
Sources	(1)	(1)	(1)	(2)	(3)

Sources: (1) Committee of Inquiry into the Conduct of Local Authority Business, Vol. 2, 1986, Cmnd. 9799; (2) K. Young and N. Rao, *Coming to Terms with Change, The Local Government Councillor in 1993*, Joseph Rowntree Foundation and LGC Communications, 1994; (3) LGMB, *First National Census: Survey of Local Authority Councillors in England and Wales*, 1997.

Only 18 per cent of minority ethnic councillors are women, and there is particular under-representation among Indian, Pakistani and Bangladeshi women (LGMB, 1998). In Scotland women made up around 17 per cent of regional councillors and 22 per cent of district councillors prior to local government reorganisation in 1996. Following reorganisation around 22 per cent of councillors in the new Scottish unitary councils were female and this proportion did not change after the second elections in 1999. No party or council comes close to achieving gender balance and less than a dozen of Scotland's councillors are from minority ethnic backgrounds. In Northern Ireland, women are around 14 per cent of councillors (Brown et al., 1999). Although proportions of women are low, these figures compare favourably with those for most European municipalities, with women constituting less than 25 per cent in most countries. The exceptions are Finland (31 per cent), Denmark (28 per cent) and Sweden (41 per cent).[5]

Equalities: the current agenda

For a start, there is clearly more than one equalities agenda operating in English authorities. There is enormous variability in terms of where authorities are now with regard to equal opportunities approaches and where they are headed. Almost all authorities have equal opportunities policies, but size, type of authority, political control and other factors all affect the type and extent of equalities practice. At the minimal end of the scale are authorities in which policies exist on paper but have little impact on practice, or where equalities have been marginalised; at the other end of the scale are authorities who have adopted a pro-active managing diversity or mainstreaming approach. Some have done very little, others have 'tried everything'. Some authorities still have equalities advisers, but most never did.

This variety in part reflects the range and variety of local authorities in England. Unlike Scotland and Wales which each now has a relatively small number (32 and 22 respectively) of similarly structured unitary authorities, the 388 English authorities are made up of 33 London boroughs, 36 Metropolitan authorities, and 46 new unitary authorities, 34 county councils and 238 district councils. All but the county and district councils are all-purpose authorities, while county and district councils are in a two-tier system, with the county councils providing major services such as education and social services and district councils providing more locally based services such as local planning, housing, environmental health and refuse collection.

English authorities also vary in political control and in size, ranging from those with populations of as little as 25,000 and only 150 staff to those with populations of over a million or more and more than 30,000 staff. These differences have been significant in how authorities have addressed equalities. With the initial lead coming predominantly from urban London and Metropolitan authorities, much of what has been portrayed widely, if not always accurately, in the media was based on the activities of relatively few Labour councils. In the absence of recent survey data, it is difficult to be precise about how many and which kinds of councils have done what.[6]

There has been relatively little rigorous evaluation of what actually happened and how it has worked, particularly within councils themselves. Nor have practitioners always been aware of or used external research findings. If we use Teresa Rees' tinkering, tailoring and transforming typology then it is apparent that authorities mostly 'tinkered', a minority 'tailored' whilst 'transforming' is still a new idea (Rees, 1998; Jewson et al., 1995). Most authorities adopted an equal opportunities approach in employment policy and altered their selection procedures. A relatively small number of mainly Metropolitan and London authorities took more positive steps to eliminate discrimination against women by removing barriers, accommodating women's caring responsibilities and adopting positive action training programmes in some cases. Few focused on service delivery. In Wales, as late as 1997, a survey by Breitenbach et al. found only a quarter of Welsh authorities had policies that addressed services as well as employment. (Breitenbach et al., 1999).

These approaches did not deliver cultural or organisational change in the main, leaving authorities largely untouched by the experience. Although more women did make progress in terms of careers, it was largely as individuals. Furthermore as they gained promotion they discovered that jobs nearer the top were still based on male expectations and a culture of long hours. There is also some evidence that authorities who had made some gains were finding it hard to hold onto them when managers locally were given more responsibility as a result of decentralisation or CCT. Faced with scarce resources and pressures of work, equalities procedures and gains sometimes suffer (Beddington et al., 1997).

After an initial flowering in the early 1980s, growing pressures on local authorities from central government and its lack of support for equal opportunities inevitably had an impact. The fear of being labelled a 'loony left' council after the media's less than fair coverage of many of the early initiatives on equalities meant that some elected members were (and still are) not as willing to champion equalities work. Over the years that the Conservatives were in power (1979–97) there often was a sense that little could be done and that change was unlikely. This pessimism sometimes meant that councils went backwards or simply failed to do more with the powers and rights they had. Even with the return of a Labour government, New Labour's efforts to distance itself from old Labour concerns has not helped to make equalities really 'respectable' again.

Some councils, often those Labour councils who have invested resources and time in equalities, report that their initiatives have 'ground into the sand'. They can't seem to get the issue moving again, or to make any further headway after the high-profile initiatives and the big strides made in the 1980s. Some others argue that equalities work is a luxury that they can no longer afford. With constant cuts and low recruitment, there is little they feel they can do to change the profile of their workforce. Other councils feel there is no need to do more – 'we've done it', they say, and point to the increased number of women in higher graded jobs. While gender remains a key issue for some councils, the achievements that have been made have generated complacency elsewhere with senior managers arguing that 'we have no glass ceiling here'. The fact that, for example, the position of many manual women, worsened as a result of CCT, passes them by (Escott and Whitfield, 1995). The failure to systematically evaluate progress and achievements means that perceptions rather than facts may determine policy.[7]

Equal opportunities recruitment procedures have been criticised by some authorities and commentators for being too rigid and procedure-bound.[8] It is argued that they neither deliver the best person for the job nor contribute to the recruitment of a more diverse and representative workforce (Hunt and Bundred, 1998). They have also been criticised for being too time-consuming, particularly in situations where council service departments are competing against the private sector. At the same time, equalities have remained a priority in some authorities such as Hounslow and Lewisham in London, where good work has continued and developed, and equal opportunities recruitment practices have become well established in most authorities, regardless of political control. Overall the picture is of quiet, low-level progress in most authorities, innovative work in some others (still mostly urban and Labour authorities), and real pessimism or negative views in others. This contrasts with both Scotland and Wales where there appears to be a real sense of excitement about new possibilities in a post-devolution context.

There are significant differences in the salience of different equalities groups for different councils with gender less prominent in some.

Disability issues are generally recognised as pressing because the legislation is relatively recent and makes new demands on the way councils offer and deliver services. Also, the disability lobby is active and often very vocal. In many authorities, elected members are also keen on tackling ageism. This may, in fact, reflect the over-representation of older people among councillors themselves (LGMB, 1998).

Race, until recently, was seen as important for urban authorities with sizeable black and minority ethnic populations, but not elsewhere. Indeed, some councils with very small black and minority ethnic populations argued that there were other groups with greater needs in their community – for example unemployed white working-class youths. Any such complacency has been shaken by the Macpherson Report into the death of Stephen Lawrence (see Introduction, n. 3) and the subsequent Race Relations (Amendment) Act which has placed a duty upon public bodies including councils to promote good race relations and equality of opportunity. As many councils address gender, race and disability together, these race equality developments have heightened the profile of and interest in equalities work more generally.

Sexuality however, remains a 'no-go' area for many, probably most, councils as a result, in part, of controversial legislation enacted by a past Conservative government. Section 28 of the 1998 Local Government Act prohibits local authorities from intentionally 'promoting' homosexuality. The Labour government had pledged to repeal Section 28; however their move to repeal it as part of the Local Government Bill was defeated in the House of Lords in July 2000. Subsequently the government dropped the repeal of Section 28 in order that other measures contained in the Bill might go ahead. Whereas Section 28 remains in force in England and Wales, it should be noted that the Scottish Parliament overwhelmingly voted to repeal Section 28 (called Section 2a in Scotland) in June 2000. It remains to be seen whether this will result in Scottish local authorities taking a more proactive approach in this area.

Resources for equalities work generally have decreased after initially increasing. The number of equalities units have dwindled, as have the number of specialist equalities staff. Where there were once separate race and women's units, these have now become 'generic' and usually have been reduced to one adviser, perhaps working in a central policy team. Separate Women's Committees have often been disbanded and it seems likely that very few remain. However, the disbanding of units and committees has had some positive outcomes, with women moving into mainstream management and policy jobs, taking their equalities knowledge and commitment with them. A number of women from the

Greater London Council, for example, went on to become Chief Executives or Chief Officers elsewhere, and continued to raise issues concerning women and other groups in their new posts.

Recently there has been a noticeable shift in focus from employment to service delivery. Despite the early interest in influencing council services, equalities work in many councils has in fact largely been the concern of personnel and focused on the Council's workforce. Now it is being argued that meeting the needs of women and other groups is an essential part of delivering a quality service. Services must not only be accessible to all, but they must be appropriate and meet the diverse needs of different groups and individuals. This change offers real opportunities to affect council services. With the increasing focus on customer service; consultation; service and community plans, standards and performance indicators; and on outcomes for council residents, women's needs and views should be on the agenda in all authorities if, and it is a big if, the process is carried out properly.

New initiatives and approaches to equalities work

Some equalities practitioners have begun to feel that the old ways of approaching equalities work are no longer effective, and perhaps never were for many authorities, and that, in any case, changes in the context within which authorities operate mean that new ways must be tried. This may be because some practitioners now share the managerialism which has overtaken local government, but I would argue that equalities staff and supporters have perhaps above all been very pragmatic in responding to changing pressures. If they had not done so, equalities work might well have fallen even further down the agenda, or fallen off the agenda entirely.

Currently, a number of authorities are developing new ways of addressing the equalities agenda. Some are taking a managing/valuing diversity approach; others are adopting a 'mainstreaming' approach; and some are combining both. The 'social exclusion' model is gaining ground, as is what could be called a standards-based approach. A few have taken a social justice approach.

Managing diversity ('the business case')

Certainly the terminology of diversity is creeping into many authorities' policies and documents, but probably relatively few have adopted and understood the full implications of the approach. The diversity approach is critically examined by David Mason (chapter 5). From a local authority's point of view its appeal lies in greater acceptability and inclusivity. Given the negative image that traditional equal opportunities often attracts, the diversity approach, with its origins in the US and its focus on the business case for equalities and the need for organisational and cultural change, has been helpful in reviving interest in equalities work.

The way diversity is used varies. Some authorities have used it as a new label to overcome hostility to traditional equalities approach and to engender new interest, but without significantly altering procedures and practices ('old wine in new bottles'). Others have adopted it, almost unconsciously, and done it without naming it. These (few) examples involve women Chief Executives who bring an equalities perspective to their work, and whose management styles are based on drawing out the best from each of their employees.

The London Borough of Camden has adopted a 'valuing diversity' approach which has led them to review their procedures for recruitment and selection. The job description/person specification process, now common in most authorities, has not yielded a (sufficiently) diverse workforce and Camden is considering a process based on setting minimum standards combined with an assessment of each individual's contribution to the (existing) team. Through this, they hope to promote diversity which in turn will contribute to better decisions and services (Hunt and Bundred, 1998).

There has been relatively little awareness and use of the notion of becoming an 'employer of choice', a useful aspect of the managing diversity approach which explicitly recognises that often competitive advantage comes from having the best staff. This means that an organisation will want to make itself attractive to the best and brightest. Given the public image of local government, this aspect would be useful not just for equalities purposes.

However, there has been some resistance and hostility to the diversity approach, with authorities arguing that its focus on the individual rather than the group diverts attention from the most disadvantaged groups and that it is inimical to positive action (Kandola and Fullerton, 1994). Some of this hostility seems to arise from a misunderstanding about what managing diversity is meant to involve. In particular, US firms often operate affirmative action alongside it, recognising that they need to have a diverse workforce if they are to benefit from diversity. The business case argument, with its US management connotations, may in any case need adapting for public services. Recognising that a diverse workforce can contribute to improving service delivery seems valid, and indeed crucial to improving service delivery. But whereas better decisions and services should lead to higher sales and profits for companies, higher demand for public services simply creates greater pressures on those services where there are not enough resources to meet those demands. The Government's 'Modernising Government' White Paper (Cabinet Office, 1999) argued the need for a more diverse workforce to ensure that good quality services are delivered to an increasingly diverse population, and the Macpherson Report referred to earlier has also recommended training on valuing diversity in all public services. These may provide a catalyst for this approach.

Mainstreaming

There is considerable interest in mainstreaming equality in the work of councils. In part this results from the European Union's promotion of the approach and recent moves to make certain EU funding conditional upon mainstreaming equal opportunities within plans. In addition, the Equal Opportunities Commission has been an active champion (EOC 1997). Rees (1998 and this volume) provides a detailed description and analysis of mainstreaming and of its origins. Unlike the business case argument, it has its roots in the world of policy and politics and explicitly addresses the way decisions are made in public sector organisations and the ways in which organisational change can be achieved.

There are different definitions of mainstreaming, ranging from gender impact assessments of policy changes, and making equalities the responsibility of every member of staff, to the EOC's definition, the one largely used by local authorities in the UK: 'the integration of equal opportunities into all policy development, implementation, evaluation and review processes' (EOC, 1997). The attraction for local government of mainstreaming is that it appears to address the perceived failure of previous approaches and the marginalisation that many equalities staff feel because it offers a way of tacking organisational culture and practices from inside. For example, Best Value (see Kelly, chapter 11 this volume) and the local government improvement model are both part of a framework within which all services are reviewed and delivered and which require customer-focused corporate objectives and processes. If these are the key drivers of local authority practice, it will be essential to integrate equalities. Carried out effectively, mainstreaming equalities into Best Value in particular should result in the delivery of more appropriate and accessible services for women (Baldwin and Foot, 1998).

The EOC mainstreaming work highlighted the STEPS (Strategic Equality Plans in Service Delivery) approach at the London Borough of Hounslow. Hounslow has developed a model for building equal opportunities into performance management by involving users and front-line staff in reviewing services and establishing service requirements. Each service area develops an equality strategy statement and performance indicators which are regularly monitored.[9] Watford Borough Council has mainstreamed equalities into the heart of the decision-making structure of the council by using the budget process to ensure prioritising of equalities.

However, there are some very real problems with making mainstreaming happen. First, most council officers do not make the (common-sense) connection between quality of service and equality – that quality services must be accessible and appropriate to all. Second, there is still insufficient recognition that council citizens are not monolithic groups. Needs are diverse and one size does not fit all. Even where authorities have taken women's needs on board, they often fail to see the differences among women – in terms of race and age, and also needs. Thus, for example, some councils provide child care and sessions aimed at women during the day at leisure centres, but provide little for full-time working women in the evening.

A further barrier is the lack of good information on different groups in the authority. Unlike Sweden, which has developed a very full information base which is used to inform decisions and priorities (EOC, 1997), authorities in the UK often make decisions without full information on who uses and does not use services. This position is changing with the emphasis on performance indicators and targets, but although data are increasingly collected on complaints and customer satisfaction, this information often is not broken down by gender, race or disability.

There is also a fear among those working in equalities in authorities that a move to mainstreaming will be used to carry out 'backdoor cuts', as it provides an excuse to get rid of specialist equalities staff. While cuts may be one factor, the lack of recognition that equalities staff actually have the knowledge and experience needed to reach different groups in the community and to develop more appropriate services is another. These concerns are borne out to some extent. Authorities trying to pursue mainstreaming without any specialist help find that, where equalities is the responsibility of everyone but no one's actual job, it is hard to keep the momentum going in a context of heavy workloads and long hours. Sometime authorities depend on a key manager who happens to have a particular commitment to and knowledge of equalities for expertise and advice, only to find that the initiative founders when the individual leaves. The EOC research on mainstreaming concluded that 'expert equality advice and support' was required throughout the process to support effective mainstreaming and that specialist teams and units should be available to advise key corporate committees (EOC, 1997).

Another problem is that Britain does not have the strong national legislation or central government direction to underpin a mainstreaming approach. The importance of a supportive national framework emerged from the transnational comparisons done as part of the EOC's research (EOC, 1997). Italy developed a national plan to implement the Beijing Platform in public bodies and has a Ministry of Equal Opportunities which develops, coordinates and monitors progress. In Sweden the national government takes a lead in promoting equal opportunities practice by establishing a five-year action plan with quantitative and time-based goals against which progress can be monitored. County Administrative Boards are required to produce an equalities strategy which addresses national equal opportunity goals at regional level.

In England and Wales, authorities now are asked whether they have an equalities policy, follow codes of practice and monitor as part of the indicators which they are required to publish annually by the Audit Commission, but they are not required to actually show progress against targets, nor is there any specific pressure, as yet, on local authorities from Government departments or the Government Women's Unit. However, the performance indicators for 2000/2001 include the percentage of senior management posts held by women (Audit Commission, 1999). In addition, although the DETR (now DTLR) has been reluctant to include equalities as a central requirement in Best Value, the guidance on requirements for Best Value Reviews under the Local Government Act 1999 refers to equity considerations in terms of setting 'targets to redress disparities in the provision of services to those that are socially, economically or geographically disadvantaged' and requires that authorities explicitly consider whether their services comply with equalities legislation (DETR, 1999: 7–8; see also DETR 2001).

Finally, there is still a lack of practical tools to help authorities carry out the integration that mainstreaming requires. The EOC framework and the equalities toolkit from Wales (Welsh Local Government Association, 1999) are a start, but most authorities still do not know how to 'do' mainstreaming and want more detailed guidance and more examples of concrete practice.

Social exclusion/inclusion

This is another concept which has been adopted from Europe and is based on the view that all people should have access to the social, cultural and material resources which will enable them to achieve the best for themselves and allow them to play a full part in the community as a whole. Strongly adopted by the New Labour government when it came into power, it recognises some of the concerns of elected members and authorities about poverty, homelessness and disadvantage, and the way in which different factors such as age, social class and unemployment combine to cause the disempowerment and isolation of communities and groups. In practice, however, the government's concern still tends to focus on exclusion from the labour market and not to make the links between disability, race and gender, and poverty and exclusion.

Structurally, some authorities are combining work on equalities, anti-poverty and social exclusion in their central policy units and calling the new units social inclusion/exclusion units. In part, this is another example of the pragmatic way in which local authorities adapt to changing fashions and terminology, but there is some concern that, as with the other new approaches, there is a danger that the needs of traditional equalities groups will be lost in these wider approaches.

Social justice

This approach is used explicitly by only a few authorities and concentrates on the rights agenda rather than the arguably less political and more pragmatic, business-oriented approaches. These authorities argue that equal opportunities and access to appropriate services is a right.[10] The disability movement, in particular, has been lobbying for a civil rights model. The Human Rights Act and the case law it is bound to engender may lead to a resurgence of interest in this approach.[11]

The standards-based approach

This approach combines a pragmatic response to current initiatives with mainstreaming. Successive governments have instituted requirements for local government to be performance- and standards-driven with a strong focus on outcomes and results. National performance indicators were established for local government services which are audited annually and published nationally in 'league tables'. The new Best Value regime also requires public targets in the form of a community plan and authorities will be required to publish their performance against the plan. There are a number of examples of initiatives which are adapting the standards-based approach to equalities considerations. The Employers' Organisation for local government has been working in partnership with the Commission for Racial Equality (CRE), the Equal Opportunities Commission (EOC) and the Disability Rights Commission (DRC) to produce a generic equalities standard to feed into Best Value processes. The standard which is currently being finalised is based upon the CRE racial equality standard (CRE 1995). In addition, specific equality performance indicators have been developed for services, and efforts are being made to influence the design (in the longer term) and the implementation of the Local Government Improvement Model to ensure equalities is addressed.

Lessons

What have we learnt after almost twenty years? Local government is essentially pragmatic, with a bias towards procedure, but lately we have been rather inclined to follow management fashions. Our collective failure to evaluate what has been done before moving on to the next management fashion or the latest 'good idea' from government or the US means that we have not always seen what has been achieved, and that we have some times been in danger of throwing the baby out with the bath water. Despite some very real pessimism in authorities in recent years, equalities work has survived through a very difficult period and developed and moved forward.

What is clear is that there is not one easy, simple solution. What seems to work in practice involves elements of all the approaches, including the procedural approach. Probably the key factors remain the same, whatever the approach adopted. First, high level, visible commitment from elected members and Chief Officers, ideally captured in the local authority's vision, values and objectives, and supported by the authority's performance management system, is clearly essential. Elected members need the capacity to ask the right questions, to scrutinise service outcomes and to ensure the right processes are in place. Both service managers and equalities staff need to be knowledgeable about the communities they serve and their needs. Equalities' expertise is essential in this to make links with groups and communities and to help service and other managers understand the diversity and needs of the people the authority serves.

Second, structures, processes and procedures are important. Integrating equalities into Best Value reviews, consultation with the public, the development of organisational objectives, performance plans and local performance indicators, business planning, performance management, and so on ensures that progress and performance on equalities is not just reliant on the commitment and interest of key individuals who may leave.

Third, information, hard and soft, is needed, with a focus on outcomes and performance rather than process. What difference do various initiatives and approaches make? Who are our services-users and what do they think of our services? Do services meet their particular needs? How do we compare with similar authorities? Who works for us? Using benchmarking, targets, performance indicators, customer surveys, focus groups and feedback (or making sure that equalities is being addressed in these processes) is just as relevant for assessing the authority's performance on equalities as for any other key policy objective. External views are also important and can be used constructively to reflect upon performance. Community groups and voluntary sector organisations have views and ideas which can be built into the Best Value process. Finally, reviewing and evaluating progress more generally on a regular basis is needed to help practitioners, elected members and senior officers to make informed decisions about how to take equalities work forward. In doing so, councils can benefit from the work of academics and central local government bodies.

The future

In the period between starting this chapter and finalising it, there has been what feels like a significant change in the seriousness with which equalities work is being taken by central and local government. In response to the Stephen Lawrence Inquiry, there is increasing pressure from central government on itself and on local government to set targets for equalities, and a renewed interest in making equalities work more effective, which is beginning to show up in mainstream processes and key initiatives such as Best Value. The death of a young black man at a bus stop in South London may prove to be the most powerful factor in getting equalities for women, black and minority ethnic people and disabled people back on the agenda at the start of the new millennium.

Notes

1. In the GLC, this focused on supporting initiatives by and for women. Consultation meetings were held in every borough in London, women's groups were set up for key services and key groups, and women in the community were supported in setting up child care and other projects.

2. The views which follow are very much my own, based on my personal experience and work, and on impressions gained from the contacts, queries, seminars and so on which arise in my current job, rather than on more quantified data. While more systematic information on race initiatives in councils is kept centrally, information on gender is not kept in the same way.
3. Figures here and in the following tables are taken from Employers' Organisation for Local Government surveys and the Labour Force Survey, unless otherwise indicated.
4. The Employers' Organisation's Future of Work Programme has been supporting action research which is testing out ways of both improving service to customers and giving employees more flexibility through changing ways of working. Details of publications and the research are available from the Employers' Organisation on 0207 296 6756.
5. Figures supplied by the Local Government International Bureau.
6. An earlier LGMB/SOCPO (1993) study of equal opportunities in employment in England and Wales found that more than 80 per cent of authorities had adopted policies and altered their selection and training procedures. However, when broken down by the type of authorities, the figures showed that shire districts were less likely to have equal opportunities policies and procedures than other types of authorities.
7. Sweden assesses progress against specified national goals, using performance indicators. Particularly interesting is the Three Rs method developed by the Swedish Association of Local Authorities where quantitative data are collected on representation (for example, who speaks most at council meetings and who is in contact with citizens in the community), the distribution of resources (for example of use of space in school yards by boys and girls) and on 'realia' (assessing whether the norms underlying service provision are based on men's or women's needs).
8. For example, there is some evidence of overly rigid application of procedures where interview panels literally read out the agreed questions and are told not to ask any follow-on questions or to probe for fear of discriminating.
9. London Borough of Hounslow, 1993, Strategic Equality Plans in Service Delivery. For further details, contact Bernadette O'Shea or Michael Spooner on 0208 862 5035.
10. The London Borough of Waltham Forest has adopted a social justice approach. For further details, contact the Social Justice Unit at the Town Hall, London, EH7 4JF, 0208 527 5544.
11. The Human Rights Act (1998) allows individuals, whose rights under the European Convention have been infringed, to pursue their claim in a court or tribunal in the UK, as opposed to having their case heard in the European Court in Strasbourg.

References

Audit Commission (1999), *Best Value and Audit Commission Performance Indicators for 2000/2001: Volume 1*, London: DETR.
Baldwin, P. and Foot, J. (1998), *No Quality Without Equality – Best Value and Equalities*, London: LGMB.

Beddington, R., Foreman, J. and Coussey, M. (1997), *Decentralisation and Devolution*, Hertfordshire: Wainwright Trust.

Breitenbach, E., Brown, A., Mackay, F. and Webb, J. (1999), *Equal Opportunities in Local Government in Scotland and Wales*, Edinburgh: Unit for the Study of Government in Scotland, University of Edinburgh.

Brown, A., Jones, A. and Mackay, F. (1999), *The 'Representativeness' of Councillors*, York: Joseph Rowntree Foundation

Cabinet Office (1999), *Modernising Government*, CM 4310.

Cabinet Office/Home Office/Department for Education and Employment (1998), 'Policy Appraisal for Equal Treatment', available from Women's Unit at the Cabinet Office, 0207 273 8831.

Collier, R. (1998), *Equality in Managing Service Delivery*, Buckingham: Open University Press.

Commission for Racial Equality (1995), *Racial Equality Means Quality: A Standard for Racial Equality in Local Government in England and Wales*, London: CRE.

DETR (1998), *Modern Local Government: In Touch with the People*, Department of the Environment, Transport and the Regions, CM 4014.

DETR (1999), *Local Government Act 1999 Part 1: Best Value*, Department of the Environment, Transport and the Regions Circular 10/99 December.

DETR (2001), *Best Value and Procurement: Handling of Workforce Matters in Contracting*, Department of the Environment, Transport and the Regions Circular 01/01.

Employers Organisation for Local Government (formerly the Local Government Management Board (LGMB) (1999), *Employment Trends in Local Government*, report to Policy Panel, 7 April.

Equal Opportunities Commission (1997), *Mainstreaming Gender Equality in Local Government*, Synthesis and Framework reports, Manchester: Equal Opportunities Commission.

Escott, K. and Whitfield, D. (1995), *The Gender Impact of CCT in Local Government*, Manchester: Equal Opportunities Commission.

Home Office (1999), *The Stephen Lawrence Inquiry: Report of an Inquiry by Sir William Macpherson of Cluny*, CM 4262-1.

Hunt, J. and Bundred, S. (1998), *Equal Opportunities Recruitment: Fairness or Failure?*, London: LGMB.

Jewson, N., Mason, D., Drewett, A. and Rossiter, W. (1995), *Formal Equal Opportunities Policies and Employment Best Practice*, Research Series No. 69, Sheffield: Department for Education and Employment.

Kandola, R. and Fullerton, J. (1994), *Managing the Mosaic: Diversity in Action*, Institute of Personnel and Development.

LGMB (1998), *First National Census: Survey of Local Authority Councillors in England and Wales*.

LGMB and Society of Chief Personnel Officers (1993), *Equal Opportunities in Local Government*.

Rees, T. (1998), *Mainstreaming Equality in the European Union*, London: Routledge.

Welsh Local Government Association (1999), *Equal Opportunities Toolkit*, Cardiff.

11
Equalities Work: The Implications of 'Best Value' Requirements

Ellen Kelly

As for the local authorities, schools and hospitals, if they do not deliver according to the standards required of them by UK plc, hit squads will arrive from headquarters to replace them. (Barnett, 1998)

That's one view of Best Value, which is one of the Blair government's key tools for bringing quality, efficiency and effectiveness to the business of local government. In the rather more prosaic language of the Scottish Office (1997), Best Value is described as 'the basis of sound government', as a 'process rather than a product' which 'is descriptive rather than prescriptive' and as being grounded in sound operational and strategic management with a clear 'customer and citizen' focus. Prosaic language or not, if 'management' were substituted for 'government' one could easily imagine that the Scottish Office document was written by Tom Peters or some other guru of modern management, rather than a civil servant.

Laying aside discussion of the validity of the claims made for organisational efficiency by Peters and others of his ilk, there can be little doubting the determination to modernise how both central and local government works. The detail of this is laid out in the White Paper 'Modernising Government', published in March 1999, which sets out the government's programme of renewal and timetable for reform. Among many proposed changes to the policy making process, 'Modernising Government' is at pains to talk about 'making sure policies are inclusive' and 'involving others in policy-making'. The White Paper also sets out in some detail how these aims will be achieved.

So, are we in at the beginning of a revolution in local government whereby outcomes and results are what matters, and the views of service users are what counts, or is Best Value simply another strand of a thick rope of bureaucratic processes which central government is placing around the neck of local government? And what is the likely fate of the feminist and equalities agendas in the process?

It is important to understand that Best Value is not a stand-alone concept. The Blair administration has four key and overlapping agenda items for local government. These are Best Value, Social Inclusion, Public Performance Reporting and Community Planning. Best Value has been defined as a quest for affordable services of the highest possible quality, underpinned by performance measurement, independent inspection and audit. Social inclusion is less easy to define in a sound-bite, but is potentially a very far-reaching concept, which starts with the recognition that there are groups within the community which, because of their life circumstances, are liable to experience continued poverty and unemployment. Whole communities can be socially excluded, for instance ex-mining areas or large run-down local authority housing estates in poor areas of the country, or classes of people, for example lone parents or disabled people reliant on benefits. To misquote Sam Goldwyn, the purpose of social inclusion is to 'include the excluded'.

The purpose of Public Performance Reporting (PPR) is to make local authorities more accountable. It means that local authorities have a duty to report in as clear and intelligible a manner as possible on their performance to electors and other stakeholders (for example, local businesses and trade organisations) in their area. The idea behind Community Planning, which is still in its very early stages, is that members of local communities should be as fully involved as possible in decisions which affect their lives. All the statutory agencies within a given area, which may be quite small, say a village and its hinterlands, or a specified area within a large town or city, will be expected to work together with panels of local citizens and businesses, in order to develop cost-effective forms of service provision appropriate to that area.

All four policies are different facets of a single theme: bringing about real and meaningful change in the culture and balance of power within local authorities. All represent the determination to make local government both more accountable to local communities and more efficient. The impact of these four priorities is likely to change the face and style of local government on a scale that the Thatcher administration could only have envied. In effect central government has set the strategic agenda for local authorities for the foreseeable future.

It should also be remembered that central government has set this agenda in the context of an intention to keep taxes down, limit the spending of public bodies and still maintain a commitment to a more inclusive and equitable society. It could be argued that the Blair programme for local government, perhaps more clearly than in any other area of activity, shows the inherent difficulty in attempting to maintain control though the use of performance management measures – which by their nature need considerable and skilful adjustment if they are ever to be effective measures of qualitative change – whilst speaking the language of radical partnership between communities, local and central government.

Best Value is a bundle of processes, none of which are in themselves new. Performance monitoring, service review, consultation and the use of contractors to deliver services are hardly ground-breaking techniques. What is ground-breaking about Best Value is the way that it links these well understood (if not always well practised) techniques in a systematised way. It incorporates requirements for continuous improvement in the quality of service provision, insists on incorporating the views of existing and non-service users within review and performance appraisal and demands far more openness and transparency from local authorities. This is combined with a no nonsense message that there can be no presumptions as to the best way to deliver a service.

To understand Best Value, a quick glance into the not too distant past is helpful. Best Value's immediate precursor was the much disliked Compulsory Competitive Tendering (CCT). The purpose of CCT was to obtain better value for money. It was intended to make local authorities more efficient, obtain lower costs and challenge local monopolies. CCT was also a contested policy, introduced as a key plank of Conservative policy and bitterly opposed by the Labour Party in opposition.

Introduced by the Conservative government in 1980, as part of the Local Government Planning and Land Act and greatly extended by the Local Government Act 1988, the theme of 'quality' did not enter the lexicon of CCT. In other words, CCT was a bottom-line issue, in which 'defined areas' of local authority work were put up for tender, in a process whereby the key and deciding factor was cost. The areas initially selected were those parts of local government which were viewed as easy to hive off, i.e. those areas with very clearly defined service parameters, where the bottom line could easily be calculated. Thus Street Cleansing, Building Cleaning, Catering and Refuse Disposal were all early targets, shortly followed by Leisure Services. More rigour was undoubtedly required in many local authorities to achieve value for money. Unfortunately, CCT did not distinguish between those services that were delivering the goods and those that were not. All had to be put to contract, with cost as the sole arbiter. It should also be noted that the areas first selected for CCT are the very areas of activity where low pay is most prevalent and where there is high representation of both women as well as black and other ethnic minority workers. In fact many bids were won by in-house local government contractors, known as Direct Service Organisations (DSOs), but at the cost of lost jobs and lower wages.

The outcome was all too predictable, with service quality often taking a hammering and low-paid workers either losing their jobs or being forced into the private sector, with a resultant loss of job security. A study of CCT by Kerley and Wynn in 1990 found that it was unskilled female workers in the poorer regions of the UK who had most to lose. A report commissioned by the EOC on the impact of CCT noted that low-paid women had suffered disproportionately and that equalities staff were generally not involved in the CCT processes (Escott and Whitfield, 1995). A 1998 survey of local government finance professionals in the north-west of England concluded that, in terms of blue-collar CCT, savings had been achieved, but through the reduction of the work force and a deterioration in conditions of employment for those who remained (Wibie, 1999). Whatever its success in developing a more cost-aware culture and setting defined standards for performance, with a background like this it was hardly surprising that abolishing CCT was seen as a prime objective by local government and was duly included in the Labour Party Manifesto for the May 1997 General Election.

The government moved very quickly after the Labour Party won the General Election in May 1997 and it was announced by late May that CCT was to be replaced by 'Best Value'. In a process which, for some at least, had uncomfortable overtones of that utilised for the Poll Tax, Scotland was to have a 'big bang' approach. The Scottish Office (now the Scottish Executive) announced that all CCT timetables were to be suspended, to allow all Scottish local authorities to proceed with Best Value by July 1997. It should be noted that suspension is the operative word. Post-devolution, the Scottish First Minister has kept the right to reintroduce CCT if he is not satisfied that Best Value processes are producing the required results. Scottish Office Ministers and more recently Scottish Executive Ministers have made it clear that Best Value is not a soft option. 'The manifesto was quite clear that authorities which fail will be subject to sanctions. I know that this is not a popular message but I should leave you under no illusions about it' (Malcolm Chisholm, Scottish Local Government Minister, July 1997). In England and Wales a different methodology was initiated, with Best Value introduced via a series of thirty pilot areas, prior to being launched for all local authorities.

In Scotland the Best Value Taskforce, with staff from the then Scottish Office, the Convention of Scottish Local Authorities (CoSLA) and the Accounts Commission of Scotland, was set up with a remit to develop the essential elements of Best Value. These were defined as resting on the four key principles of:

- accountability;
- transparency;
- continuous improvement and a planning framework;
- ownership.

The Taskforce also identified four key elements within the Best Value system. These were:

- sound governance, identified as encompassing:
  - consumer/citizen focus
  - sound strategic management
  - sound operational management
  - sound financial management;

- performance measurement and monitoring;
- continuous improvement though competition and other tools;
- long-term planning and budgeting.

The Department of Environment, Transport and the Regions (DETR) has set out three key 'E's' for Best Value in England and Wales: economy, efficiency and effectiveness. These three factors are now enshrined in the Local Government Best Value Bill for England and Wales. There was no requirement for a Best Value Bill for Scotland, since Scottish local authorities already have a duty laid on them to achieve effectiveness, efficiency and economy by the Local Government (Scotland) Act 1994. Moreover, section 211 of the 1973 Local Government Scotland Act gave the Secretary of State for Scotland sweeping powers to intervene in the running of a local authority's affairs, if there was sufficient cause for concern. (Post-May 1999 these powers transferred to the First Minister of the Scottish Parliament.) This power is not available to the Ministers responsible for local government in England and Wales. Thus the process of introducing Best Value in Scotland has been able to move at some speed. At the time of writing, Scotland is approximately two years ahead of England and Wales.

How then is Best Value different from CCT? The most immediate difference is that there are no 'defined areas'. All parts of every service are up for review via a rolling five-year programme. Local authorities select key areas, with priority given to those areas of provision seen as most problematic – i.e. known to be inefficient or not to be meeting the needs of their target group (for example, services for older people, housing services, legal services, the provision of school meals). In Scotland, England and Wales all Councils must show clear commitment to the 'Four C's' in carrying out the reviews. The 'four C's' are to Challenge, Compare, Consult and Compete.

Quality is a key component of Best Value, as is a 'customer/citizen' focus. If these requirements are to be properly met, local authorities will be forced into effective consultation with the full spectrum of the community. Partnership working, along with the wide-spread use of Citizens' Juries, focus groups and user panels will be the order of the day. As an example, my own authority, the City of Edinburgh Council, currently has over 100 recognised partnership bodies, as well as a Citizens' Panel of 1,800, weighted to ensure adequate representation of women, people from minority ethnic groups, people with disabilities and a cross section of income and employment bands. Although the City of Edinburgh may be early in the field and is also one of the areas in which the Scottish Executive is piloting Community Planning, there is little doubt that Best Value will demand this sort of attention to consultative processes. Otherwise local authorities will be unable to prove that they have carried through adequate consultation. Failure to do so will undermine one of the key tenets of Best Value and lay the authority open to the imposition of sanctions, such as the re-imposition of CCT.

Consultation must be on-going, both in the course of service review and in regular progress checks with user groups. There is also a requirement to monitor satisfaction through the use of complaints systems, surveys and other methods. Interestingly, the Best Value draft Bill for England and Wales specifies very clearly who an authority must consult. The list is very wide-ranging, including existing or possible future service users and representatives 'of persons appearing to the authority to have an interest in any area in which the authority carries out functions'. Just in case any local authority is still misguided enough to see consultation as a soft option there is a requirement for authorities to have regard to written guidance to be issued by the Minister for Environment, Transport and the Regions in terms of both the persons to be consulted and the form, content and timing of consultations. The guidance issued for Scotland is somewhat less prescriptive but only marginally so: 'the Best Value Framework needs to ensure ... all relevant people are consulted. For example customers, authority taxpayers, other organizations such as local businesses, suppliers or interest groups' and that 'consultation is effective. For example, the authority has followed up the key issues raised by consultees; and, where people are not consulted but have a legitimate reason to contribute their views, there should be some kind of recourse open to them' (Best Value Taskforce, 1999). Both in England and Wales and Scotland this is a change from the White Paper which stated that the government would not prescribe when and how consultation is done. It provides another indicator of a steadily increasing concern on the part of central government that local authorities approach Best Value in an equitable manner. Taken together, the dual focus on 'quality' and 'customer/citizen' concerns within Best Value are likely have great importance for the future of equal opportunities.

In England, Wales and Scotland, Best Value is to be monitored through two types of performance indicators. A small group of Key Performance Indicators, KPIs, has been developed, by the Audit Commission in England and Wales and its sister body the Accounts Commission in Scotland. (The remit of both Commissions is to provide an external auditing and performance monitoring function for public bodies, including local authorities, local health trusts, the fire brigades and the police.) In both instances the KPIs have been drawn up through a consultative process involving the private sector, the Audit or Accounts Commission and local authority representatives. A key purpose of KPIs is to enable comparisons to be drawn between the performance of local authorities. Although not their prime purpose, they will almost inevitably be used by central government to develop performance 'league tables' as a spur to improvement. The KPIs are also intended to focus attention on 'outputs', that is, the achievements (or lack thereof) of local authorities, unlike CCT where the emphasis was on inputs, due to the focus on cost.

Each local authority must also develop extensive local Performance Indicators to suit its circumstances. Guidance on their development is supplied by the DETR for England and Wales and the Scottish Executive for Scotland. Local authorities have to develop two different types of indicators. One set will be used in new annual Public Performance Reports and needs to be meaningful to the public. Another set of local PIs will be used for the management of processes.

Although there was no initial commitment to the development of equality as a stand alone concept within Best Value, a number of pointers indicate a developing consensus on the part of central government that equalities issues must be included within the development of both KPIs and local PIs. Not least among these were conference speeches by both Tessa Jowell and Henry McLeish, previously responsible for local government in England and Wales and Scotland respectively, to predominantly local government audiences, attesting that equalities are integral to Best Value and that a Fair Employment agenda is also part of Best Value. Despite the reference to a Fair Employment agenda by both Ministers there was no indication as to what that might mean in practice. At the very least a commitment to uphold the legislative requirements of civil rights in employment and to meet the requirements of the national minimum wage would seem to be the least that could be expected. This is already par for the course among local authorities, but not within private sector companies where the most severe transgressions continue to take place. Extending what is already usual practice in local authorities to all contractors as part of the Best Value process would have considerable impact in supporting the Fair Employment agenda.

In Scotland the hopes for development of KPIs and local PIs that incorporate meaningful reference to equalities issues were given a boost by the report of the Consultative Steering Group on the Scottish Parliament (1998). One of the four key principles identified was that the Parliament should, in its operation and its appointments, recognise the need to promote equal opportunities. This was backed up by a recommendation for mainstreaming of equal opportunities into the work of the Parliament and the Scottish Executive. To support work on equalities issues the Consultative Steering Group also recommended that the Parliament should have an Equal Opportunities Committee.

The recommendations of the Consultative Steering Group were adopted by the Parliament in 1999. Even with the caveat that the Scottish Parliament and Executive now have to show that they can effectively deliver on equal opportunities issues, it would be surprising if anything less than a full-blooded commitment to equal opportunities work, and a consequential expectation that equalities issues will be fully integrated into the core of their day to day working, will be demanded of local authorities in Scotland. What is already evident is energetic lobbying by women, black and other ethnic minority groups and the lesbian, gay, bisexual and trans-gender communities of members of the Parliament demanding that their voice be heard and needs reflected in the work of the Parliament. As yet, perhaps unsurprisingly due to the considerable difficulties faced by its members in joining together to form a lobby group, such activity is not so evident from disabled people, but this can only be a matter of time.

Perhaps in anticipation of similar developments within the Welsh Assembly, the Welsh Local Government Association has produced an

Equalities Toolkit for Welsh local government. This is explicitly linked to the development of Best Value: 'in the wider context of the democratic responsibilities of local government, the legal and social obligations of councils and the Government agendas of inclusiveness, equity and social justice, equal opportunities must surely be regarded as an implicit principle of Best Value' (Welsh Local Government Association, 1999).

Inherent in the development of both KPIs and local PIs is the use of benchmarking to ensure cost-effectiveness against other Councils, the private sector, other services and external databases. As with the introduction of quality and the customer/citizen focus, the use of KPIs and local PIs has considerable potential for a much more stringent approach towards integrating the needs of equalities groups and communities of interest within service delivery and for the development of effective methods of monitoring progress on the equalities agenda.

Ongoing reviews of equality legislation are also likely to result in local authorities being required to pay more attention to the effective intergration of equal opportunities within their work. The Race Relations (Amendment) Act 2000 responds to the Macpherson Report into the murder of Stephen Lawrence by strengthening the duties imposed on public bodies to promote good race relations and equality of opportunity. It includes a requirement that public authorities proactively assess the implicatiions for racial equality of all policies and services and monitor the ethnic composition of their workforce. Review of the Sex Discrimination Act and Equal Pay Acts has stimulated speculation that similar provisions may be incorporated into unified sex discrimination legislation. Best Value contracts by extension, would need to take account of such duties.

Despite some concerns by local government politicians that Best Value is simply CCT in sheep's clothing, there are some important distinguishing features. Best Value, though sharing some parts of the CCT agenda – specifically those of financial stringency, service specifications and performance monitoring and competition, as well as a background of real constraints on local government expenditure – is not of itself anti-equalities. Both the DETR (1998) and the Scottish Office Circulars (Scottish Office, 1997) stress that Best Value is essential to delivering the key corporate objectives of a council. If the pursuit of equal opportunities and addressing the needs of equalities groups (often defined as women, black and other ethnic minority groups, disabled people and lesbian, gay and trans-gendered people; sometimes with the addition of older people as well as, less frequently, children and young people) is a key corporate objective, as is the case with many councils, then equalities and equal opportunities issues must be addressed at every stage of the Best Value process. The Best Value Taskforce interim guidance (1999) specifies that authorities will incorporate equality issues within the Best Value framework. Moreover, it is in a local authority's best interests to do so, since failure to comply may well result in the imposition of sanctions.

Given the clear emphasis on quality, accountability, transparency and the requirement for meaningful and on-going consultation, it is clear that the potential is there within Best Value for a serious engagement with a specifically feminist and also the broader equalities agenda. This results from the observation that, if the requirements for effective and inclusive consultative arrangements and quality services to be delivered are to be met, women's voices and those of other equalities groups must not only be heard, but must be given due attention.

Thus far, there has self-evidently been a highly variable approach to the integration of equalities issues within Best Value. This is due to the highly variable nature of local authorities, rather than any real barriers posed by the requirements of the process. Moreover, it can be argued with some justice that many of the people within local authorities who implemented CCT are the same people who, at least initially, have been given responsibility for implementing Best Value. This group are, in the main, technicians, primarily concerned with developing contract conditions and quantitative performance measures. By its nature, the inclusion of equalities considerations in contracts demands a qualitative approach, which in turn pulls direct contact with service users into the process and is inevitably more demanding than simply developing numeric performance measures.

The technicians involved may well previously have had little need to deal with service users in this way and may well not be comfortable with the process. Some may even question the validity of including qualitative performance measures within the Best Value process. Certainly, many will need to develop new approaches in order to do so. In consequence, at the time of writing there is an observable tendency to focus on cost as the primary and deciding element, rather than as one of a group of key elements within Best Value. As already noted, equalities staff were not usually included in CCT processes. The outcome, with some honourable exceptions, was that equal opportunities issues were usually notable by their absence. In many councils, it has taken some time for the message to penetrate that equality is an integral part of quality – and Best Value – not a bolted-on optional extra.

There has been considerable effort on the part of CoSLA, the LGMB, the WLGA and, where they exist, equalities officers and committees, to get over the message that quality cannot be achieved without serious consideration of equalities. To those not engaged in the issue it would seem axiomatic that for service provision within local government to be of an acceptable quality, it must be appropriate to the needs of local communities and communities of interest, and must be equally accessible to all and of the same (good) quality for all. This self-evident truism has taken some time to establish itself within Best Value processes. An off-the-record comment by a Scottish Executive official is very revealing: 'We thought that saying Councils must focus on meeting customer and citizen needs would be enough without having to spell it [the equalities agenda] out.' It was the undoubted evidence of the lack of consideration of equalities issues in early Best Value work in Scotland which persuaded the Best Value Taskforce to include unequivocal guidance on the need to integrate equalities issue within the interim guidance.

The Department of Environment, Transport and the Regions was not so trusting. Whilst not making equalities issues a key principle of Best Value, its written guidance can have left English and Welsh Councils in little doubt of the need to integrate equalities from the outset, when it stated that local performance plans had to 'reflect authorities corporate objectives, including those of sustainable development and equal opportunities' (DETR, 1998). There is equally little doubt that the message from central government about the need to integrate equalities issues within Best Value has slowly amplified as the process gets underway.

There is also a parallel 'mainstreaming' agenda which is integral to Best Value. This was instigated by the European Union and has been adopted with some enthusiasm by both the EOC and the CRE. In its submission to the Consultative Steering Group on the Scottish Parliament, the EOC defined mainstreaming as requiring the following:

- determination to pursue equality of opportunity and outcome through all policy development, practices, legislation and implementation;
- commitment to scrutinise *before adoption* [EOC emphasis] all legislation and its implementation to identify potential for discrimination;
- commitment in all legislation and its implementation to promote equal opportunities in the relevant areas and to redress inequality and/or differential impact;
- an effective mechanism to gather data, evaluate and monitor services; and a commitment, where there is evidence of inequality and/or

differential impact, to assess what changes are required to achieve greater equality and, where possible, to implement these.

Mainstreaming has been adopted as a key strategy of the Scottish Executive and is a key principle of the Scottish Parliament (Mackay and Bilton, 2000). This has very real implications for the way local authorities in Scotland conduct their business, although it is still too soon to evaluate the substantive changes likely to take place.

In terms of local government, mainstreaming got off to a rather shaky start, especially in London, where it coincided with reductions in funding and the abolition of Women's and Race Equality Units and Committees. This led to understandable suspicion, and it is only since the late 1990s that the potential of mainstreaming for achieving the objectives of the equalities agenda has been recognised, albeit with some caveats as to the necessity of retaining sources of expertise on equalities issues within local government.

The need to have these caveats clearly stated attests to the struggle for recognition that has been the lot of equal opportunities activists within local government since Lewisham set up the first Women's Rights Working Party, as a Subcommittee of its Policy and Resources Committee, in 1979. (A full Women's Committee had to wait until one was set up by the now defunct Greater London Council in 1982.) It is tempting to speculate that, even allowing for the societal values inherent in the operation of hegemonic culture, this constant struggle for recognition relates to the 'people-centred' and qualitative agenda of equal opportunities.

The feminist and equalities agendas do not, of themselves, require large capital programmes. They do not require thousands of staff to provide services. Unlike other specialisms, such as law or accountancy, there is not one, single recognised qualification, the possession of which entitles an individual to state that they are a qualified expert. The core concern of both the feminist and equalities agendas, at least in local government terms, is to change the culture of local authorities to one which is inclusive, both within employment and service provision, of the needs of all sections of the community.

The outcome has been that, until very recently, there has been an unfortunate tendency for senior officers and elected members to assume that 'anyone can do it' and to disregard the need for specialists who have the skill and expertise to support a local authority in its efforts to move towards more equitable ways of working. This may also help to explain the inescapable fact that there are very few dedicated equalities staff, despite the intensity of interest in the subject.

Although no official figures are available, a survey undertaken shortly after local government reorganisation in Scotland and Wales in 1996 indicated that twelve Scottish local authorities and seven Welsh local authorities had specialist staff in post (Breitenbach et al., 1999). At the time of writing informal sources suggest that there are about 20 dedicated staff within Scottish local authorities (concentrated mainly in the Central Belt, Dundee and Aberdeen) and less than ten in Welsh local authorities, concentrated in three Councils. There are a rather larger number who have equalities issues within their remit, mainly those at Chief Officer level, or within their area of responsibility, or as personnel/human resource managers or as managers of decentralized services. Even including these, the number of staff in Wales and Scotland with a direct remit to action Equalities issues is very unlikely to exceed 100, at a generous estimate. With such a paucity of resources, it is obvious that the battle is far from won in terms of mainstreaming equalities into the Best Value agenda and, indeed, the work of local government in general.

Despite the paucity of resources, the concept of mainstreaming is gaining ground within Scottish local government. Recent Convention of Scottish Local Authorities (CoSLA) guidance defines mainstreaming as 'the integration of an equalities dimension into policy development, implementation and appraisal. It involves integrating equality considerations into mainstream council activities so that these wider processes are influenced ... mainstreaming means thinking about the needs of different groups in the community, consulting and explicitly addressing diverse needs when producing policies and delivering services' (CoSLA, 1998). The guidance makes it clear that mainstreaming should be firmly embedded within Best Value, Community Planning and Civic Governance. Just how closely this mirrors central government's stance was shown at the conference to launch the report. This was hosted by the Scottish Office and the key speaker was Henry McLeish, then the Minister for Local Government in Scotland. In his speech Mr McLeish gave a very clear example of how 'joined up' government works, as he linked the new Social Inclusion Strategy for Scotland with the need to modernise local government and highlighted Best Value as an essential part of the Government's modernisation programme. In the course of his speech Mr McLeish noted that a three-way working group, composed of the Accounts Commission, CoSLA and the Scottish Office, had been set up to look at the long-term development of Performance Indicators to better reflect Best Value. He also added that he had requested that 'this should include the development of indicators on equality of opportunity'.[1] This sent a clear signal to those local authorities in Scotland which have not yet engaged fully with the equal opportunities agenda that opting out or pleading poverty of resources is not an option and that such a stance will not be acceptable to the government.

Both the CRE and the EOC see mainstreaming as an ideal tool for placing equalities issues at the heart of government, instead of at the margins. If mainstreaming achieves its objective it will lead to profound change in the operation of both central and local government. Mainstreaming provides an opportunity to bring both the feminist and equalities agenda to the fore by positioning the issues within the heart of policy-making and service provision. Best Value provides an excellent launch platform to support the development of mainstreaming.

It is important to remember that the process of integrating equalities issues within Best Value should not be seen as hitherto unknown ground. There is a wealth of existing knowledge and experience on how equalities issues and specifically feminist initiatives can be integrated into the work of a local authority. Suffice to say that even the most inexperienced officer or elected member can, with a modicum of diligence, access a wealth of publications that cover the issues. Unlike the pre-GLC Women's Committee period, i.e. pre-1982, where, generally speaking, little was known and less cared about the needs of equalities groups and communities of interest within government, knowledge of equalities issues is now disseminated throughout central and local government. (Making this statement should in no way be confused with a presumption of a general depth of understanding. That happy position is still some way in the future.) Expanded knowledge of the issues in no way precludes continuing opposition from the beneficiaries of hitherto predominant hegemonic, societal ideologies.[2] It must be expected that for many years to come, carrying through the changes necessary to achieve a more equitable distribution of resources will continue to meet pockets of entrenched opposition from within both central and local government. Change is never easy, especially when it necessitates change in the balance of power within governmental organisations.

It remains one of the wonders of late twentieth-century European culture, a testimony to the pervasiveness of white, heterosexual male values, that the interests of the majority of the population represented by women, people from black and other ethnic minority groups, disabled people, older people and young people, as well as lesbians and gay men should previously have been so easily dismissed as marginal and not worthy of serious consideration. Even now, change to a more equitable agenda is by no means assured. There has been considerable progress in some areas and little in others. Whilst remaining hopeful about the potential of Best Value to bring about real change and to support the full integration of equalities throughout local government, it is as yet much too soon to tell the eventual outcome. Travelling hopefully to an unknown destination is probably the best that can be said at this point.

Notes

1. This point was made in a speech at a joint Equal Opportunties Commission (EOC)/Convention of Scottish Local Authorities (CoSLA) conference, hosted by the Scottish Office in February 1999.
2. In this instance 'hegemonic' is used in Gramsci's sense of an all-prevasive, saturating view of social structures which favour a specific group, in this case, white, able-bodied, heterosexual men as being 'the norm, simply the way things are' in relation to the most every day facts of life. Any viewpoint which is not that of the favoured group is positioned as 'other', therefore alien and contrary to societal norms.

References

Barnett, A. (1998), 'All Powers to the Citizens', in *Marxism Today*, Special Issue.
Best Value Taskforce (1999) *Best Value in Local Government, Long Term Arrangements, Interim Conclusions*, Edinburgh.
Breitenbach, E., Brown, A., Mackay, F. and Webb, J. (1999), *Equal Opportunities in Local Government in Scotland and Wales*, Edinburgh: Unit for the Study of Government in Scotland, University of Edinburgh.
Consultative Steering Group on the Scottish Parliament (1998), *Shaping Scotland's Parliament: Report of the Consultative Steering Group*, Edinburgh: The Stationery Office.
CoSLA (1998), *Mainstreaming: Integrating equality into all council activities*, Edinburgh: Convention of Scottish Local Authorities.
DETR (1997), *Press Release on Government's Preference for Public or Private Sector Provision of Service*, London: Department of the Environment, Transport and the Regions.
DETR (1998), *Modern Local Government: in Touch with People*, Department of the Environment Transport and the Regions, CM 4014.
Escott, K. and Whitfield, D. (1995), *The Gender Impact of CCT in Local Government*, Manchester: EOC.
Kerley, R. and Wynn, D. (1990), *Competitive Tendering: the Transition to Contract Tendering in Scottish Local Authorities*, Glasgow: Strathclyde Business School, University of Strathclyde.
Mackay, F. and Bilton, K. (2000), *Learning from Experience: Lessons in Mainstreaming Equal Opportunities*, Edinburgh: Governance of Scotland Forum, University of Edinburgh.
Macpherson, Sir W. (1999), *The Stephen Lawrence Inquiry*, London: The Stationery Office.

Scottish Office (1997), 'Best Value', Scottish Office Development Department Circular, 22/97.
Scottish Office (1998), Scottish Office Development Department Circular, 12/98.
Welsh Local Government Association (1999), *Equalities Toolkit for Welsh Local Government*, Cardiff: Welsh Local Government Association.
Wibie, J. (1999), 'Compulsory Competitive Tendering and Local Government Financial Services: an Analysis of the Views of Local Government Accountants in the North West of England', in *Public Administration*, Vol. 77, No. 3.

Index